Editor **Rick Wilks**
Illustrator **Gram Campbell**

Researched, written, printed and bound
in Canada.
First Printing.

Trade Distribution by:
Firefly Books Ltd.
3520 Pharmacy Ave., Unit 1-C
Scarborough, Ontario, Canada
M1W 2T8

Canadian Cataloguing in Publication Data

Argue, Robert, 1950-
The super-insulated retrofit book

(Sun builders series)
Bibliography: p.
ISBN 0-920456-45-6 (bound). — ISBN 0-920456-43-x (pbk.)

1. Dwellings — Energy conservation — Amateurs' manuals.
2. Dwellings — Remodeling — Amateurs' manuals.
3. Dwellings — Insulation — Amateurs' manuals.
I. Marshall, Brian. II. Renewable Energy in
Canada (Firm). III. Title. IV. Series.

TJ163.5.D86A73   693.8′32′028   C81-094992-X

Renewable Energy in Canada is a
registered non-profit organization
dedicated to the dissemination of
information about renewable energy
sources, technologies and related
environmental concerns.

The Super-Insulated Retrofit Book
A Homeowner's Guide To Energy-Efficient Renovation

Brian Marshall   Robert Argue

Publisher Renewable Energy in Canada 107 Amelia Street, Toronto, Canada M4X 1E5

Introduction

Recently there has been a drastic escalation in the development of energy-efficient housing. As the western world became increasingly cognizant of the economic and political realities of a finite and controlled fossil fuel dependency, new sources of energy supply were sought. Initially the "supply mentality" approach was seen as an answer. When energy supplies became scarce and expensive, new sources of fuel were seen as a salvation (the environmental implications rarely counted in this approach). This entailed developing more exotic (also disruptive and expensive) energy sources such as arctic gas, tar sands, oil shale and hydrogen from nuclear electricity.

At the same time activities were underway that had their beginnings in the environmental and back-to-the-land movements, which were exploring the use of renewable energy sources of supply. Solar heating was one of the basic principles. At first the use of active systems was encouraged. Later passive solar heating systems that allowed the direct access of light and heat into the home achieved popularity as a means of space heating.

However, the most promising source of supply is conservation: doing more with less, increasing the efficiency of what we have and reducing to an absolute minimum the supplemental energy requirements. At the point of articulating our lowest heating needs, we have reached the time to examine various supply options. An examination of the costs and benefits of new supply versus conservation will inevitably favour the latter. It is cheaper to save a barrel of oil than to extract, process and burn that barrel. It is cheaper (and less environmentally disruptive) to save a kilowatt hour than to have to build the capacity for supplying that energy.

There are additional arguments for conservation that extend beyond economic considerations. The conservation option can create more jobs, promote a more stable society and is less disruptive environmentally.

In the residential sector, the response to conservation has taken the form of the super-insulated house. By incorporating the three basic strategies of increasing the insulation, and by using air-tight construction and directing windows to the south, houses are being built with a close to zero heating load.

A house built to super-insulated standards will generally have a heating load of about 10 per cent or less of a conventional house of similar size and location. If the neighbours' heating bill is $1000 a year, the super-insulated house can get by on less than $100 worth of fuel.

These remarkable savings are based on solid, well-proven and economical building techniques. Hundreds of super-insulated houses have been built. Thousands more will be built over the next year or two by dozens of small, medium and large builders. Extra costs are incurred for increased insulation and careful air-vapour barrier detail. Generally, a super-insulated house will cost little more (around 5-10 per cent) than a conventional house, but the savings more than make up for any added costs.

In addition to the economic benefits of lower heating bills and the environmental and political advantages of a reduced dependence on fossil fuels and electricity, super-insulated houses are also super-comfortable. Time and time again new owners are surprised and pleased with the comfort level of their new homes when compared to conventional houses. There is a uniform temperature throughout the house. They are draft free, quiet, and there are no cold spots or cold walls that will make you feel uncomfortable. Some owners have enthusiastically compared the comfort of moving into their new energy-efficient house as equivalent to moving from outdoor to indoor plumbing.

Most of us, however, will not have the opportunity of designing and building a new house. Rather we, individually and as a society, are stuck with the existing housing stock. Over 80 per cent of the houses currently standing will still be here at the turn of the century. The issue then becomes how to upgrade these grossly under-insulated, leaky and expensive houses to some semblance of energy-efficiency. This is the subject we have endeavoured to cover.

To date attempts at upgrading our houses can only be described as band-aid measures. Increased insulation in the attic, turning down the thermostat at night and weatherstripping the front door are all good measures, but they will reduce your heating requirements by only 10 to 20 per cent. Each new "retrofit" activity will reduce the necessary heating further, but before long the marginal cost and benefit will make new one-shot efforts unattractive.

This book looks at the total transformation of your home to a super-insulated, air-tight house. The measures are drastic. They demand the total conversion of either the inside or exterior of your house. If the efforts are large, the rewards are great — in this case a 70 to 90 per cent reduction in heating bills. If you super-insulate your house in conjunction with any renovation work, such as new interior walls or re-siding, the economic return is very positive. At the same time you're developing a comfortable and secure house.

The steps to achieve a super-insulated retrofit house are similar to those mentioned earlier in connection with super-insulating building techniques. They call for increased levels of insulation, tightening up your house, and upgrading your windows. This very comprehensive approach is described in detail in the following chapters: the *Primer*, which examines the why's and what's of the super-retrofit; the *Manual*, which presents step-by-step instructions for both interior and exterior retrofits; a *Survey* which looks at selective examples of what has been done and the *Appendix* which offers further reading, technical summaries and sources of materials.

One final word before you undertake your project. Every super-insulated retrofit will have its own problems and special circumstances. Each house has its unique shape and structure, door and window details, uses one of a variety of construction materials and has survived the years with varying degrees of health. We have tried to cover these contingencies as thoroughly as possible, however, there are still a number of considerations that only the homeowner can evaluate. These include the condition of the house, both inside and outside; the implications of reducing your interior space or extending your house dimensions; what other retrofit activities you will undertake at the same time and how they will fit together; the aesthetics of your house, inside and out, and what changes will enhance or detract from its appearance; and, of course, the economics of the various options. The ideal house for the super-retrofit is one that is already undergoing extensive renovation. While gutting the inside of a home to upgrade the wiring, plumbing and/or walls, is an ideal time to make the house air-tight and increase the insulation levels. If you are re-siding, take the opportunity to do a good energy-efficient job. The super-insulated retrofit is a major project, but one that will continue to pay dividends far into the future.

Robert Argue
Brian Marshall
November, 1981
Toronto, Canada

Contents

Primer

Site

We have little control over the macro-climate features of our environment. Temperature regimes, cloud, sun and wind are given characteristics. But when it comes to the micro-climate, the particular effects of the sun, wind and temperature on our own home and its immediate vicinity, we do have more control.

When designing a new house (especially for a rural setting) you can exercise great control over your micro-climate. But when it comes to existing houses in urban and suburban areas, that control is greatly diminished. The first step is to understand how the various forces work.

The Sun

You want the sun to have access to your house in the winter for its light and heat. You want to control its influence during the summer so that overheating does not become a problem.

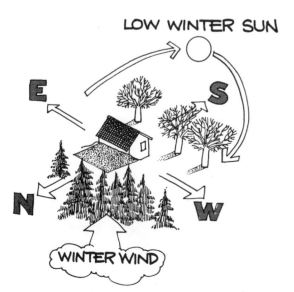

In the winter the sun rises in the south-east, climbs only about 20° in the sky (at latitude 45°) and sets in the south-west. Ideally, nothing should block this winter sun from entering the house. Morning sun is preferable to afternoon sun so you should orient the windows more east of south if due south is not possible.

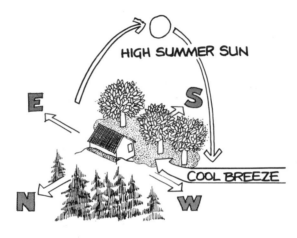

During the summer the sun rises in the north-east, climbs to about 70° in the southern sky (at 45° latitude) and sets in the north-west. You don't want this sun shining directly into the house so some shading device is required. Architectural features such as overhangs and awnings will allow the low winter sun to penetrate, while blocking the higher summer sun. Vertical glass (such as windows) naturally allow more sun in the winter than in the summer. Sloped glass can lead to over-heating problems and should be either avoided or handled with caution. Greenhouses, however, are an exception and require sloped glass to maintain adequate light levels.

Landscaping features such as deciduous trees and vines can also be used. They too will let the winter sun through while providing welcomed shade in the summer.

In general, north-facing windows are to be avoided since they contribute to heat loss but not to solar gain. West-facing windows should also be minimized since they let in too much afternoon sun for much of the year, thereby contributing to overheating.

The Wind

You want to reduce the chilling effects of the winter wind, while inducing the cool summer breezes. It is common for the winter wind to come from the north and west. This is where it is best to plant coniferous (evergreen) trees to act as a buffer. If they are placed at a distance equal to one and a half times the height of the house, and if they are not packed too

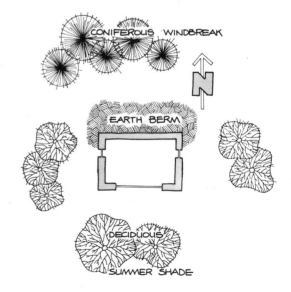

Insulation

tightly, a barrier which deflects rather than absorbs the wind is created. This will reduce the effect of the wind. The wind contributes to energy loss not only by increasing the convection loss of the shell of the house, but also by substantially increasing the air infiltration rate. If the windows are recessed, as in an exterior retrofit, the wind's effects will be lessened considerably.

You can use architectural features to reduce the wind chill. Locating garages and porches on the north and west sides reduces the wind's effects. Placing "cold" rooms such as storage, stairs, halls and laundry on the north side of the house is also useful.

Summer breezes are to be encouraged. By having a window pattern that allows cross breezes through the house, cooling is provided. Windows opened high on the south side of the house and low on the north side will expel excessive heat build-up while inducing cooling breezes.

Many of the preceding features are difficult to implement in existing houses. If you are making extensive renovations keep them in mind. If you only have minimal control over the micro-climate the best approach is to develop a landscape plan. Prepare a bird's-eye view of your house and surrounding property. Put all the features on, including trees, fences, bushes, grass and other buildings. The object is to block the winter wind and summer sun, and to allow summer breezes and winter sun. Any changes you wish to make, such as planting trees, should be plotted on your overall plan to see if they contribute to a more efficient micro-climate.

Insulation is used to prevent or reduce heat loss from your house. The effectiveness of most insulation is due to thousands of small air pockets. It is the still air that provides the insulation and not the material. That is why you get reduced insulating capacities from compressed insulation. The material is still there, but the air pockets have been reduced.

Heat flow by conduction is slowed by insulation. Heat also travels (escapes from your house) by convection and radiation. While many insulations reduce convection loss, you still require a good air-barrier to properly seal your house. Similarly, the insulation should fill the cavity and not leave gaps around the sides, face, top and bottom. Gaps encourage convective heat loss.

Some insulation, such as aluminum foil, works by both trapping air and decreasing the radiative losses because of the shiny surface. An air gap must be kept beside a reflective surface for it to be effective.

Insulation should be continuous. The studs in your wall reduce the insulating value of that wall by creating a thermal bridge the heat can pass through. While the insulation value of fibreglass in a 2 x 6 stud wall is R-20, the studs are only R-6 or R-7. Cross-strapping is one method to reduce the amount of thermal bridging by minimizing contact area.

Adequate insulation is half of the battle in keeping out the cold. Air-leakage control is the other half. Virtually all existing homes have inadequate insulation. In some areas,

YOUR BASIC HOUSE IS PRETTY POORLY INSULATED

AN AIR-TIGHT VAPOUR BARRIER KEEPS THE COLD WIND OUT AND YOUR HEAT IN… LIKE A NYLON SHELL

POORLY FITTING INSULATION LETS COOL AIR CIRCULATE AND LETS HEAT ESCAPE

A GOOD SNUG FIT WITH A MINIMUM OF GAPS KEEPS YOU WARM AND COMFORTABLE such as the attic and basement, it is relatively easy to add insulation. When it comes to the walls, your best bet is generally to build a new wall from either the inside or the outside.

Most houses are insulated to abysmal standards: from R-0 to R-12 in the walls, R-12 to R-20 in the attic, R-0 to R-8 in the basement. New houses built to air-tight, super-insulated standards are achieving, depending on climate, R-25 to R-40 in the walls, R-40 to R-60 in the ceiling and R-20 to R-30 in the basement. Duplicating these levels in a retrofit can be difficult. The techniques discussed in the "How-To" section upgrade walls to at least R-20, the attic to R-40, and the basement to R-20. Combined with the air leakage control measures taken at the same time and an improvement in the windows and doors, there should be an energy saving of 60 to 90 per cent.

The old adage *"if a job is worth doing..."* is certainly true when it comes to insulation. Already your house has been built and insulated far below proper standards for comfort, and dollar and energy conservation. Don't make the same mistake again.

Types of Insulation

Dozens of types of insulation are on the market today, providing an extensive range of advantages, disadvantages, best applications and, of course, costs. This book favours glass fibre insulation. Fibreglass, loose, or more commonly in batts, is inexpensive, versatile and not overly prone to fire or water damage. On the other hand it is awful to handle, so a

mask and gloves should always be worn. It is recommended for attics and ceilings, walls (inside or out) and inside basements. For outside basements (below grade), extruded polystyrene (styrofoam) is recommended. Other insulations have specific applications that depend on the conditions, such as available space.

Fibreglass — used extensively in walls and ceilings: not an expensive option

Cellulose — good for blowing in existing cavities and flat areas where there will be no moisture.

Rigid fibreglass — good for exterior sheathing or shutters.

Extruded polystyrene (blue styrofoam) — best used exterior, below grade and under slabs.

Expanded polystyrene (beadboard) — can be used for interior ceilings (light weight), and basement walls.

Urethane board — good for basement walls, expensive but high insulating value.

Polyisocyanurate board — best for insulating shutters; light weight and a high R value.

Fine-tuning

When adding insulation to the house the attic is generally the first place to begin. This is because it is often the easiest place to work in rather than the most cost-effective.

Adding an R-20 fibreglass batt, perpendicular to the existing insulation is one approach. Another is to blow in loose glass fibres or cellulose to a uniform level of 6 inches or more.

Adequate ventilation above the insulation is necessary to prevent moisture accumulation. One square foot of vent space for each 300 square feet of attic area is adequate. The best vent system allows a circulation of air in at the soffit and out through a ridge cap. Too much ventilation (i.e. power vents) will actually increase heat loss by increasing air leakage through the ceiling.

The basement is often a prime candidate for re-insulation. Strapping a stud wall to the walls or hanging a curtain wall a few inches out will allow for high levels of fibreglass to be put in place. Empty stud walls can be filled with blown cellulose or fibreglass. Blocks between studs often prevent the gap from filling completely and must be bypassed.

When re-insulating it is always important to remember to create an air-vapour barrier. An air barrier is created to reduce air leakage. All cracks and holes should first be filled with an air-tight seal. A vapour barrier is placed on the warm side of the insulation to prevent moisture entering the wall, condensing and causing settling and rot. A 6 mil polyethylene vapour barrier is commonly used. It must be lapped and sealed at all seams. Where it is impossible to place a poly vapour barrier, vinyl wallpaper or a vapour barrier paint can be applied directly on the wall.

The Super-Retrofit

In the super-retrofit the entire house is wrapped in an air-vapour barrier and levels of super-insulation. There are two distinct approaches to the super retrofit: working on the exterior, and from the interior.

Exterior Insulation

We think the exterior insulation is far superior. It allows for an unbroken layer of insulation and an air-vapour barrier. However, exterior insulation is not always possible because of lot lines or aesthetic considerations.

Exterior insulating techniques are fast, efficient and relatively inexpensive. The only tricky part comes when fitting the new air-vapour barrier and siding into the existing windows and doors. The "How-To" section provides the details.

The roof can be re-insulated in the same manner. First a continuous vapour barrier is installed over the existing roof. Next a new layer of joists is installed, insulated and new roofing put on. If the whole house is retrofitted in this way, a continuous air-vapour barrier and continuous insulation can be wrapped around the entire house.

The basement can be insulated from the exterior by digging a trench next to the house. Styrofoam (extruded polystyrene) is placed next to the foundation and laid horizontally (tilted down slightly away from the house to allow for drainage). Back filling holds the insulation in place.

Advantages and disadvantages of exterior super-insulation retrofits

Advantages
— Exterior insulation allows for a complete and continuous air-vapour barrier and insulation around the house. It bypasses problems created by wall and floor partitions.

— It is a relatively easy job which creates a minimum of disruption within the house. It does not remove any interior living space from use.
— Insulating on the exterior of masonry and brick houses increases the mass within the house, making it more suitable for utilizing passive solar energy.
— Its best application is in situations where re-siding is desirable or necessary, since much of the cost can be borne by the re-siding. The added cost of a curtain wall and insulation is minor.

Disadvantages
— Exterior insulation is not appropriate if you want to maintain the exterior face of the building.
— In stone or brick houses it changes the look and the texture quite radically.
— It is sometimes difficult to add the 6 to 8 inches of thickness to the wall, as it can interfere with lot lines or other uses of the space next to the house.

Interior Insulation

Insulation and air-vapour barrier can be installed from the interior. Generally this involves removing the existing dry wall or plaster and building a new wall. This new wall can consist of either horizontal and then vertical strapping, or a vertical stud wall hanging a few inches out from the old wall. Fibreglass batts fill the space. Then a continuous air vapour barrier is put in place. The wall can be built out to any dimension, achieving insulating values of R-20 and greater.

If space is a consideration, a high density insulating material can be used which will give the same insulation property as fibreglass, but use only half the space. Of course, it will cost more for the materials.

Variations on interior insulation include fastening insulation directly on the old plaster and applying a new drywall layer over the insulation and air-vapour barrier.

Generally it is better to remove the old plaster. You then expose areas which otherwise may be difficult to seal and insulate, such as behind window and door trim. Basements can also be built up from the inside. This is especially convenient if you have an unfinished basement.

Attics are usually easy to seal and re-insulate, although cathedral ceilings present difficulties.

Advantages and disadvantages of interior super-insulation retrofits

Advantages
— Interior insulation is best used when exterior insulation is not practical because of aesthetic or exterior space considerations.
— It is very appropriate when major interior renovations are already planned.
— Adding extra insulation when the walls are already exposed is a simple and inexpensive task.

Disadvantages
— Interior insulation can not always achieve a continuous air and insulation barrier due to problems posed where the wall partitions and floors meet the wall.
— The vapour barrier is penetrated by electric wiring and plumbing.
— If no interior renovation is planned, then interior insulation can be a messy and costly job.

Those hundreds of small air leaks in your house account for between 30 and 40 per cent of the heat loss of a house. These leaks can occur wherever different materials meet and wherever you put a hole in the house.

Air naturally flows in and out of these holes, powered by various causes. The wind creates variations of pressure on the house: a higher pressure on the windward side and a lower pressure in the wind's shadow. This works like a bellows — sucking in and blowing out air. There is also the stack effect which brings air into the lower portions of the house and expels it in the upper regions. It is caused by temperature differences inside and out. In the winter the heated house air wants to rise up and out.

Even without the forces of wind and the stack effect, the air inside wants out, and the outside air wants in due to gaseous diffusion.

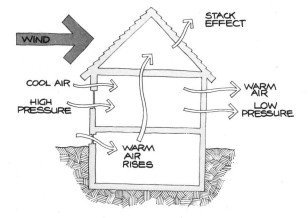

Typical sources of air infiltration include:

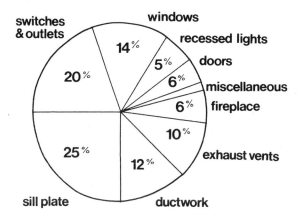

Installing a tight, secure air barrier is essential. Just adding the insulation will not substantially reduce infiltration. (Stuffing a hole with fibreglass won't necessarily reduce air leakage either. That same material is used in furnaces as an air filter. At best you'd get cleaner air leaking into the house.) With a decreased overall consumption, infiltration could account for up to 60 per cent of your new fuel bill.

Traditionally, the vapour barrier prevents water vapour from penetrating the insulation. When it hits the "dew point" the vapour condenses into water droplets or, if it is cold enough, into ice. This is because cold air holds less moisture than warm air. As the temperature drops the relative humidity, the per cent of possible moisture at a given temperature, increases until it reaches 100 per cent. This is the dew point. The vapour barrier must be placed such that the dew point is on the outside.

This has traditionally been interpreted that the vapour barrier is on the warm side of

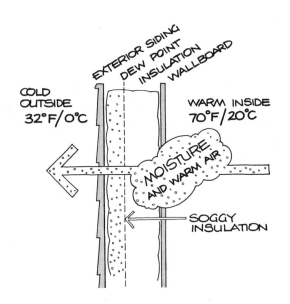

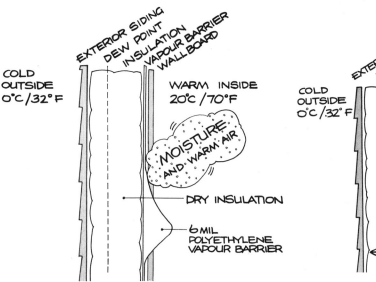

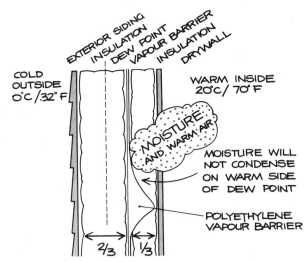

the insulation. It is possible, however, to place the vapour barrier within the insulation. As long as at least twice the insulation value is on the cold side of the vapour barrier, and one third or less is on the warm side, the dew point will exist outside of the vapour barrier. This 2/3 to 1/3 rule allows the vapour barrier to be protected within the wall.

Care must be taken when re-insulating a wall that this rule is maintained. If your wall has an existing vapour barrier you should never add more than one-half the walls insulation value on the interior unless you first remove or destroy the old barrier.

Similarly, exterior retrofits should have at least twice the insulation value added outside the vapour barrier than exists inside. If your old wall has R-10 (without a vapour barrier) and you want to add an

exterior 6 mil polyethylene barrier and exterior insulation, the exterior insulation must be at least R-20.

The super-retrofit requires a continuous air-vapour barrier. Vapour is prevented from entering the walls by a non-permeable material. Six mil polyethylene is recommended or, if it cannot be applied, a vapour-barrier paint. Air is prevented from flowing in or out by the vapour barrier and the liberal application of weatherstripping and caulking. The house should be considered as a hot air balloon, or an upside down boat. No leaks should be tolerated.

Fine-tuning

Before adding insulation, identify and seal all air leaks. This is best accomplished through the "flutter test". A suspended

tissue or candle flame or smoke from incense or a cigarette will flutter, revealing air leaks. Do this on a cold winter's day. Testing a wall when the wind is blowing directly on it will give best results.

Caulking: Use a quality caulking compound that will stay flexible over time. Silicone is best, but expensive. A butyl rubber is also a good choice. Caulking should be done on the inside of the house to prevent moisture from becoming trapped in the walls. Outside caulking should be done wherever water may enter the wall.

Weatherstripping: If the joint moves, weatherstrip it. This means all windows and doors. Also milk chutes, cat doors, attic hatches, etc.

Chimneys and vents: Use two metal chimney firestops to seal chimneys. A muffler cement can be used to seal the chimney to the firestop.

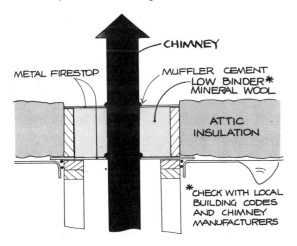

Recessed Lights: They cannot be well sealed or insulated due to the fire hazard they pose. They are best replaced with surface mounted lights which can be sealed and insulated.

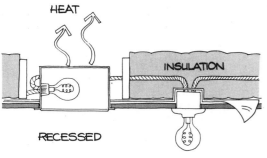

Fireplaces: If you have a fireplace ensure that the damper seals well and is used. Adding glass doors and outside combustion air also reduces the amount of air lost up the chimney. Sealing off the fireplace is the most efficient solution. An air-tight stove can be added connected to the flue.

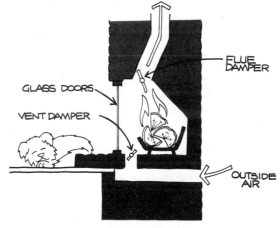

Sill Plate: If the sill plate (where the foundation meets the walls) is accessible, it should be caulked at all seams. Another method is to fit styrofoam pieces between the joists and caulk around the edges.

The Super-Retrofit

During the super-retrofit an air-vapour barrier is put in place. This usually consists of a continuous, overlapped and caulked 6 mil polyethylene sheet. By wrapping the entire house in plastic uncontrolled air change is kept to a minimum. Some of the characteristics of a well installed air-vapour barrier include:
— continuous between floors and around partitions wherever possible.

— continuous bead of caulking (non-hardening such as acoustical sealant) between sheets overlapped on top of a stud for support.
— tied-in and caulked to window and door frames, as well as any holes for vents, chimneys, etc.
— some means of maintaining continuity around electrical boxes, wires, plumbing and other potential holes.
— minimum number of holes and tears.

The furnace and the hot water heater can be placed in a separate air-tight room fed by outside combustion air through a 5 or 6 inch vent. The room is sealed and insulated from the rest of the house. Having two-thirds of the insulation on the outside wall and one third on the inner wall will prevent pipes from freezing. All water pipes and hot air ducts should be insulated within the furnace room.

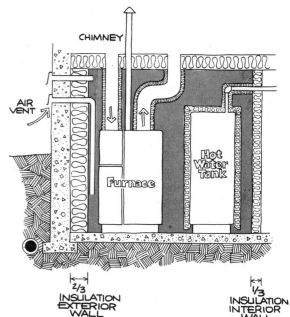

Air Quality

If you have done a good job of sealing the house and reducing air infiltration, your house will now be too tight. It may be so tight that you will have to induce ventilation. This is a good position to be in because controlled ventilation is preferable to uncontrolled ventilation.

A conventional house will have an air-change rate (the rate at which the entire volume of air in a house is replaced) of about one change every two hours (.5 ac/hr). Sealing a house well may reduce this rate to as low as one change every 10 hours (.1 ac/hr). By comparison, some new houses are being built with an air change rate as low as 1 air change every few days. Air quality suffers at such low air change rates.

Potential problems of poor ventilation include accumulation of contaminants from household products; pollution from smokers, gas stoves and furnaces; accumulation of radon gas emitted by some construction materials; build-up of lingering odours; depletion of oxygen in extreme cases, such as a smoldering fire that feeds on the oxygen supply. The most serious problems are caused by excessive humidity.

Most potential air quality problems disappear when the air change rate is .2 ac/hr and greater. However, humidity control requires an air change rate of .3 or more.

Humidity is increased due to people breathing, cooking, washing and cleaning, and because of plants and damp materials. Altogether a typical household will introduce 25 pounds of water vapour into the home every day.

Humidity is kept down (often quite low) by a high air change rate that lets in cool and dry air. However, when air change is minimized, humidity starts to build. The first sign is usually excessive frost build-up on double-glazed windows during the winter. If this moisture penetrates the walls, due to an inadequate air-vapour barrier, the resulting condensation can eventually lead to dry rot in the framing and settling of insulation. The following chart gives the ideal humidity levels indoors at different outdoor temperatures.

Outdoor Temperature		Maximum Humidity Level	Desirable Humidity Level
°C	°F	%	%
-35	-31	20	15
-29	-20.2	25	20
-23	-9.4	30	25
-18	0	35	30
-12	10.4	40	40
-7	19.4	45	40
-1	30.2	50	40

Humidity levels are a good indicator of how tight your house is. If the levels exceed those recommended, you must take appropriate action. The first thing to look for is whether you are producing excessive humidity. You can not do much about people breathing, but over zealous washing and cleaning, or a damp basement may be the culprit. Also make sure that your old humidifier attachment on the furnace is disconnected. You will no longer need it.

Source	Amount
Cooking	2.2 lb/day
Washing Dishes	1.1 lb/day
Washing Clothes	4.4 lb/week
Drying Clothes (in home)	26.4 lb/week
Bathing — showers	0.4 lb each
— baths	0.1 lb each
People	2.8 lb/person
Plants	1.1 lb/plant/week

Sources of Moisture in the Home

Sometimes spot ventilation, such as a slightly opened window in the bathroom while showering, will reduce humidity. Dehumidifiers are not effective at reducing humidity to the necessary levels.

In some cases a necessary technique is to leave two windows open a crack — one upstairs and the other downstairs. This method is not very desirable since you relinquish control over the heat loss. Another technique calls for installing a vent from the outside to your basement or return air plenum, with an operable damper. The vent allows outside air to enter and the damper can be adjusted so it is just slightly more open than the point at which humidity builds up on the windows on a cold day.

By far the best technique, the one that gives you the most control and the least heat loss, is an air-to-air heat exchanger. This device exhausts stale, humid indoor air to the outside, at the same time bringing in fresh, outdoor air. The two streams of air run past each other, divided by a (usually) thin plastic membrane that allows the heat to transfer from the outgoing air to the incoming air. In this way fresh, indoor air can be maintained without the associated heat loss. Air exchangers must have a drain incorporated to deal with the moisture that condenses and have an anti-freeze mechanism for use in cold climates. Systems typically operate at 80 to 100 cubic feet per minute of air flow. They can be set for continual running or to operate from a humidistat.

You can build your own air exchanger (see bibliography) or have it commercially made and installed. The cost runs from $250 to $1000. If your house is tight enough to require an air-to-air heat exchanger (generally .3 changes per hour or less), they represent a good investment for energy savings, as well as an improved environment for the health of both you and your house.

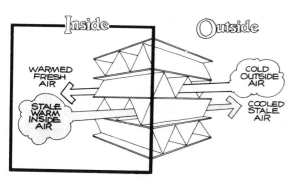

Windows provide natural lighting and a view of the world. In terms of energy, they act as both heat gainers and heat losers. The goal is to maximize the heat gain throughout the heating season while minimizing heat loss.

Minimize Losses

A double-paned window will have an insulating value of up to R-1.8. Compared to a wall's insulating value of R-12 to R-40 windows can represent a significant heat loss. They also contribute to discomfort due to radiant heat loss. They lose heat through direct conduction, radiation and infiltration around poorly sealed panes and frames.

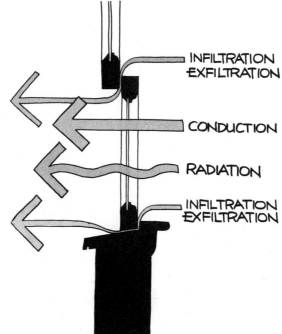

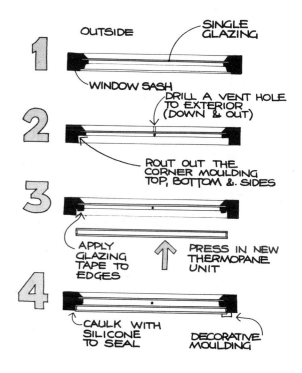

Options to decrease heat loss include:
— Make windows more air-tight. Sealed units (with separate ventilators) are best. Casement and awning windows are the second choice and should be well weatherstripped (a vinyl V works well). Sliding and double-hung windows are more difficult to seal.
— Make windows double or preferably triple-glazed. This way they lose less heat. They can either replace old units or be added to existing windows. Route out a grove to fit the units on the inside of single-pane windows. Weep holes should go from between the old and new panes to the outside. Seasonal glazing can be added by using storms or securing plastic on the outside or inside.

— Have smaller and fewer windows. Decrease the window area of your house, especially the ones to the north, west and east (in that order). Windows facing these directions can be removed either permanently or seasonally. Semi-permanent insulated shutters can be secured over windows that are rarely used for their light or view in the winter. Windows in storage rooms, basements or spare bedrooms may fall into this category.

— Provide movable insulation for all windows. Insulating shutters and shades can substantially reduce heat loss. Movable insulation should be:
• insulated to at least R-5
• sealed, to prevent air convection around the insulation
• reflective, to reduce radiant heat loss
• non-permeable, to prevent water vapour passing through to condense on the cold window.

Movable insulation should also be easy to handle, store, operate and look attractive. It can be installed indoors or outdoors, although inside is preferable as it offers ease of access and protection from weathering. Storage, however, can sometimes be a problem. Movable insulation can be made as shades, curtains or shutters. Shades and curtains generally present problems because it is difficult to seal the edges and obtain high R values, although some commercial units perform well.

Insulating shutters are the most effective and easiest to make. A light-weight rigid insulating board (such as Thermax) can be framed and covered with a designer fabric. Magnetic strips, Velcro or tabs can secure the shutter on to the window frame. It can be stored on the wall next to the window when not in use.

Maximize Gains

All houses receive passive solar heating through the windows. The object is to maximize the gain during the heating season but prevent overheating problems.

Insulating Shutter

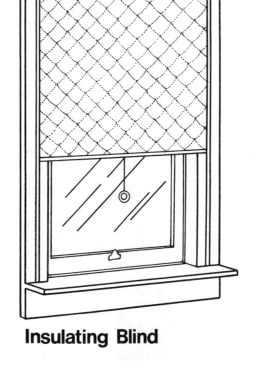

Insulating Blind

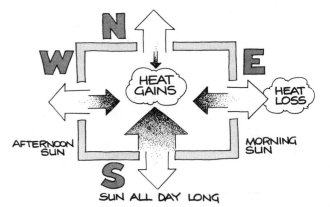

South is the optimum direction for windows to gather heat. Moving one square foot of window from the north to south side of the house saves a gallon of fuel oil a year. As you move east of south you pick up less total heat, but more is collected in the morning when houses need it most. As you move west of south the heat is concentrated in the afternoon, a situation that can lead to overheating problems. Variations of ± 30 degrees from due south have virtually no impact.

Windows are effective heating sources if used properly. The low winter sun can stream through windows (reflection off snow enhances this collection). During the summer the higher sun misses much of the window. In fact, a south-facing window will receive only half as much sunlight in July as in January! The summer sun can be reduced further by the use of overhangs, shades, trellis work or deciduous trees.

A typical frame house that has been super-retrofitted can accommodate a southern window area equivalent to about 6 or 7 per cent of the floor area. A greater window area will lead to overheating problems unless additional thermal mass is added to soak-up and store the excess heat.

Most existing houses require that over 80 per cent of their heating needs come from non-renewable energy sources; generally gas, oil or electricity. The remaining few per cent come from internally generated heat and unintentionally trapped solar energy. A super-insulated retrofit can reduce the total fuel demand by 70 to 90 per cent. The following is a list of traditional heat supply sources.

Internal Gain

A typical family produces over 25 kilowatt-hours of heat energy per day. Appliances such as the dryer, refrigerator, and water heater account for the largest percentage. Cooking, lights and people (who generate about 100 watts each) provide much of the rest. Because this heat energy will become a major heat source, activities should be modified to suit the season or time of day.

Solar Heat

Passive solar energy gains, most notably direct sunlight through south-facing windows, can become a major factor in space heating. Double-glazed, south-facing windows, if unshaded, provide a net heat gain through the heating season. If they are protected with night-time insulation their benefits are that much greater. North-facing windows are, of course, the main agents of heat loss. East windows help to heat the house during the morning; west windows during the afternoon.

Because of the greatly reduced heating demand of a super-insulated retrofit, windows have a much greater effect. While windows can contribute a large portion of the heat requirements, they can easily lead to excessive heat loss and overheating. If south-facing windows amount to more than the equivalent of 6 or 7 per cent of your heated floor area, you may either have to provide some shading or add additional mass to your house to store and use the passive solar heat. Concrete and tiled floors, masonry walls, double drywall and fireplaces will contribute additional mass to your house.

Furnaces

The furnace in most homes is oversized. It spends too much time turning on and off, even on cold days. This means it rarely achieves its top burning efficiency. A typical oil or gas furnace runs at a seasonal efficiency of only 50 to 65 per cent.

Once you have reduced the heat load substantially because of the super-insulated retrofit, the existing furnace should be upgraded or replaced.

Oil furnaces can be installed with a smaller burning nozzle, but the achievable size reduction is marginal. Replacement is often the best move. Not only will your new

furnace be sized more correctly, but you can buy a furnace with many of the energy-conservation features that are available today. The only difficulty in replacing your furnace may be finding one that is small enough for your new energy-efficient house.

Gas Furnaces

These are available with electronic ignition (no wasteful pilot light) and automatic flue dampers which reduce heat loss up the flue. Gas furnaces are now available with condensor heat exchanges. These do not require a chimney, only a plastic hose which exhausts warm air (113°F) out of the side of the house. They will operate at a seasonal efficiency of 90 to 95 per cent.

Oil Furnaces

These are now available with more efficient nozzles, electronic ignition and an automatic flue damper, all which improve the efficiency of the system.

Electric Heating

Electric baseboard heaters are often installed in low energy buildings. They offer zone control possibilities and lower capital costs. In addition fossil fuel furnaces are often not available in a small enough size. Electric furnaces are also used with a conventional forced hot air distribution system. However, electricity is, in most regions, an expensive method of space heating. (We also have a prejudice against electric space heating since its use reinforces the nuclear option by increasing the demand for electricity.)

Wood Stoves

Many low energy buildings receive much of the required back-up with an air-tight wood stove. The decision to heat with wood is based on the availability of wood

and lifestyle considerations. It may be necessary to provide outside combustion air for wood stoves. Traditional fireplaces, even with improved efficiency provided by outside combustion air and glass doors, are just too inefficient to be considered a viable space heating system.

Heat Pumps

This form of electric heating can also supply air-conditioning. Such a system is expensive and, in cold climates, a complete back-up (usually electric resistance) is necessary. Heat pumps are not recommended for low energy buildings.

Solar Heating

Certainly passive solar heating is valuable, provided potential overheating problems are dealt with. Active solar heating, with its associated collectors, storage and controls, is generally too expensive to be used as a back-up for a low energy house.

Domestic Hot Water Heaters

Some houses, both new and the super-retrofits, rely on the domestic hot water heater for space heating. The sizing and capacity of water heaters is adequate for heating a low energy house. Heat is extracted from the tanks on demand using either a fan-coil unit connected to an air-distribution system, or by using baseboard radiators. A solar hot water heater feeding into such a system makes sense since the unit would be small, relatively inexpensive and fully utilized throughout the year.

Appliances, both major and minor, can account for a major portion of your home's energy bill. The greatest user of energy (aside from the furnace) is your hot water tank. Hot water heating will account for 20 per cent of your total energy bill. In a super-insulated house hot water heating can use more energy than space heating! There are three approaches to reducing energy requirements for hot water:
1) reduce your hot water consumption,
2) reduce the heat loss of the system,
3) improve the efficiency of the operation.

Reducing Water Use

Minor changes in habits will go far in reducing hot water consumption. Don't run the hot tap unnecessarily. Use full loads for dishes and laundry. Use the light cycle and cooler water wherever possible. Shower

rather than bathe. There are a number of gadgets on the market that will make saving easier. The most common are the faucet aereators and water-saving shower-heads. A normal shower uses about 8 gallons of water a minute. A water-saving showerhead can reduce this to 2 gallons a minute while maintaining a skin-tingling shower. These devices cost between $15 and $20 and will pay for themselves within the year. It should be emphasized that no number of gadgets will conserve energy if you choose a wasteful lifestyle.

Reducing Heat Loss

Generally hot water systems are not designed with efficiency in mind. They usually have only 1 inch of insulation. The new "energy saving" tanks may have 2 inches! There are many low cost or zero

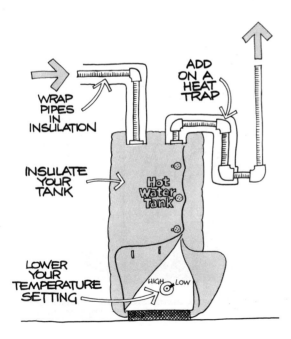

ADD ON A HEAT TRAP

WRAP PIPES IN INSULATION

INSULATE YOUR TANK

Hot Water Tank

LOWER YOUR TEMPERATURE SETTING

HIGH LOW

cost changes you can make that will reduce your fuel bill substantially.

Lower the thermostat: The typical tank is set high, around 150° F. This is too hot to use directly so you always mix it with cold water. This wastes water and the tank loses heat. Lower the temperature to a point where it is hot enough for normal use and you still have reserve capacity. One hundred and twenty degrees farenheit may be a good temperature. Lower temperatures will increase tank life. Automatic dishwashers generally require a higher temperature (140° F) to dissolve fats.

Increase the tank insulation: Add a blanket of fibreglass insulation to your existing tank. Prepared packages are available for under $30 that do an effective and neat job, but any insulation will do. Just be careful to leave junction boxes clear, as well as the air intake and the top of gas heaters.

Pipe insulation: Insulating your pipes will reduce heat loss and sweating problems in the summer. At least the first metre of the hot and cold pipes, where they join the tank, should be insulated. Insulating more of the pipes generally is not worth it unless you have heavy hot water use.

Heat trap: This is a U-shaped bend in the hot water pipe where it leaves the tank. It prevents hot water from convecting throughout the pipe and increasing heat loss.

Efficient Operation

Proper operation and maintenance of your water heating system will mean more efficient operation.

Servicing: Just like your gas space heater, a gas water heater should be serviced every two years. Every few months drain your tank from the bottom valve until the water runs clear. Fix dripping taps. A 7¢ washer, replaced, can save you over $20 a year.

Operation: If you are going to be away for a couple of days or more turn off your tank. Turn it on as soon as you get home and hot water will be ready for you by the time you are ready for it. If most of your hot water use is in the early morning (showers, washing, etc.) and in the evening (cooking, cleaning), then you may want to consider an automatic timer that will turn the heater on only as it is needed.

Preheat tank: You can install a preheat tank for your system. An uninsulated tank is placed next to your water heater. Mains water first enters the preheat tank, allowing the water to rise to room temperature before entering your water heater. For most of the year (especially in super-insulated houses) this will provide a net energy savings.

There are also methods for recycling the heat from your waste water. These systems are often too difficult and costly to retrofit.

Alternatives

There are many alternatives to the conventional gas or electric heaters available for heating hot water.

Wood Water Heaters: They are on the market and will provide a tankful of hot water after about 30 minutes. If a wood stove is part of your house heating system, there are a number of ways of adapting it for water heating. A copper coil in the fire box allows heated water to convect into a nearby tank, while various systems of transferring heat from the flue to the water are also available.

Instantaneous Heaters: Both gas and electric heaters are available. These devices heat the water only where and as you need it. They are especially appropriate if you have a bathroom that is far away from the water heater, or if you have an alternate source of heating, such as wood or solar, that may require topping up.

Solar Water Heating: This can supply 50 to 70 per cent of your hot water needs. You require suitable space (around 100 square feet) that has access to the sun throughout most of the year, and faces south (± 30°). The collectors should be at an angle equal to your latitude. There are a great many approaches to the design and installation of solar heating systems. The bibliography lists good books on the subject.

Other Appliances

The efficient use of other major and minor appliances relies a great deal on the homeowner's common sense. Don't leave appliances on when they are not being used. Don't use them unnecessarily. When you do use them, use them to their capacity.

The greatest savings can occur when you buy a new appliance (or decide that you don't really need another gizzmo). In Canada many major appliances come with an *EnerGuide* energy rating, usually expressed in kilowatt hours consumption per month. Compare ratings before you

buy. Energy is still the hidden cost. What you pay in energy costs can be many times more than the original purchase price.

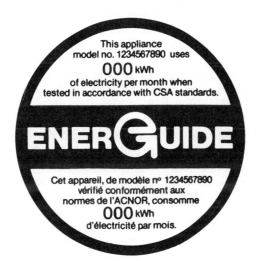

It is not enough to have extreme levels of insulation and an air-tight vapour barrier if you leave windows and doors ajar all the time or set your temperature at 75° F. You have to understand how your house works and how your activities affect it. Great lifestyle changes aren't necessary to live in a super-insulated house, but sensitivity to the house and how it functions is an integral aspect of a successful project. A study was made of the heating requirements of several identical passive solar heated homes. The back-up energy required varied by as much as 10 times from one unit to another. Some of the occupants were indifferent to the workings of the building; they would leave windows and doors open, wouldn't use the insulated shutters at night and they kept the thermostat high all day and night. This last habit rendered solar heat absorbed by the thermal mass within the house insignificant, as it couldn't be released at night since the furnace kept the room at a high temperature. This nullified much of the benefit of passive solar heating and thermal storage. On the other hand, some of the units were occupied by energy conscious homeowners.

They turned down the thermostat at night and used the insulating shutters. In the early morning they put on sweaters until the sun heated the rooms rather than turn the thermostat up immediately. They were aware that the air-lock entrance works only when one door is closed all the time. These small habits added up to 90 per cent savings in the auxiliary fuel they required over the winter.

There are many books on the market which detail the one hundred and one tips and habits that will reduce your energy requirements for space heating, water heating and electricity. Here are some of the common suggestions.

Appliances: Run appliances only as they are needed. (The "off" switch is a great energy saver.) Machines (washers, dryers, etc.) should be run as full as possible and not used for only a few items. Washing machines can also be run in a "cool" mode which saves hot water costs.

Lights: Again, the "off" switch is a great energy saver. Task lighting, using the light where you need it, at the table, over the counter, etc., is efficient. Florescent lighting (the tubes) is much more efficient than incandescent lighting (the bulbs) and should be used wherever the quality of light (garage, laundry room) is not important. Use low wattage bulbs when possible, but remember that one high wattage bulb is more efficient than several of low wattage.

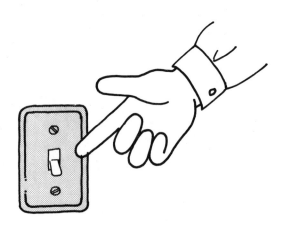

Hot Water: Hot water use can be reduced considerably with one or more of the water saving devices currently on the market. Flow-restricting showerheads allow a tingling-feeling shower but require one-quarter of the hot water used by regular showers.

Much wasted energy can be saved by insulating the hot water system. Insulate the tank with a batt of fibreglass (kits are available for this job). Do not cover the junction box or the air intake and the top on gas heaters. You can insulate the hot water pipe, or better yet, install a heat trap. This is a U-shaped configuration where the hot water pipe leaves the tank. Energy is prevented from convecting away. Turning the tank thermostat down will also save money as well as increase the tank's life. They are always turned too high. Turn it as low as you are comfortable with. Houses having a dishwasher require higher water temperatures (140° F) for safe and efficient operation.

Heating System: Your furnace will work more efficiently if it is kept in shape. Clean (vacuum) or replace the filters in forced-air systems at least once a month. The whole furnace should be tuned and the efficiency determined by a service representative once a year for oil furnaces and once every two or three years for gas furnaces.

Any duct work through unheated space should have all the joists sealed with duct tape and be insulated.

The operation of the thermostat is critical. If your house has a passive solar heating system it will work best if you allow the temperature to rise a little in the daytime

and fall somewhat at night. This lets the thermal storage mode work to its advantage. Even without a passive heating element, your house will operate more efficiently if you turn the thermostat down at night or when you are away.

Windows: Whether part of a passive system or not, they will perform better if they are insulated at night. South window curtains or shades should be open during the winter's day and closed at night. Reverse this order in the summer to keep the house cool. Other windows should be insulated at night or whenever they are not being used for the view or light.

Other Holes: Your house is full of many small holes and these should be plugged, sealed, weatherstripped or caulked. The dampers in vents should close with a good seal as should cat doors. Milk chutes and attic hatches should either be removed (or relocated on the outside if necessary) or weatherstripped and insulated. Fireplaces should have a good damper. An insulated plug that is fitted into the opening can reduce both the heat and air that escapes the house.

Maintenance

When you understand how your house performs as an energy-efficient system and how your lifestyle affects its operation, you should become aware of the regular maintenance your house requires. The parts of any system, whether a car or a house, tend to wear over time. A regular maintenance schedule will help identify and solve potential problems before they seriously affect the structure or efficiency of your house. The following list indicates

some of the regular checks you should perform.

Windows and Doors: At least once a year check the weatherstripping for wear along windows and doors, including the door threshold. Check the caulking to ensure it has not cracked or shrunk. Install storm windows and doors in the fall, as well as any window awnings. Keep the glass clean.

Walls: exterior: Repair cracks or loose joints where water may penetrate. Check vents for smooth, tight operation, as well as the condition of the caulking. *interior:* Check for air leaks around vents, baseboards, electrical outlets, doors and window trim.

Roof: Check flashing around chimney and vents.

Ceilings and Attics: Check on the condition of the insulation for tight fit and any signs of moisture damage or settling. Ensure that the vents are not blocked.

Crawl Space or Unheated Basement: Close vents to the crawl space in the fall. Open them in the spring. Check for dampness and the condition of exposed wood. Check taping and insulation on any heating ducts. Check condition of insulation on floor.

Furnace: Clean or replace filters and oil the fan motors. Continue furnace service schedule.

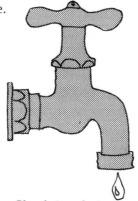

Hot Water: Check insulation around tank and pipes. Fix dripping taps (usually a 7¢ washer). Drain the tank until the water runs clear to remove sediments.

Vacations: Turn off hot water tank. Turn down the house furnace (high enough to ensure pipes will not freeze). Unplug any power-drawing appliances.

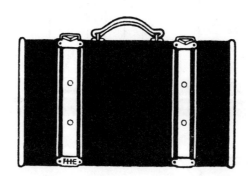

All our houses use energy from the sun to some extent. All light that enters the house contributes to heat gain (though windows, compared to walls, are great heat losers). In almost all homes the loss is greater than the gains.

Solar retrofitting increases the solar gains to the house while minimizing the heat loss. There are many methods of achieving this, all of which rely on understanding the sun and its seasonal cycles.

In the winter, at northern latitudes, the sun rises in the south-east to a high point of only 12 to 25° above the southern horizon, and sets in the south-west. The higher your latitude the smaller and lower the arc the sun makes.

SOUTH

In the spring and fall the arc widens until the sun rises due east (the equinox) and sets due west. During the summer the arc is very large. The sun rises in the north-east, moves around to the south at a high angle (65 to 75° above the horizon) and sets in the north-west.

These movements of the sun affect both the tilt and orientation of the solar devices you install. In northern climates a vertical (90°) surface, such as windows and walls, serves as an ideal collector. It will collect light from the low winter sun when it is needed,

but will avoid much of the higher summer sun. In fact, a south-facing vertical surface at northern latitudes (say 45°) will receive twice as much sunlight during February as in July!

As you tilt back the surface, you increase the sunlight received during the rest of the year. Generally, tilted passive solar heating devices are to be avoided as they may lead to excessive overheating. The primary exception is the greenhouse. This is due to its light requirements throughout the year.

Orientation

A surface which is oriented due south will generally receive the maximum amount of energy. Precision is not required since variations as large as 30° east or west of south will not seriously affect performance. The ideal orientation varies from site to site. If there is a large building that blocks the morning sun, then an orientation west of south is desired. For passive solar systems, an orientation east of south is generally preferred. This allows the room or greenhouse to receive early morning light at a time when heat is most required. It also avoids too much afternoon light which can often result in uncomfortable overheating.

If your house orientation is already fixed, much of this discussion is not relevant.

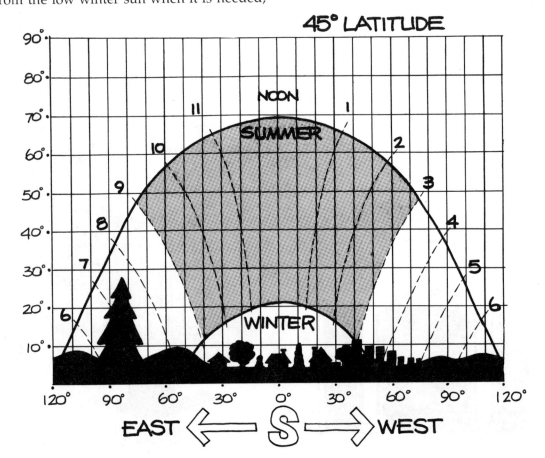

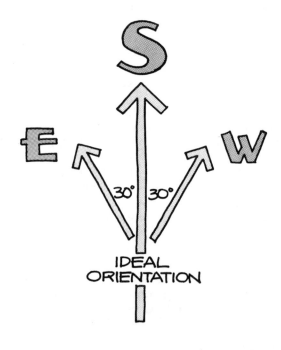

IDEAL ORIENTATION

Mass

When employing passive solar heating you must provide enough thermal mass within the house. Thermal mass absorbs and stores heat. This helps to prevent over-heating and allows the house to remain warm overnight.

Ideally sunlight hits the mass, turns to heat and is soaked up by the system. The temperature of the room neither rises too fast nor too far. At night, as the room starts to cool, the mass gives up the stored heat. These slow temperature swings, a slight rise in the day followed by a slight fall at night, are a natural part of any passive solar system. The trick is to have enough

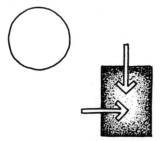

THERMAL MASS ABSORBS HEAT DURING THE DAY. KEEPS TEMPERATURE DOWN

THERMAL MASS RELEASES HEAT DURING THE NIGHT. KEEPS TEMPERATURE UP

mass (or a small enough glass area) to prevent the large temperature swings that make the house uncomfortable.

Mass is found everywhere; in the wood structures of the house, in the drywall, furniture, concrete floors or blocks, bricks and tile. A super-insulated frame house normally contains enough thermal mass to handle the solar energy collected by a south window area equal to about six or seven per cent of the house's floor area. Larger glass areas require additional thermal mass. This mass can be situated in the living space or located in an isolated storage. A simple fan/duct system can blow heated air into the storage.

Air Circulation

You may find that your new energy-efficient house has different air circulation characteristics. There tends to be less circulation and mixing. This is because circulation induced by infiltration has been substantially reduced. Also temperature differentials are decreased because of warmer walls and window area. The convective circulation caused by the temperature differences no longer operate.

When you introduce passive solar energy into a house with reduced air circulation you can get hot spots. An open concept floor plan helps to reduce them as the air and heat naturally circulates. However, if your house consists of a number of closed rooms you will have to induce circulation. The most common solution is using the air circulation of your forced-air heating system. Many systems have the fan running continuously on low speed, moving to high speed when the furnace

turns on. Return air vents located at high points of the house will reduce hot points and make more efficient use of collected solar energy.

Overheating

Ensuring that there is enough thermal mass is only one measure to prevent overheating. Too many homeowners have built half a solar house — there is no provision for solar control. The result can be as disastrous as the second story of a house reaching 120°F during the winter!

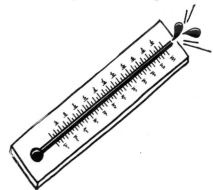

Some mechanism for rejecting the sun is important.

Shading is one such mechanism of solar control. Deciduous trees are often used since the leaves block the summer sun, while the bare branches let through the winter light. The problem with using trees is that often even the bare branches can block 50 per cent or more of the winter sun.

Awnings that can be seasonally adjusted are another control mechanism.

Fixed overhangs will also work, except that the sun cycle and the heating cycle do not occur simultaneously.

Shades, curtains and shutters can be used to repel the sun when it is not desired. If made correctly (insulated, sealed at the edges and impermeable to water vapour), shades and shutters will insulate during winter nights as well as reject the sun during summer days.

Ventilation is another mechanism of solar control. Venting high on the south side and low on the north will draw in cooler air and exhaust the rising heated air.

Avoiding windows that face west helps to prevent overheating. Even overhangs are ineffective for the low western sun.

Finally, do not allow too much glazing in the first place. It may be tempting to make the whole south face one big solar collector, but this can result in a very uncomfortable place to live.

The Retrofit

Windows provide an excellent source of view, light and heat. Be sure to take maximum advantage of south-facing windows. The section on windows documents this in detail. There are two other major approaches to passive solar heating; mass walls and attached greenhouses.

Mass Wall

Sometimes called a *Trombe Wall*, the mass wall is an isolated passive solar heating system. The heat collection and storage is isolated from the living space. Sunlight passes through glazing, strikes a brick or concrete wall and turns into heat energy. The heat is trapped by the glass. Some of the heat energy heats the space between the wall and the glass but most of it is absorbed by the wall itself.

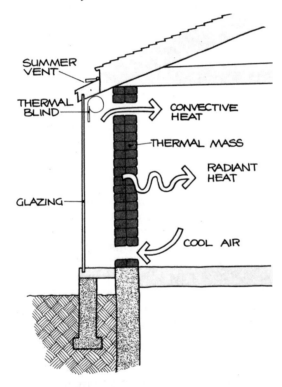

Heat enters the house by one of two mechanisms. The majority passes slowly through the wall (in 8 hours) and radiates into the room. Because of the time-lag involved, this is usually in the evening. Some of the heat can enter the house by convection. If vents or windows are opened to the house at the top and bottom of the wall, the heated air will circulate into the house through the top opening. Cooler house air enters the bottom opening. The advantage of a mass wall, instead of windows for passive solar heating, is that it takes advantage of the built-in storage capacity of the brick or concrete. The heat energy comes slowly into the house through the wall, preventing large temperature swings. The wall also acts as a sound or sight buffer if you do not want a large window area to the south.

Mass walls are appropriate for brick or masonry houses with a large exposed southern face. A glazing system is erected over the wall. Often a gap of about 18 inches is left between the glass and the wall to allow a passage for cleaning.

In most climates erecting a mass wall is a better option than re-insulation. If designed properly the mass wall will add net heat to the house. One of the key aspects of a properly designed mass wall is providing for night-time insulation, generally within the cavity. The mass wall on Ecology House in Toronto (see Survey) was erected on a ledge built on concrete foundation piles. The framing was built on the ground (to fit thermopane "seconds") then lifted into place and attached to a ledger plate at the top. The glazing was held on by glazier's tape. The cavity in the wall was made air-tight and insulated at the ends. Windows on the two stories provide vent openings. Large diameter ducts (24 inches) provide summer-time exhaust.

Labels on diagram: SUMMER VENT, THERMAL BLIND, GLAZING, CONVECTIVE HEAT, THERMAL MASS, RADIANT HEAT, COOL AIR

The Solar Greenhouse

One of the most attractive options for the solar retrofit of an existing building involves the addition of an attached solar greenhouse. As well as providing heat to the home, it can be a source of year-round food production. It will also add considerably to the market value of a home. To ensure that the attached greenhouse does not constitute a drain on the fuel bill, several design criteria must be followed.

Orientation

To maximize the amount of sunshine entering the attached structure, the greenhouse should be oriented within 20° of due south. While ideally the structure is attached to the south-facing side of the house, several effective structures have been attached to the east or west face of a building. In this case the-best-of-all-possible orientations was not permitted because of shading or local zoning restrictions. By orienting the greenhouse structure to the south, solar gains are maximized during the winter months and minimized during the summer.

Slope

The slope of the south-facing glazing is also an important function of energy-efficient design. To maximize solar gains in the winter months the glass should be at a vertical tilt, thus gaining both direct sunshine from the low winter sun and reflected sunshine off the snow cover prevalent in most northern locales. However, the vertical glazing will provide inadequate light levels for the greenhouse

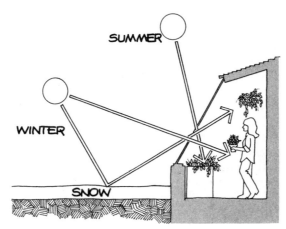

during the remainder of the year. The photosynthetic process — the lifestream of plant growth — depends upon significant quantities of light. To provide this requirement the glazing should be installed at a low angle; witness commercial greenhouse design. We must look at some form of compromise between the desired slope for heating and growing requirements. This compromise will result in the glazing being titled at an angle between 45° and 55° from the horizontal.

Thermal Mass

A well designed solar greenhouse minimizes the severe temperature fluctuations which can occur in a poorly designed structure. By storing the large amounts of solar energy entering the greenhouse during the day, the daily temperatures can be kept to an acceptable level. When the stored heat is released to the greenhouse at night the interior temperature should be adequate enough to ensure healthy plant growth. The attached solar greenhouse must incorporate sufficient quantities of heat storing

materials into the design to serve this dual role. Materials such as water, cement, rocks and bricks will all absorb heat during the day and re-radiate it at night. The more mass integrated into the structure, the greater the ability to keep the temperatures cool during the day and warm at night. Without adequate thermal mass temperatures on a sunny January might range from 110°F at noon to 20°F at night — not ideal for plant growth.

Insulation

A prime criteria for the design of a successful solar greenhouse demands that the thermal envelope of the structure minimize the flow of heat from the interior

RIGID INSULATION

space to the outside. Not only should the walls and ceiling of the greenhouse be insulated to the highest possible levels, but the glass itself should prevent the flow of heat. Double-glazing is a fundamental component in the design of a solar greenhouse, and the structure should be equipped with movable insulation to reduce the losses through the glass at night.

Air Movement

If properly designed the attached solar greenhouse should be able to provide heat to the house throughout the year. Provision should be made for allowing the heated air to enter the home, either through a convection loop or with a fan located at the peak of the structure (to blow heated air into the house). The convective loop can be designed to draw cool air from the house into the greenhouse at its lower level, and then exhaust warmed air into the house through a vent situated at the top of the attached wall.

It is equally important to provide access for heated air to escape from the greenhouse when cooling is required. Vents should be located at the peak of the structure to allow the heated air to be exhausted to the exterior. Similarly, access should be provided for cool air to enter the structure at its lower extremities. A properly designed solar greenhouse should be able to act as both a heating supplement to the house and a source of cooling during the warmer months.

Size

The size of the greenhouse will, in most cases, be dictated by the existing structure and by the amount of money the homeowner wishes to spend. Whereas there is no real limitation to the length of the attached solar greenhouse, the width of the greenhouse should be limited to no more than 12 feet. If the structure is designed to be significantly wider, solar gains to the back of the structure will be severely limited, except in the dead of winter.

Costs

One of the joys of the solar greenhouse is that it can be constructed to meet almost any budget. Costs for a small 10 foot by 12 foot structure can range from $600 for a cheap structure using polyethylene as the glazing, to upwards of $3,000 for a durable structure built with cedar and employing double-glazed thermopane units. Costs for a greenhouse built by a contractor or prefabricated by a commercial manufacturer range from $1,500 to $15,000.

Not every homeowner will be inclined to perform the extensive job of the super-insulated retrofit. Unfortunately, by carrying out a band-aid approach now, the likelihood of re-doing the work in the future is severely minimized — "something is better than nothing". A host of books detailing re-insulation techniques are available on the market. We have chosen to focus our attention on the homeowner seeking substantial fuel savings — up to 80 or 90 per cent. However, a brief summary of half way measures is useful as a counterpoint to the more thorough job. The following measures should be viewed as little more than partial solutions to rising fuel prices.

Sealing the House

The major source of heat loss in an existing home is attributable to the infiltration of cold outside air and the exfiltration of warm house air. The sources of air leakage in the average house, if totalled, would amount to a hole in the building's structure of up to 4 square feet. Many of these leaks can be plugged through the judicious application of either caulking or weather-stripping. By recalling the major sources of infiltration in the home, you will know where the emphasis should be placed.

Sill Plates: In most houses a substantial amount of air leakage occurs between the sill plate and the foundation wall. While in some instances the sill plate may have been well installed when the house was constructed, usually no attempt to properly seal the gap would have been made. In any event, the shifting and movement of the house over the years will cause a substantial gap. This gap in an unfinished basement can be filled with a foam caulk between the plate and the foundation wall.

Electric Outlets: Another major contributor to air leakage is the area around the different electrical outlets and switch plates installed in the exterior and, in some cases, interior walls of the home. These leakages can be minimized through the installation of foam gaskets placed between the cover plates and the existing wall. As the cover plate is screwed back into place the gasketing is compressed to seal the area around the electrical box.

Attic: There are many holes and cracks to be found in the attic. Carefully caulk around the holes for electrical wiring and seal around electrical boxes. Use a 6 mil poly sheet and caulking to seal around plumbing vents. Chimneys can be sealed by cutting two pieces of sheet metal to fit around the chimney. Caulk this to the chimney using a muffler or furnace cement. Do not place any insulation within two inches of the chimney.

Windows: Depending on the type and age of the windows in the home, a substantial amount of air leakage will occur around the frame and through any of the movable joints in the window casing. Remedial measures to be considered include the removal of the interior face trim, and the application of a bead of caulking between the rough frame and the window casing. The void may be substantial, and require the use of an expandable foam caulking material. The application of weather-stripping around the movable seams of the window will greatly reduce those cold drafts. A more detailed discussion of window treatment is included in the *Super-Retrofit* section.

Doors: In the same manner in which air leakage around windows can be minimized, caulking and weatherstripping can be beneficial when used around exterior doors.

Baseboards: Cold drafts flowing around the floor generally result from cracks in the building's structure where the wall plate sits on the subflooring. This source of leakage can be reduced by removing the baseboards on the exterior walls and applying a bead of caulking between the floor and the wallboard.

Vents and Ductwork: Heating ducts running through unheated areas of a home, and exhaust vents which enable the uncontrolled movement of air into and out of the house are both problem areas which can be resolved with a minimal amount of work. Exposed ductwork in unheated areas will leak air from the seams of the ducting. By applying a duct tape to these seams air leakage, and the subsequent heat loss, can be reduced. Exhaust vents, when operating, can provide the required ventilation to clear the house of cooking odours, bathroom odours and excessive buildups of humidity in specific areas. However, these vents also allow air into the home even when they are not operating as their seal is not tight. To remedy this problem, you should install weatherstripping around the edges of the damper to ensure a tighter seal when the vents are in their closed position.

Other Infiltration Sources: Several other areas in the house's structure contribute to excessive air changes within the home. A key weak spot in many homes is the fireplace which, although providing heat when stoked with a roaring fire, exhausts a great deal of house air up the chimney. Tight-fitting glass doors can be installed over the fireplace opening to reduce this flow of air, or an insulated and weather-stripped plug can be used to fill the opening at times when the fireplace is not in operation.

Recessed ceiling lights in the top floor of a house are another cause for concern. As building codes require that these fixtures be kept away from insulating materials or vapour barriers, they constitute the equivalent of little chimneys in the ceiling, allowing easy passage for heated air to the attic. The best possible solution involves removing these fixtures and replacing them with more conventional ceiling lighting. This permits you to patch what would otherwise be a major weak spot.

As a rule, and with a conscientious effort, you should be able to reduce the infiltration rate within an existing home by as much as 20 to 40 per cent through these remedial measures. All, however, can be accomplished in a more thorough manner through the installation of a continuous air-vapour barrier.

Upgrading Insulation Levels

Some improvements to insulation levels in existing houses can be accommodated without going to the extent of tearing down or constructing walls and ceilings. The obvious spot to add more insulation is to the attic, a job which can be performed easily in a short period of time without causing any mess to the house interior.

Although this has been the predominant technique to reduce fuel consumption, its popularity results from the relative simplicity of the task rather than from its cost effectiveness. Nevertheless, the insulation levels of the attic should be

upgraded to minimum of R-40 in most areas of Canada and the northern United States. A more detailed discussion of attic re-insulation follows.

Upgrading of the insulation levels in walls demands both more care and, as a rule, more money. Without going to the levels suggested for the super-insulated retrofit, and in order not to distrub the house interior, the options are limited. In those houses with non-insulated cavity walls, insulating materials can be blown into the cavities to improve the thermal envelope of the building. Alternatively, if you can tolerate a smattering of drywall dust for a few days, rigid sheets of polystyrene can be affixed directly over the existing walls and a new layer of drywall can be placed over the insulation. In both cases the cost of the job can be restrictive for the minimal insulation levels attained. Insulating basement walls that are uninsulated is always a worthwhile task.

As an alternative to the installation of a new polyethylene vapour barrier, you can apply two coats of a low permeance paint such a Insul-Aid or vinyl wallpaper. Both of these materials will restrict the flow of water vapour from the house to the insulated wall sections, while at the same time reducing infiltration rates into the home.

The only other remedial work you perform without incurring either too great an expense or time committment relates to window treatment systems. To reduce the heat loss through windows, both at night and during the day, additional layers of glazing can be installed both on the interior and exterior of the house without causing aesthetic changes. Equally significant savings can result from the incorporation of movable insulation systems designed to reduce heat loss during the winter evenings. Many of these options are discussed in the section on *Window Insulation*.

The incorporation of these ideas into an existing house can result in fuel savings of up to 50 per cent. Until recently, most people assumed that this represented the maximum potential savings. We now know that these techniques are to be considered valuable steps, but they do not reflect the true potential savings obtained through the use of super-insulating concepts and techniques.

After you have completed a super-insulated retrofit your house will become unrecognizable in terms of both its appearance and economic performance.

But the changes are more than skin deep. New or upgraded windows, changed ventilation patterns, perhaps new landscaping, or new or upgraded heating systems and, of course, improved insulation levels and reduced air infiltration, all add up to a very different living environment.

A complete retrofit can reduce your heating bill by 80 per cent, though this figure will vary according to how well you did the work and the initial condition of your home. Depending on the size of your house, the climate and your fuel costs, savings can be in the order of $1,000 a year.

It is up to you to decide how much it is worth spending to save that $1,000 (remember that savings are tax-free). If you believe that the high interest rates are compensated for by the high annual increase in the cost of fuel, a simple payback formula can be used. Spend $10,000 and you will be paid back in 10 years. If it costs you $5,000, your payback period is 5 years.

The cost of the retrofit should not be evaluated only in terms of energy savings. The cost may amount to only a portion of the improvements you were going to make anyway; new siding, new walls, etc. Many people will be motivated by the savings they will achieve. Others will seek a home that is more comfortable, quieter, nicer looking and has a greater market value.

Some will approach the job out of a commitment to environmental issues, while others will be seeking status. (Be the first on your block to live in a super-insulated retrofit. A $100 a year heating bill makes great cocktail party chatter.)

Each section of the manual discusses the economics of the various options. The *Appendix* will show you how to assess the heat loss of your house. Armed with this information, your decision to go the super-insulated route is made all the easier.

The Super-Retrofit

Getting Underway

Performing the work required to complete the super-insulated retrofit can be very time consuming. Depending on the size of the house and the approach pursued, a thorough job can take between two weeks and two months. Minimizing the amount of work will greatly restrict the mess, boredom and bruised fingers. Proper planning of the entire job is the best means of reducing the time and expense incurred. Good planning does not refer solely to the order in which the various components of the task are performed. It starts with a well thought out decision about which options meet the home-owners economic, time and performance requirements. Later, good purchasing habits will bring about a lower overall cost and a more pleasing final result. Proper planning will minimize the amount of time necessary to break down walls or fiddle with odd shapes and sizes to make up for mistakes. Ultimately, proper planning will give the homeowner a realistic understanding of the money needed, time required and the results which should be obtained.

The most important aspect of the entire job — having decided that the super-insulated retrofit is what you want — involves a thorough analysis of your existing home to determine which approach (interior or exterior) best suits your needs. As we progress it will become evident that some houses are better suited to a particular approach. Although the two methods can be mixed together, this leads to awkward problems. As much as possible, we recommend pursuing only one approach.

Having decided which option to take, you'll need to start the specifics of planning the task ahead. In some locales this may involve drawing plans to obtain the required building permits — that is if you plan to tell the authorities about your work. Contacts may need to be made with the electrical utility if major alterations are to be made at the same time as the retrofit work, and similar contacts may be needed with local contractors for those aspects of the job which are to be fielded out.

The entire job should be properly ordered and timed so that you'll have an idea of when you can either return from your vacation or count on life returning to some semblance of order. Good planning assumes that if something can go wrong it will.

Decision Making

The interior and exterior super-insulated retrofit options are presented in detail. The job can be done from the outside with the construction of a new curtain wall that will envelope the house with an air-tight vapour barrier and a well-insulated blanket. The more conventional option presented relates to the manner in which the super-insulated retrofit can be done on the inside walls of the house. Either of the jobs can result in fuel savings of as much as 90 per cent.

Each approach has its advantages and disadvantages.

Interior
Advantages
— can be performed at same time as major renovations
— doesn't alter exterior facade of the house
— limited time on ladders, etc.

Disadvantages
— creates a mess
— complete air-vapour seal is extremely difficult
— space limitations can restrict the R values

Exterior
Advantages
— allows for easy installation of air-vapour barrier
— allows for easy installation of significant insulation levels
— work can be performed while still living at home without mess
— construction time is minimized
— best means of obtaining maximum fuel savings

Disadvantages
— demands re-siding of the house
— can pose problems of encroachment on lot line
— potential difficulties with 3 storey houses

The above chart indicates a preference for the exterior approach. This reflects the author's prejudice for attaining maximum thermal efficiency even at the expense of the altered characteristics of the building's exterior facade. The factors you must analyze include: the existing condition of your house, spatial limitations on the inside and outside, the aesthetics of the building and the amount of capital at your disposal.

The Condition of Your House

People are sometimes reluctant to re-insulate, let alone super-insulate, because of the alterations that have to be made to the existing state of the house. Many people will shy away from disrupting a house that is in good repair, even if it only involves removing baseboards and window trim to caulk leaky areas. Those are the same people who, several years down the line, will be forced to sell their homes because they can no longer afford the operating costs.

The easiest time to plan the super-insulated retrofit is when major renovation work is also being considered. If you have bought a run-down house with an eye to fixing the building up, the super-insulated retrofit can be easily integrated into your plans. Similarly, if you are considering re-siding your home, the addition of a vapour barrier and insulation can be viewed as a wise investment. The additional investment to cover the upgraded energy efficiency is easily justified in both of the above cases, and should only represent an additional 5 to 15 per cent of the total cost of the job.

One of the greatest benefits accruing from the exterior super-insulation approach relates to maintenance of the building's interior. The exterior approach can alleviate those concerns that relate to altering the desirable architectural features such as mouldings, window trim and the proportioning of rooms. Similarly, life

inside the home need not be totally disrupted if the retrofit is performed on the exterior walls.

Many of the benefits of the exterior retrofit must be set aside if the facade has redeeming aesthetic or historical features. If expense were not a concern the building's facade could be reconstructed over the newly insulated section, though if there are aesthetic concerns the interior option becomes the preferable route. In some cases the siding of the existing house can be re-used after the wall has been retrofitted. This approach will demand some care when the siding is taken down. You must be able to replace the removed siding, as the area of the outside wall will be slightly larger.

To sum up your options, we recommend that the exterior approach to upgrading the thermal envelope of the building be employed wherever possible. If, however, major interior work is required to bring the inside environment up to par, the re-insulation should be performed at the same time.

Spatial Limitations

As was previously mentioned, spatial limitations can dictate where the super-insulated retrofit will be performed. Both of the options outlined in the manual sections of the book will add close to 6 inches to either the interior or exterior of the building's shell. In many urban dwellings, especially semi-detached houses, the width of the existing house will be an argument against an interior re-insulation. In such houses which are only 12 or 14 feet wide, removing as much as 6 inches from the room can be responsible for the onset of claustrophobia.

SPACE
LIMITATIONS

Whereas the limitations affecting the interior retrofit relate to size and appearance, restrictions on the addition of insulation to the exterior can be dictated by civic authorities. Adding 6 inches of space on to the exterior shell might encroach on the lot line or restrict the access of cars to a garage in the back yard, or make a walkway between two houses prohibitively narrow. In some cases, permission to perform the exterior retrofit will need to be obtained through the local building or zoning departments. Some lobbying of local politicians may be required if you are the first person in your area to consider the exterior retrofit.

Some of the problems relating to spatial limitations can be alleviated by using higher density insulating materials. While most of these options will cost considerably more than fibreglass, as much as 2 inches of space can be saved. If, for instance, you had only 4½ inches of space, extruded polystyrene would allow for an R value of 20. The same standards using fibreglass would require 6 inches of space from the house interior. In most cases the trade-off becomes one of space for economics.

Aesthetic Considerations

While the "purist" approach to the super-insulated retrofit suggests performing the entire job from the interior or the exterior, aesthetics may often call for a mixing of the two options. If, for instance, the homeowner wanted to maintain the exterior facade to keep the streetscape consistent, yet wanted to perform the exterior retrofit on the side and end walls, the front of the building could be retrofitted from the interior. If you're considering this approach, some problems will need to be addressed where the interior and exterior insulation and air-vapour barrier overlap.

If you're considering adding rooms to the existing house, you might at the same time think of re-siding the entire building. As you will want to integrate the addition into the rest of the house, a total exterior retrofit will result in a unified exterior shell.

Thermal Efficiency

Although the interior and exterior approach to the super-insulated retrofit can result in significant fuel savings, it will generally be easier to attain satisfactory results when performing the work from the exterior. This is primarily true when one considers the installation of the air-vapour barrier. From the exterior, the entire house can be wrapped in a continuous sheet of plastic to minimize uncontrolled infiltration. This is not true for the interior because no matter how conscientious the homeowner, gaps will exist where the plastic can't extend. Cupboards, stairways and closets will all prevent the house from being totally enveloped with an air-vapour barrier, leaving weak spots in the thermal envelope of the house.

It will also be easier to install higher amounts of insulation on the exterior walls, thereby reducing conduction losses during the colder months of the year.

Overlapping Exterior and Interior Work

Ideally the entire retrofit is performed from either the interior or exterior of the house. In many cases, however, the homeowner will decide to perform one component of the job from one side and another from the opposite side of the wall. This may occur when the walls of the house have been upgraded from the exterior while the attic has been re-insulated from the interior, or where the front of the house was upgraded from the interior to maintain the existing facade of the house. Similarly, if the homeowner has already performed a section of the work in advance of the larger task, the two jobs may be performed by different means.

VAPOUR BARRIER CONTINUITY AND THERMAL BRIDGING ARE PROBLEMS HERE.

EXTERIOR INSULATION ON THREE WALLS · INTERIOR INSULATION ON FRONT WALL FACING STREET. ORIGINAL FACADE IS MAINTAINED·

The mixed approach to the super-insulated retrofit will cause some problems. Wherever the interior and exterior re-insulation overlap, a bridge will be created that will carry water vapour and heat from the inside of the building. Although the conduction of heat will cause a drain on the fuel bill, it is not the major source of concern. More severe problems can result from the movement of water vapour through the wall section to the point where it condenses in the middle of the house envelope. Unless the air-vapour barrier on the outside of the house is directly linked, overlapped and caulked to the vapour barrier on the interior of the house, there is little that can be done to totally prevent this movement.

The best stop-gap solution involves overlapping the interior or exterior insulation as much as possible to prevent heat flow from the interior to the exterior. This is especially important in solid masonary houses where the building's shell will promote heat conduction. In those houses where an overlap cannot be avoided, the interior insulation should extend beyond the exterior insulation as far as is practical. In solid masonry buildings this may involve extending the overlap the length of the interior wall (ie. 8 feet).

Preventing the movement of water vapour through the walls presents a more serious problem. Where an overlap exists, the interior walls should be provided with an effective air-vapour barrier to prevent the vapour from gaining access to the cavity sections. In most cases this can be effectively achieved by installing two coats of a low permeance paint (such as Glidden's Insul-Aid).

In most cases this weak spot will prove to be unavoidable at certain locations in the building's envelope. A thorough understanding of the concepts of thermal bridging and the condensation of cooling water vapour will allow the homeowner to best deal with these problem areas.

Cost of the Exterior vs. Interior Approach

As a rule the exterior approach to the super-insulated retrofit will involve a smaller capital outlay. This reflects both the smaller amount of labour required and the reduced material demand. The largest single expense is the cost of the siding. On a square foot basis this will average close to twice as much as for the insulation, framing and vapour barrier. The additional trim and finishing work which is needed for the interior retrofit can result in a larger expense.

In most cases the actual expense of insulation, vapour barrier and the additional framing required for the super-insulated retrofit will be small in relation to the rest of the job. Also, in

most cases the cost of labour (if contracted) will be larger than the expenses relating to material acquisition.

Conclusion

A balanced weighting of the disadvantages and advantages of the interior and exterior retrofit suggest that from most perspectives the exterior approach is the preferred option. However, each house will have its own specific requirements. A thorough analysis of your house will determine the appropriate retrofit option. You want to perform this type of job once per house — make the right decision.

After deciding which retrofit approach best suits your requirements, spend some time sketching out plans for the task ahead. This is necessary even if you are planning to hire a contractor to perform the job. Plans, be they detailed architectural drawings or your own sketches, should enable you to accurately determine the materials needed for the job. Sketching details of some of the trouble spots will help the homeowner or contractor to visualize how the job should be performed.

In some municipalities plans may need to be submitted to the local buildings' officials for approval. While permits are usually required only for major renovation and structural work, in some jurisdictions a permit may be required for the super-insulated retrofit. When re-skinning the building from the exterior, or when adding an attached solar greenhouse, some zoning by-laws may need to be contravened. In most cases where the addition of 6 inches of new wall doesn't impede traffic or block access to a neighbour, officials should bend the rules in the name of energy-efficiency. This may not be the case with the addition of a solar greenhouse as it takes up considerably more space. In some regressive jurisdictions you'll need to prepare for battle. If your plans to improve the energy-efficiency of the house are rejected on a technicality in the zoning by-laws, playing the issue before politicians and the media should result in a new hearing.

If you have plans to alter the service to the house or move the mast head to a new location on the curtain wall, you should contact your electrical utility. Both of these operations should be integrated into the planning of the job. Similarly, if major alterations or upgrading of the electrical and plumbing work is to be undertaken, approval is required and inspections will need to be scheduled into the work plan.

Purchasing the materials for the job is a major step. Good planning and purchasing habits will lead to a significant reduction in time spent chasing around and should help minimize your capital outlay. A detailed discussion of purchasing habits and material options is included in a later chapter of the book.

Plan, plan and plan. The better prepared you are for the undertaking ahead of you, the smoother the operation will be when you get to the work stage.

Exterior Retrofit

Re-insulating an existing house from the exterior holds the greatest potential for reducing the fuel requirements of today's buildings. The construction of a new, super-insulated wall on the exterior of the building's shell is the best means of redeeming the energy-inefficient construction practices which have characterized North American housing over the last several hundred years.

The exterior approach to the super-insulated retrofit most closely approaches the construction practices being employed by the leading edge of current energy-efficient builders. When completed it achieves the same impressive fuel savings. in relation to the conventional building stock. The installation of a curtain wall, or "re-skinning" an existing house, brings about many advantages. Air changes can be reduced to less than one tenth of the original rate. Conductive heat loss through the exterior of the house can be reduced to less than 10 per cent of the original factor. Both, in conjunction with treatment of windows, can reduce total fuel consumption by as much as 95 per cent. If properly performed, what was originally a leaky, poorly insulated house with a fuel bill of $1,000, can be transformed into a comfortable home with a fuel bill of less than $100.

The benefits of performing the super-insulated retrofit from the exterior are more considerable than the potential fuel savings reflect. In those cases where the siding of the building is in need of repair, the incentive to reduce the fuel bill may hasten the decision to upgrade the aesthetics of the building. The exterior approach to re-insulation allows for a considerable amount of work to be done without disrupting the interior environment. While this may remove some of the pressure to finish the task, it will do so at the expense of the potential discord among the people living in the house. Many detailed heat loss and gain calculations are thrown into disrepute when more than one of the occupants leaves the home because of the mess caused during the interior retrofit.

The re-skinning of the building is a relatively simple exercise which can be performed by anyone who is willing to tolerate bruised thumbs, sore backs and itchy arms. All of these superficial injuries can be attributed to the learning curve. A typical contractor with a good framing crew could have a thorough exterior retrofit completed on an average sized house in less than a week.

So why is it, you may wonder, that the exterior retrofit hasn't been more rapidly accepted? First, conventionally we have looked at doing major renovation work on the interior of buildings, limiting the exterior work to landscaping, gardening, painting and possibly re-siding. Second, we generally feel limited by the existing exterior dimensions of the home. Most importantly, the lack of awareness of the benefits and ease of the exterior retrofit option has impeded its implementation on the marketplace. We hope that this section and the actual operating experience gained through performing the described work will assist in introducing the benefits of the super-insulated retrofit to a broader audience.

While each job will vary according to the variables presented by each house, the trade mark of the exterior super-insulated retrofit will revolve around the installation of a continuous air-tight vapour barrier, the addition of a solid blanket of insulation around the entire shell of the house, and the upgrading of the building's windows. The various steps described in the following section may be altered according to the installation practices of the work force — especially by those innovative people who can find ever easier means of accomplishing the same or better results. We know that the steps described below will result in a well-insulated, comfortable and affordable living environment. We hope that as the field of super-insulated retrofits matures, greater numbers of affordable, easy to construct options become available.

Preparing the house

A survey of the existing shell of the building will provide you with several options. If the existing siding on a frame building is in good shape and can be easily removed without being totally destroyed, a large component of the capital cost of the job can be eliminated. This option has the added advantage of maintaining the existing aesthetics of the building, although some additional siding will need to be purchased to make up for the increased exterior dimensions of the house.

If the existing siding is badly deteriorated with rot, dry rot or other problems caused by extended aging, you should remove the siding before leaping into the heart of the retrofit. Leaving any rotted areas behind the new skin of the home will only compound the problems. Similarly, if a rural homeowner has continual problems with cluster flies or other insects breeding in the walls, the problem should be addressed before installing the new air-vapour barrier. Removing the siding and cleaning out the wall cavities, and then re-installing insulation between the existing studs of the wall should remedy such problems. The new sheet of plastic will protect the home from any further intrusion.

Protrusions around the windows and doors of the house should be considered at this early stage. Exterior face trim around the windows and doors should be pulled off to allow for easy installation of the air-vapour

barrier. Any oversized window sills, outside spot lights and electrical outlets, flower boxes and other features protruding from the exterior walls will need to be either removed or extended by several inches so that they can be remounted on the newly constructed house wall. It is advisable to contact your local electrician or electric utility to remount the main service mast outside of the new wall. The realization that any gaps in the plastic sheeting require remedial actions will lead the homeowner to remove any unnecessary holes.

To those "green thumbs" in the audience it is advisable to transplant any flowers, vegetables or ornamental ground cover in close proximity to the house. The thought of roses being bucketed away for landfill, or being downtrodden by many pairs of work boots is repulsive to even those of us

who can't grow dandelions. At the same time, if any excavation around the perimeter of the foundation wall is planned, a sheet of plastic or canvas can be laid over the ground where the dirt is to be piled. This won't guarantee the rapid renewal of grass if the dirt is to remain in place for more than a couple of days, but it will provide a short term solution if the dirt is quickly backfilled after the insulation and vapour barrier are installed.

If the homeowner has decided to upgrade not only the walls from the exterior, but also the roof of the building, some initial demolition around the soffits of the house may be required. Before resorting to a chain saw and crow bar make certain that you have a clear idea of the steps which you are going to pursue. Have a good understanding of the entire process at this stage in the job.

Excavating for Below Grade Insulation

To ensure a continuous air-vapour barrier from footings to roofline, the foundation wall should be exposed. For a hardy few, this can be performed by hand (a few friends and several cases of beer would greatly facilitate the job). Alternatively, a local contractor with a back hoe can save many hours of work and several creaking backs. A proficient operator should be able to perform the job in a couple of hours, usually for less than $100.

The width of the trenching need not be excessive, but should allow adequate room to seal the vapour barrier at the footings, and to properly install the insulating material. In other words count on a 16-inch space.

While the foundation is exposed any leakage problems can be readily fixed before re-insulating the wall. Commercially available products such as Thoro-seal and bentonite are effective for this purpose. Although the air-vapour barrier will perform the job of waterproofing the foundation wall, re-sealing is a wise idea. Also ensure that the drain tile around the building is clear to reduce the potential for frost heaving. If the excavated earth is kept close to the trench, back filling the soil can be easily completed after the re-insulation. A new layer of top soil should be added to cover the building scraps, dropped nails, etc., and new ground cover can be then planted.

Wrapping the House

One of the greatest benefits of exterior re-insulation is the possibility of installing a continuous air-vapour barrier around the existing home. The house can be surrounded with a plastic sheet reducing the infiltration of cold air into the house and the escape of warm air from the house to the exterior. This continuous seal is extremely difficult to accomplish when installed on the interior.

Six mil polyethylene sheeting should be used as the vapour barrier. The plastic will act as a good air barrier and will be effective in restricting the diffusion of vapour to the exterior. Although slightly more expensive than a thinner (2 or 4 mil) polyethylene, the 6 mil poly is significantly more rugged and thus more forgiving to harsh treatment. Nevertheless, a concerned effort should be made to protect the air-vapour barrier from flying wood, dropped tools and loose nails, all of which might puncture the material.

To seal overlapping joints and to affix the poly to the building, acoustical caulking should be generously applied. The black, gooey caulk, manufactured by Tremco is highly elastic and will not dry and crack. The material is only available in quart tubes so you will need to purchase or rent a larger, commercial caulking gun. The caulk is extremely difficult to remove from clothes, hair, etc. Work carefully.

A second-best alternative for sealing joints is subfloor adhesives. Although generally more accessible and available in regular sized tubes, these options have a shorter life cycle as a pliable air barrier.

Installing the Vapour Barrier

The initial step of re-insulating from the exterior will involve wrapping the house in a continuous air-vapour barrier which extends from below grade to the soffits of the house. This barrier will virtually eliminate any drafts of cold air into the house and will ensure the longevity of the new insulation. It is truly the most important step in the entire process.

It is important to strive for a continuous sealed barrier, void of punctures, holes or leaks in the seams. When handling the plastic sheeting, care should be taken so as not to rip the material. Similarly, when caulking overlapping seams, make sure the bead of caulking which is laid will form a tight seal between the two layers of plastic. The work load will be reduced by employing the widest rolls of plastic possible. This will mean less handling, less sealing and less expense. By minimizing the number of staples or fastening bars required, greater efficiency is attained. Not only does each staple present the possibility of being pulled out and leaving a hole in the material, but it also minimizes the room for error in putting the air-vapour barrier up.

If the polyethylene is to be installed over an extremely rough surface such as stucco, the wall can first be covered with a layer of building paper. This will reduce the possibility of perforating the air-vapour barrier when it is installed.

The sheets of plastic can be most easily installed on a vertical basis. By first affixing the barrier to the peak of the wall, the rolls can then be lowered into place and the sealing and cutting performed by a minimum of hands. This will also allow for the sheets to be hung more square, alleviating the problems of plastic buckling and leaving sources of air movement.

Starting the Job

Start the air-vapour barrier at one corner of the house to maintain square installation. Measure the height from the footings to the roof rafters following the shell of the house. Add a couple of feet for safety and cut the 6 mil polyethylene to the required length.

Apply a bead of acoustical caulking to the top of the wall the length of your plastic sheet. Using ladders, hang the plastic flush to the corner of the house and let it fall into place over the wall. Affix the plastic at the peak with a strip of wood the length of the plastic and nail through to the studs of the building. The nailing bar should be situated directly over the bead of caulking which was applied. This will result in a tight seal.

When the plastic is extended down to the footings, a double check to ensure it is flush with the corner should be performed. That having been done, the air-vapour barrier can now be sealed to the bottom of the foundation wall with another continuous bead of caulking.

Then cut the next sheet to the desired length and repeat the detail at the soffit and footings. An additional bead of caulking must now be applied at the edge of the sheet which is already hung. This will prevent any air or vapour leakage between the sheets. Be generous with the caulking. Then place the next piece of plastic in place, overlapping the seams by 3 to 4 inches. Press the outer sheet on to the

bead (which is the length of the sheet) to attain the positive seal. To ensure a long-term seal, a nailing bar should be laid over the seam and affixed to the original siding. Use scrap lumber of lengths of 1 x 2 wood nailed through to the wall of the house.

This operation should be continued around the house until you reach the starting point, at which time you will have attained a tightly sealed house. However, it will now be a little difficult to get inside the house to pour yourself a self-congratulatory beer, or to open a window to allow ventilation air. The plastic should be carefully cut around the doors and windows to minimize later work. Cut the plastic diagonally from the corners of the door and window casing in an X configuration.

To properly seal the air-vapour barrier around the doors and windows, a bead of acoustical caulking should be applied to the exterior edge of the casing. The plastic can then be compressed over the bead and stapled into place. The excess plastic can then be cut off and removed. When performing this task it is important to realize that you are attempting to reduce the chance of any air leakage around the frames of the doors and windows. By affixing the plastic directly to the casing, any potential leakage around the original frame is minimized.

A few notes of caution:
— when sealing the plastic at the top of the wall, assure that the soffits are not

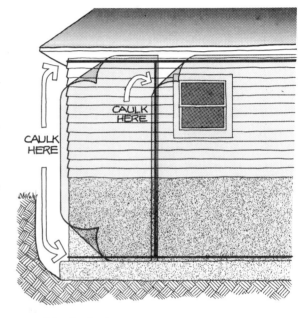

blocked. Air must be allowed to flow freely into the attic through these openings.
— take care not to shut off any vents or ducts exhausting air from the house or bringing fresh air in, unless you've decided they are no longer required. If the vents or ducts are to be maintained, seal the plastic tightly to the edges.

The problem area is the top of the wall where it is almost impossible to make the exterior barrier meet with that barrier that is used to seal the ceiling on the top floor. Some individuals have attempted to perform this feat. It involves ripping down the soffit material (plywood, aluminum), cutting the barrier to reach around each rafter, and then sealing it to the barrier in the attic of the house. The plastic would need to be caulked and taped to each rafter, and then patched to the interior barrier with more plastic and caulking. A gargantuan task.

Most individuals are content to leave the small gap at the roofline. As long as air is prevented from entering the home at its lower extremities, the difficulties should be minimized. A coat of vapour barrier paint can be applied to the walls on the top floor of the house to further reduce the effects of diffusion and the stack effect.

Framing the Insulation

Having installed the vapour barrier you can now begin framing the exterior to house the new insulation. A couple of general rules should be adhered to:
— minimize the amount of lumber required (the more wood the less insulation and the greater the cost)
— minimize the labour (more time to spend inside your newly insulated home)
— resolve details around windows and doors, etc., before commencing (fewer headaches).

Three different systems can be employed: cross-strapping of the house, rigid board insulation and curtain wall construction.

Strapping

Strapping of the house has the distinct advantage of being the most forgiving

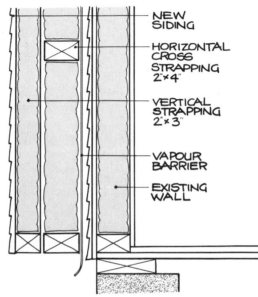

NEW SIDING

HORIZONTAL CROSS STRAPPING 2"×4"

VERTICAL STRAPPING 2"×3"

VAPOUR BARRIER

EXISTING WALL

means of re-insulating the home. Few exact measurements are required and the work can be performed by an individual as job is assembled piece by piece
Problems or disadvantages associated with this method, compared to others, involve: the relatively large amount of lumber required, the fact that the insulation has to be installed in various stages, and the relatively large number of thermal bridges from the interior to the exterior that are created.

Rigid Boards (Styrofoam, urethane foam board, thermax)

This system has the advantage of minimizing thermal bridging. Installation is relatively easy with the exception of window and door details, if the thickness

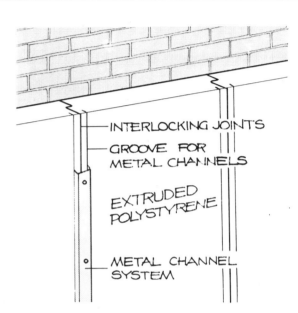

INTERLOCKING JOINTS

GROOVE FOR METAL CHANNELS

EXTRUDED POLYSTYRENE

METAL CHANNEL SYSTEM

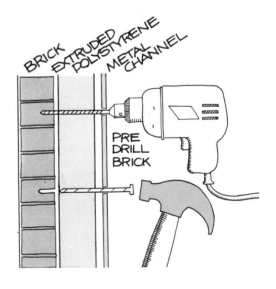

BRICK   EXTRUDED POLYSTYRENE   METAL CHANNEL

PRE DRILL BRICK

of the board does not exceed 4 inches.
Above that thickness labour time is
doubled because a cross-strapping system
is required. Rigid boards can provide an
excellent thermal blanket to a wall.

The major problem with rigid boards is
their expense. Both the insulation material
and the fastening devices are very
expensive in relation to wood and
fibreglass. A less significant problem will
result from the difficulty encountered in
affixing a new siding. As a rule, the siding
materials will need to be screwed to the
metal channeling systems.

One other problem can arise from the
relative lack of impermeability of rigid
boards. As the board prevents the
movement of vapour to the exterior, frost
may build up and associated problems
could result if there has been improper
installation.

A compromise between the continuous
strapping of a wall and the installation of a
curtain wall (to be described later in the
chapter) has been developed in
Saskatchewan. The process eliminates the
need for a continuous ledger plate around
the perimeter of the house. In its place the
curtain wall is hung from spacer blocks that
are nailed to the structural wall of the
building. The process resolves some of the
problems inherent in the cross-strapping of
exterior walls. On the other hand, it does
involve a greater investment of time than
simply installing the curtain wall onto a
pre-assembled plate.

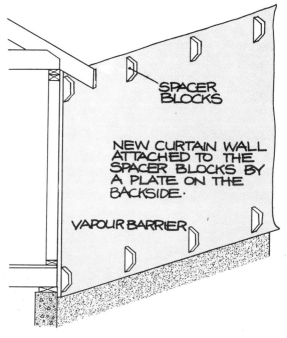

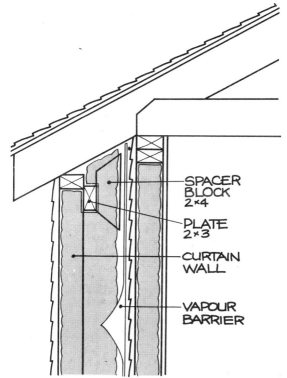

The Saskatchewan system involves nailing
spacer blocks to the studs of the building at
the base and peak of the existing wall. To
ensure that the blocks are solidly tied to the
existing studs, the location of the studs
should be marked before the air-vapour
barrier is installed. This may pose
considerable problems in older homes
where the spacing of the structural studs is
often quite irregular. Should a search and
destroy mission be required, make sure
that the work is performed prior to the
installation of the polyethylene. Otherwise
your air-vapour barrier may resemble a
chunk of Swiss cheese.

Once the air-vapour barrier has been

carefully installed, the spacer blocks can be
nailed through to the structural wall of the
building. Depending on the amount of
insulation which you plan to install in the
new exterior wall, the spacer blocks will be
either 2¹/₂ or 3¹/₂ inches. By using either 2
X 3's or 2 X 4's nailed on edge, the
necessary space can be obtained. It is
important that a strong mechanical bond be
obtained, so the the nails must be at least
1¹/₂ inches longer than the spacer blocks.
The blocks should be nailed to each stud at
the same level from the peak and base of
the wall.

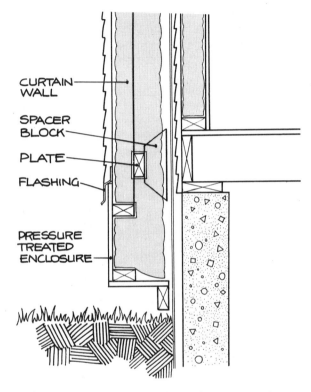

CURTAIN WALL

SPACER BLOCK

PLATE

FLASHING

PRESSURE TREATED ENCLOSURE

The new exterior curtain wall can now be assembled on the ground in front of the existing wall. The studs should be laid out at 24 inches on centre. Then they are nailed together with a continuous plate affixed to the back of the wall assembly. Either a 1 X 3 or a 2 X 3 can be used to hold the studs in place. The plate should be affixed at the location of the spacing blocks. When both plates have been nailed to the studs at the predetermined locations, the new wall assembly can be lifted into place. Then the horizontal plate can be nailed intermittently to the spacing blocks.

Once the new wall has been firmly affixed to the spacing blocks the insulation, building paper and new siding can be installed. The only job remaining is to box in the newly assembled wall. If your plans require that the new wall be brought within several inches of ground level, pressure-treated wood will be required to ensure the longevity of the section. A vertical section of the wall should be extended from the existing curtain wall, and then a horizontal section should be tied from the new wall to the existing foundation.

This system of re-insulating the exterior of the building will result in the optimal thermal performance of the newly insulated structure when performed in conjunction with a sound air-vapour barrier. The sole problem with the system, from the authors' perspective, relates to the additional time required to ensure a strong bond to the existing shell. In cases where the location of the studs is easily identified, this option will not be as restrictive. Keep in mind that the time required for the cutting and installation of the strapping bars might still be substantial.

Curtain Wall

This is the preferred means of exterior re-insulating. This system, which involves hanging a new frame wall away from the existing shell, results in a minimum of thermal bridging, requires less lumber, limited labour and it can provide the greatest freedom in design.

R values from 12 to 40 can be attained by simply altering the ledger plate detail upon which the newly framed wall is constructed, without adding to the cost of lumber. The majority of the work can be performed at ground level, thereby facilitating the construction process. In addition, a minimum number of perforations are required in the newly hung vapour barrier. This method is applicable to most housing types, locations, etc. and details around the windows, doors, etc., can be dealt with in a conventional manner.

The major difficulty arises with the design of an adequately strong ledger plate to withstand wall loading and possible pressures exerted by frost heaving below grade insulation. If proper care is shown for these concerns no problems should arise.

A minor problem will be encountered by those wishing to put up a vertical siding. This would require an extra layer of strapping running horizontally over the new frame, adding to the cost and the labour.

Constructing the Curtain Wall

Having properly installed the vapour barrier to the existing shell, the first task involves applying a ledger plate around the perimeter of the building. Several options are available depending on the house, amount of insulation required and type of siding to be installed.

You could use a small steel angle iron lagged into the building. This might be the preferred option when working with masonry buildings. The problem of direct thermal conduction from the warm house wall to the cold exterior can be overcome by placing a thermal break between the angle iron and the house. A strip of neoprene rubber would suffice — another possible material is a $1/2$ inch of styrofoam SM30. Have holes pre-drilled into the angle iron at 16- or 24-inch centres on both flanges so that the iron can be easily affixed to the house and the plate can be tied down to the iron using bolts. The length of the bolts holding the plate to the masonry wall will vary according to the sheer strength of the bolt and the strength of the masonry.

It is important that the curtain wall be tied directly to the structural wall of the existing house. In frame housing the ledger plate supporting the curtain wall should be directly affixed to the vertical studs of the house or to the header of the joists. If a brick veneer has been installed, it must be remembered that the brick has no structural role and the ledger plate must still be affixed directly to the wood frame of the house.

In solid brick or other solid masonry construction, the ledger plate can be bolted directly to the exterior of the wall. Similarly, if the ledger plate is to be located below the joists on the first floor of the house the plate can be lagged to the foundation wall.

An option more readily used by the average homeowner involves constructing your own ledger plate from wood. Using a 2 x 4 as the nailing edge to the house, a 2 x 6 or 2 x 8 can be lagged into the 2 x 4 at the bottom, then braced with plywood and 2 x 4's. This option is most easily used when affixing the curtain wall to frame buildings.

A much stronger bottom plate detail can be installed with an additional 2 x 4. To achieve this the 2 x 6 plate is inverted so that it sits on top of a series of 2 x 4's affixed to the wall. Initially a chalk line is drawn to indicate the location of the plate to be affixed to the wall. A 2 x 4 is then pre-drilled (use a $3/8$ inch bit) at 24-inch centres or at the studs. The plate is then lifted into place ageinst the chalk line, the location of the holes is marked, and the 2 x 4 removed.

Holes are then drilled through the exterior shell of the building on the marked locations. If you're drilling into a masonary structure, a lead shield will need to be installed to fit over the bolt. This will necessitate drilling a larger hole using a masonry bit. If you're affixing the plate to the studs, the $3/8$ inch bit can be used to drill through to the structure of the house.

Once the holes have been drilled, the pre-drilled plate can be lifted back into place and the $3/8$ inch bolts can be lagged into the structure. The bolts should be at least 3 inches long to ensure that there is enough strength to the assembly.

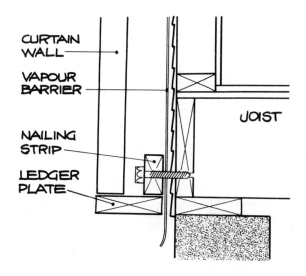

CURTAIN WALL

VAPOUR BARRIER

NAILING STRIP

LEDGER PLATE

JOIST

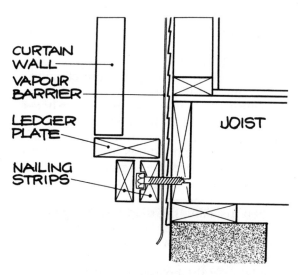

CURTAIN WALL

VAPOUR BARRIER

LEDGER PLATE

NAILING STRIPS

JOIST

The next step calls for nailing a second 2 x 4 on top of the initially installed plate. Use 3 inch nails and be sure that the top edge of the plates are flush.

The assembled section now provides the bearing for the 2 x 6 plate which is installed on top of the above-mentioned plate. The 2 x 6 should be solidly nailed to the 2 x 4's to create a very strong bottom plate.

Should you require this procedure at an intermediate stage, the entire process can be duplicated at the mid-point of the wall.

The horizontal plate should be sized to the thickness of the insulation required. If R-20 is being added to the outside, a 2 x 6 will be required; R-28 a 2 x 8, R-32 a 2 x 10. Although a 2-inch board as the horizontal plate is suggested, you could use a ³/4-inch plywood plate, especially when adding very thick amounts of insulation. Should you employ this option, use an exterior grade CDX and ensure that adequate bracing is provided. Loading might amount to as much as 50 pounds per linear foot, so design accordingly.

Bracing can be provided by plywood gussets at the end of each section of the ledger plate, cut at right angles. Two by four braces can be nailed into the horizontal plates, then affixed to the frame of the house.

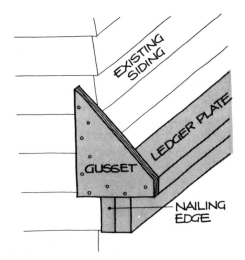

Below Grade Insulation

Once the ledger plate has been installed around the perimeter of the house, a measurement can be taken to size the below grade insulation. Measure from the bottom of the plate to the footing and cut styrofoam. Care should be taken when backfilling. Ideally, gravel should be used as a backfill to prevent soil from clinging to the foam, but this will not always prove practical. On newer buildings constructed with concrete block foundations, the styrofoam will sit flush to the basement walls. On older buildings this will become more difficult because of uneven stone wall foundations.

When installing the rigid boards against concrete block foundation walls make certain the fit from the footing to the newly installed ledger plate is accurate. A slight wedging of the boards will ensure its

permanence when backfilling is performed. Boards should be fitted tightly together to reduce heat loss and potential leakage problems.

With the older, uneven foundation walls, attaining a tight fit might prove more difficult. Styrofoam should be fitted as snugly as possible and the gaps filled with Perlite or vermiculite to reduce any potential spaces between the insulation and the foundation wall.

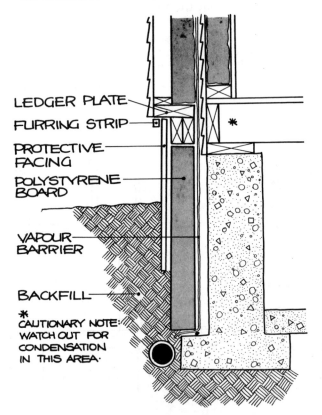

Styrofoam or any polystyrene breaks down under exposure to sunshine (ultra violet deterioration), so any rigid insulation which projects above the ground should be covered with a protective surface. This should also assist in reducing damage from dogs scratching, balls bouncing or rain splattering against the insulation. A strong weathering material, such as cement millboard, can fulfil this function.

The best means of affixing the protective board involves backfilling the board. This should extend more than 6 - 12 inches below grade. At this point you should nail a small furring strip to the bottom of the ledger plate to wedge the board onto the insulating board. This will provide a sturdy, long lasting means of protecting the insulation.

Installing the Framing

At this stage the framing of the above grade walls can begin. This is perhaps the easiest step of the entire process, as long as the ledger plate(s) has been carefully installed and squared. The majority of the work can be performed at ground level by prefabricating framing sections. These sections can then be lifted into place on the ledger plates and anchored, allowing for easy installation of the insulation and new siding.

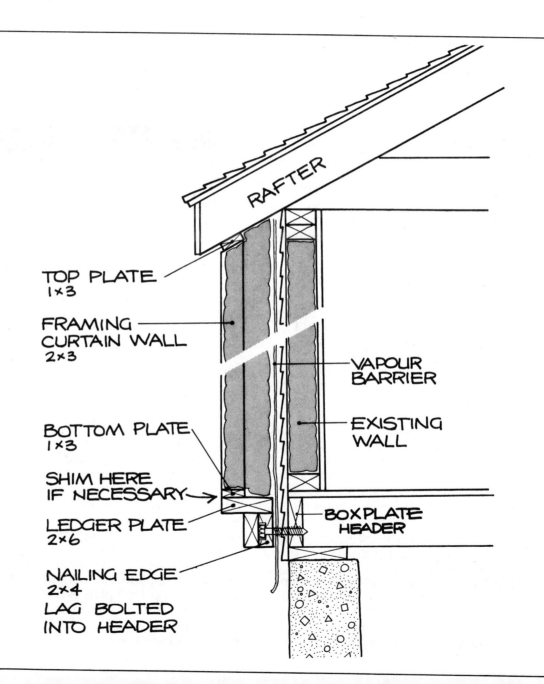

TOP PLATE 1×3

FRAMING CURTAIN WALL 2×3

BOTTOM PLATE 1×3

SHIM HERE IF NECESSARY

LEDGER PLATE 2×6

NAILING EDGE 2×4

LAG BOLTED INTO HEADER

RAFTER

VAPOUR BARRIER

EXISTING WALL

BOX PLATE HEADER

Prefabricating the Sections

One of the advantages of the curtain wall method lies in the reduced requirement for lumber. Independent of the amount of insulation to be installed, the wall can be constructed with 2 x 3's hung at the outside edge of the ledger plate. Assuming that 6 to 8 inches of insulation is to be installed means that as much as 3 to 5 inches of insulation will be placed between the existing wall of the house and the framing sections themselves.

Construction is simple: Measure the height from the ledger plate to the ledger plate or to the roof rafters. Cut the 2 x 3 studs 1⁵/₈ inches shorter than the required height. The studs can then be laid out on the ground in front of the wall. They should be spaced at 24 inches on centre which will provide the required space for friction-fit fibreglass batts.

Once laid out, a plate of 1 x 3 can be nailed into the studs at the top and bottom using galvanized 2¹/₂-inch nails. A 1 x 3 plate can be used at top and bottom in lieu of a heavier piece of wood as the 1 x 3 is not a structural member. It simply allows for easier and faster installation. Once the section has been constructed it can be lifted into place on the ledger plate. The measurements allow for a ¹/₈-inch leeway and, if found to be excessive, small shims should be wedged between the 1 x 3 ledger plate. If the square of the ledger plates has been checked and double checked, the new framing section will fit snugly. The section

can then be nailed into the ledger plate below and either the ledger plate or rafters above with 2-inch galvanized nails.

Top Details

Affixing the section at the roof line will be dependent on the type of house under renovation. A typical peaked roof extending over the walls of the building only requires locating the existing roof rafters. The studs need to be cut at an angle to meet the rafters. Use a bevel to check the angle. Then test your cut in place along the length of the wall. Once you are certain that you've got it right, use the piece as a template and mark the rest of the studs. The top 1 x 3 plate is then nailed on to the studs at the same angle, and the section lifted into place and nailed through to the existing rafters.

On gabled roof housing the end walls can be constructed in a similar fashion except that more intricate measurements will be required. Perform the first measurement from the peak of the roof and then work towards one side. If the spacing of the studs remains at a constant width (16 or 24 inches), each stud will be lower than the next stud by a constant amount. Ensure that your measurements are correct.

Once the pieces have been measured and cut, the sections can be assembled using 1 x 3's for the top and bottom plates. As in the previous examples, the sections can then be nailed to the ledger plate and to the roof overhang.

Flat roofed housing will present the fewest difficulties as the framing sections can be assembled with a minimal amount of measuring and cutting of angles. Simply nail the curtain wall into the ceiling joists and the ledger plate.

Framing Around Windows and Doors

Although it would be easiest and quickest to assemble the curtain wall with all of the studs at 24-inch on centre, windows and doors do not necessarily conform to this frame. It is best to alter the stud spacing to accomodate these openings before prefabricating. In most cases it will prove easiest to frame the window and doors and work the rest of the curtain wall from these fixed spots.

One should remember that studs spaced at 24 inches on centre will house friction-fit fibreglass batts. Any spaces wider or thinner will demand that the batts be cut to fit. The more cutting required, the more itching and cursing will result.

When framing for windows and doors, think the entire process out before actually constructing it. Make sure you are aware of what steps will be involved in the finishing details, including the aesthetics of the job and waterproofing aspects.

The method of rough framing the windows and doors will differ according to the siding to be re-installed, and the thickness of the new curtain wall. On the sides (vertical edge) of the windows the studs should be lined up flush to the existing window casing. This will allow for easy installation of the new exterior window casing, nailing it to the curtain wall stud and the existing casing.

The horizontal framing piece can most easily be installed after the studs are in place. The top framing piece should be installed in the same manner as the side studding — flush with the existing casing. The bottom framing piece poses a slightly more difficult problem. To ensure proper drainage from the exterior window sill, the new sill must be installed at a slight angle tilting away from the window. To allow for this, a straight line should be drawn from the existing sill and marked on the vertical studs. The framing piece is then nailed between the studs at an angle flush to the

existing sill, resulting in the window being entirely rough framed.

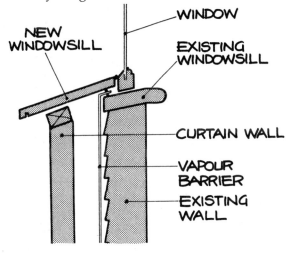

Framing of doors can be performed in a similar manner, although additional bracing may be required at the threshold to accommodate the heavier traffic. When working on windows and doors, be sure to look ahead several steps to ensure that the new work will not interfere with the operation in any way.

When two framing sections meet at the corners of the house, the corner pieces should butt together and be affixed with nails. This will allow for more secure nailing of the siding when it is installed. If, when all of the framing has been completed, the wall seems less rigid than required, additional bracing can be added to the mid-sections of the frame. This should not be required if the 2 x 3's are spanning less than 10 feet. It should also be

rememberd that the wall is not a bearing wall, and thus some deflection due to wind loading can be accommodated. Finishing work around windows and doors will tie the curtain wall to the existing house frame and provide more strength to the assembly than might initially seem apparent.

If required, additional bracing can be provided by tying the curtain wall to the house. This bracing can be attained by toe nailing 2 x 3 sections into the house and nailing the angled piece to a plate affixed to the back of the curtain wall studding. This will require a certain amount of dextrous nailing in a very small space, so try to determine the real need for bracing in advance, and if needed, put the plate onto the back of the studs before the section is raised into place.

Insulating the Curtain Wall

Now that the framing is in place, the itchy job of insulating can begin. Even if you're working on a warm sunny day, protective clothing is a necessity. Long sleeved shirts and pants will prevent the loose fibres from causing mayhem with arms and legs, and gloves can ease the burden of wear and tear on hands. A mask should be considered a necessary component of any insulating job using fibreglass or mineral wool, as loose fibres can cause serious respiratory aggravations. To top things off, a hat is a useful addition. Now you're ready for the job, uncomfortable as it may seem on a warm day.

The manner in which the insulation is to be installed will depend upon two things; the amount of insulation allowed for, and the amount of work you are willing to perform. The curtain wall should be assembled on at least a 6-inch plate allowing for the installation of R-20 6-inch fibreglass insulation. The curtain wall should be assembled 8 inches or more from the existing siding to increase R values to R-28 and higher.

For the best possible job, the insulation should be installed in two stages. An initial layer of insulation should be placed between the framing and the vapour barrier covering the existing house. The insulation should be sized to fit snugly against the framing. If using the 2 x 3 framing spaced 5½ inches from the wall, 3½ inch insulation (R-12) can be installed horizontally from the ledger plate, stacking up the wall to the house rafters. This provides a solid blanket of insulation to the wall with no thermal breaks in the material. The second layer of insulation is then installed vertically between the studding, friction fitting between the wood. This second (or exterior) insulating layer should be an R-8 batt and fit tightly between the studs. Friction fitting batts will not slump or compact if properly installed. If the space between the existing house and studding is enlarged, wider batts can be employed.

The double layer approach is thermally the most efficient, yet involves a bit more materials handling. The easier approach is to install the thicker batts vertically

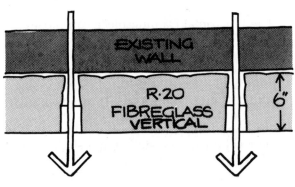

between the studs. Six-inch fibreglass batts would be the preferred choice, sized to meet 24-inch on centre framing. The main problem with this approach is that a gap will exist between the insulating batts. An uninsulated space may exist between the studs and the house, leaving a weak spot in the wall section. This will decrease the effective R value of the entire wall assembly, resulting in a less efficient installation. By understanding the trade-offs, you can make your own choices.

Sheathing

To protect the insulation from the elements, especially in those cases where the siding material employed is relatively loose, a protective layer should be applied over the framing. Usually a layer of builders' paper will suffice as a water shield, but you can use materials such as Tentest or Fibreclad (additional insulation) as a sheathing. This sheathing is the preferred option when additional support against wall racking is needed, but in 9 cases out of 10 this isn't required. The option does exist to add more insulation to the exterior of the curtain wall (rigid fibreglass, styrofoam), but the expense of such measures is somewhat prohibitive. If extra R value is needed, attain the levels by extending the thickness of the curtain wall.

Builder's paper (25 pound) can serve as a weatherizing surface. Install the paper horizontally from the bottom up, overlapping the sheets to prevent any

potential moisture penetration. The recessed windows and door frames should be similarly covered with the paper. The easiest way to affix the paper is with a staple gun. Air tightness is not a concern.

Siding

Once you're at this stage, most of the work has been completed. The remainder of the job, with a few exceptions, is a standard siding installation.

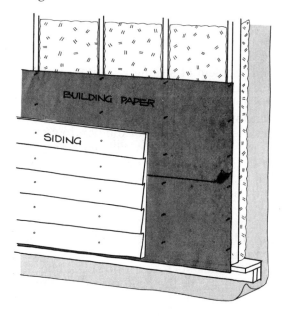

In only one case is an additional amount of framing required — if the exterior cladding is to be installed on a vertical plane. Any type of horizontal siding can be affixed to the curtain wall studs which are placed at 24-inches on centre allowing for an easy

installation. If, however, you are re-cladding the house with a vertical siding, such as board and batten, horizontal strapping must be nailed to the 2 x 3 studwork of the curtain wall.

This strapping should start at the bottom with the first piece of wood nailed to the edge of the ledger plate. Then, 24-inches on centre higher, the remainder of the strapping continues up the face of the curtain wall to the rafters of the house.

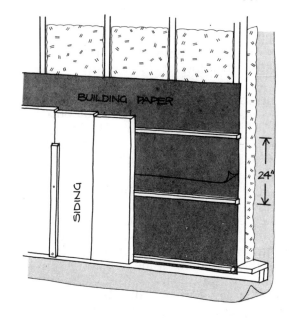

These cross-strapping members provide some additional strength to the framing of the curtain wall and allow for easy installation of the vertical siding. Make sure that you have something to nail each end of every piece of siding into. This demands some additional strapping around window and door frames, both horizontally and vertically. If working with mitered corners it would be worthwhile to nail the strapping vertically on the butted corner studs as well.

Whether installing vertical or horizontal siding, you must attend to the finishing details around windows and doors. Installation of the siding is facilitated by constructing the 2 x 3 rough stud framing of windows and doors flush to the existing window sill and casing. In most cases, you will still be left with an interesting detail where the new siding butts up to the existing window.

This aspect of the job requires pre-planning. Performing the job once is a cause for great satisfaction. Having to perform the same job on the same window because of lack of foresight is cause for headaches, backaches, alcoholism, etc. Before doing the finishing details on windows and doors, make sure that you are accommodating your future plans. Even better, make the alterations to the windows and doors before doing the finishing work on these sections of the house.

With a new curtain wall extending out from the existing house by as much as 6 to 8 inches, the sill plate, running from the window casing to beyond the siding, may need to be as much as 12 inches wide. Two important concerns must be addressed when installing the new sill plate. First, a water-tight seal between the new plate and the window casing must be attained. Otherwise rain, melting snow and sleet will leak into the wall behind the siding causing problems. Second, a drip edge must be cut into the exterior edge of the sill to prevent water from running back up the bottom edge of the plate through capillary action.

The latter problem is the easier to resolve. The drip edge demands little more than a saw cut on the bottom edge of the plate, approximately $1/4$ inch deep, running the length of the piece of wood. This kerf will prevent the movement of water from running back up the sill.

The problem of sealing is a bit more difficult to resolve. To obtain the best possible fit of the sill to the existing window casing, the sill plate should be bevelled to the angle of the window casing. In most instances, this will be an angle of 5 to 10°. The better the cut and the tighter the fit, the less time required for caulking and sealing the joint.

The caulking bead will be required to provide a weatherproof seal between the existing casing and the new sill. A high quality caulk such as Mono should be employed with the bead placed on the butt edge of the window casing. As the new sill is slid into place, the bead should be compressed to fill spaces between the wood. The new sill should then be nailed into place and the excess caulk removed from the joint, with the remainder being smoothed out to prevent ridges or pools from forming.

In the same manner the vertical casing pieces and top casing should be installed and sealed. The sill of the window should extend beyond the new cladding of the building by $3/4$ to 1 inch.

The vertical and top casing should be installed so that they run flush to the exterior siding. This will allow for the exterior face trim to be nailed over the edge of the casing, resulting in a neat finishing detail. With a litte more work the exterior edge of the casing and the edge of the face trim could be mitered to provide a seamless joint between the two pieces.

The 'Cadillac Version'

The best possible exterior retrofit would involve the thorough job of installing a new vapour barrier and re-insulating the structure from the footings of the building, up beyond the roof rafters to the peak of the roof. While this type of job poses some interesting construction difficulties, it resolves the major weakness in the structure's new insulated shell (the gap between the exterior wall insulation and the interior ceiling insulation). Most people are willing to allow this relatively small problem to go unresolved, but some get around the difficulties by performing the re-insulation of the roof from the exterior. This method is relevant if you seek to substantially increase the insulating levels in sloped or cathedral ceilings which have a limited amount of space in which insulation can be installed.

If you have an accessible attic, it will almost always be easier and cheaper to install the additional insulation there. The only other time at which the exterior approach might be considered would be if a re-roofing job were required.

The section referring to vapour barrier installation and the "theoretical dew point" is useful. (See page 13). This theory accounts for the manner in which condensation forms in newly insulated wall or ceiling sections if the vapour barrier is not properly installed. If warm moist air is allowed to cool too much, the water vapour will condense into droplets of water. As a rule of thumb place the vapour barrier no more than one-third of the way into the insulating level of the wall or ceiling section. If you are striving for an insulating value of R-40, the vapour barrier should be inside the R-12 level. In many cases the insulation levels in the attic already exceed the point at which a new vapour barrier can be installed. For a safe installation of a new vapour barrier on the roof exterior make sure that you either remove some of the existing insulation in the attic or that you apply adequate insulation over top of the vapour barrier on the exterior to meet the rule of thumb.

In most attics there is an area of heat loss through the ceiling equivalent to the exterior dimensions of the house. If you live in a home with simple exterior dimensions of 30 feet by 40 feet, no matter how many stories, you have 1200 square feet of attic space. However, as soon as you consider the installation of an exterior re-skinning of the roof, depending on the pitch of roof, the area of heat loss can be increased to as much as 1800 square feet — a 50 per cent increase. This means that the exterior insulation would need to total R-60 to reduce the equivalent heat loss met by an insulating level of R-40 placed on the attic floor. Not only a more difficult, but a more expensive proposition.

However, there are many cases when exterior re-insulation of the home's roof is the preferred option. The job itself is not dissimilar from the exterior re-cladding of the walls of the building mentioned previously, with two major exceptions. First you will be working higher in the air under more difficult conditions, and second more attention must be paid to the venting of the newly insulated sections. Let us progress from the initial stages of the wall re-insulation.

Rather than stopping the vapour barrier which is installed over the existing wall of the house at the roof rafters, the 6 mil polyethylene sheeting is continued directly around the soffits and carried up to the peak of the roof. The easiest way to perform this aspect of the job involves starting from the peak of the roof and simply unrolling the plastic down the roofline and the walls and cutting it to stop at the house footings. To ensure that the plastic stays in place and is not blown about, some small pieces of strapping can be nailed into the roofline over the air-vapour barrier. Once the initial sheet of

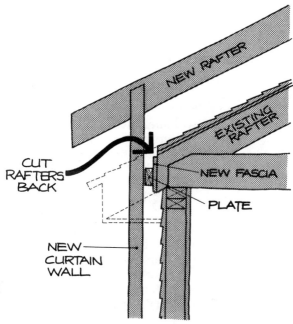

poly has been put in place extending from the roof peak, a bead of acoustical caulk should be put on to the edge of the plastic to provide an air-tight seal next to the sheet. Once the caulking has been performed the next sheet can be unravelled. Apply some pressure over the bead to ensure positive adhesion from one sheet to the next. This isn't difficult to perform on the walls of the house where the seams can be reached from a ladder, but you won't find the same ease when working on the roof. Walking on plastic will cause several problems. The integrity of the newly installed vapour barrier can be negated by walking on the plastic, causing puncture holes or rips in the material. Also, it is almost impossible to stand on the plastic without slipping.

Several options are available. To compress the bead of caulking which has been applied, the sheet of poly laid over the bead can be rolled back to allow access to the seam. This will alleviate problems at this early stage. A more comprehensive solution is needed so that the remainder of the work can be performed on the roof without destroying the air-vapour barrier. By nailing a series of 2 x 4's horizontally across the plastic at 24-inches on centre, a foot-hold is provided that can double as a means of holding the vapour barrier in place. The other option involves placing a layer of Tentest or another inexpensive sheathing material directly over the vapour barrier so that it is totally protected.

Detail at the end of the roof rafters also affects vapour barrier installation: substantial overhang might pose problems as the job progresses. Before installing the vapour barrier it might be advantageous to cut the roof rafters back to the level where the new curtain wall will extend, and by nailing a new fascia piece to the end of the rafters, use that as the top brace for the curtain wall. The studs used for the curtain wall construction would extend beyond the roof line by 10 to 16 inches, depending on the amount of roof insulation required. A plate would be affixed to the back of the prefabricated wall sections which could then be nailed into the newly installed fascia .

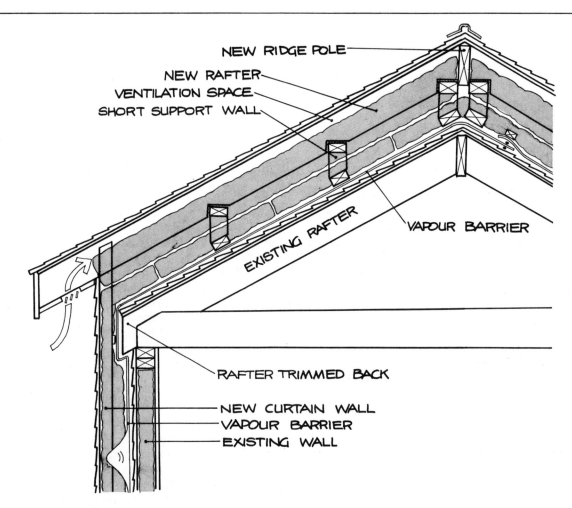

NEW RIDGE POLE
NEW RAFTER
VENTILATION SPACE
SHORT SUPPORT WALL
EXISTING RAFTER
VAPOUR BARRIER
RAFTER TRIMMED BACK
NEW CURTAIN WALL
VAPOUR BARRIER
EXISTING WALL

The extended studs would then be used as supporting braces for the new rafters to be put in place over the existing roof. Support for the new rafters at the peak of the roof can be provided by constructing a short support wall constructed from 2 x 4's extending to the required height. If you are looking to re-insulate the roof with an additional R-40, space must be allowed for the 12 inches of insulation, as well as some additional space to allow for proper venting of the roof. The new roof needs to be situated approximately 16 inches above the existing roof line; therefore the curtain wall studs would extend 16 inches higher than the roof line and a supporting wall extending 12½ inches above the roof would be needed on either side of the peak of the roof.

You will also require an intermediate bracing for the rafters. This can be accomplished either through construction of additional supporting sections placed at the quarter points of the rafters, or through individual bracing of each of the rafter sections. Although continuous supporting walls will require additional lumber, the assemblies can be prefabricated at ground level and lifted into place over top of the vapour barrier in a manner which demands a minimum amount of work on the roof. The major drawback is the extra notching required for each of the rafters.

To provide stability to the newly installed rafters, a new ridge plate can be put in place employing a 1 x 6 into which the rafters extending up either side of the roof are nailed. Once the shell has been completed the re-insulation can be performed. Over the existing vapour barrier two 6-inch fibreglass batts can be laid perpendicular to each other. The first layer of insulation should be placed horizontally (lying flat on the roof). The second layer of batting is placed on a vertical plane running between the newly installed rafters and the first layer of insulation. This will allow for adequate air movement from the soffits of the building over top of the insulation. To ensure this air movement, it must be remembered not to extend either the roof or the wall insulation too close to the roofline.

At this point the job becomes a standard roofing job. A layer of sheathing must be placed over the rafters providing a new diaphragm to the house. This sheathing could be either a Tentest layer or an exterior grade plywood. Once this sheathing has been installed from the peak of the roof to the ends of the rafters, the new roofing material can be applied over top. The remaining work required will involve installation of the new soffit at the bottom edge of the rafters, allowing adequate screening or venting so as not to impede the flow of air. If ventilation problems are seen as a major concern, a ridge vent can be installed at the peak of the roof.

Several notes of caution are offered. First, this is a relatively serious approach to re-insulating the home. It will demand a considerable amount of work, and possibly some greater expertise in working with tools than the other approaches offered in this book. Secondly, you should be concerned about the additional loading which you are adding to the roof structure. It is recommended that before progressing with this job you consult a structural engineer, or at least your local building inspector to ensure that you don't end up with a well-insulated rubble pile. In most cases the addition of several pounds per square foot will not pose a problem, yet in some buildings it won't be allowed.

Aesthetic Considerations

At the front and back of the house this is not a concern as the newly installed walls and roof can be maintained in proportion to the rest of the house. However, the gabled ends of the building will demand some ingenious solutions, as you will now be looking at as much as 16-inch spaces between the new roofline and the original gable.

The benefits to be accrued from this approach, however, are significant. Extending the vapour barrier continuously from the footings of the building over the entire house will resutt in an installation which is unattainable through any other approach. The building can be made entirely air-tight if care is taken during installation. This will obviously result in a draft-free living environment, as well as long term security for the structural integrity of the building.

Note: An intermediate approach to trimming the existing rafters of the house requires installing the roof and wall air-vapour barriers independently of each other. Use extruded polystyrene between the roof rafters as the linking material. In this approach the curtain wall extends up to the rafters and is affixed to their underside. Between each set of rafters a chunk of extruded polystyrene is installed sitting tight to the rafters and roof boards. The polystyrene is then caulked to the wood to ensure a good air-vapour seal. The vapour barrier extending up the wall would be caulked to the siding and sealed with the acoustical sealant. The vapour barrier extending down the roof from the peak is then caulked to the roofing materials at a spot directly above the styrofoam boards. As the extruded polystyrene acts as an effective vapour barrier, when coupled with an effective caulking job, major problems are overcome.

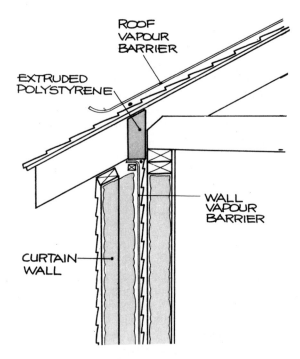

ROOF VAPOUR BARRIER

EXTRUDED POLYSTYRENE

WALL VAPOUR BARRIER

CURTAIN WALL

Economic Considerations

As a general rule, the exterior approach to the super-insulated retrofit will be the most cost effective means of attaining significant energy savings. In many ways the exterior approach is less complicated. Interior variables to consider include the type of construction, the degree of difficulty encountered when installing the air-vapour barrier and the specific finishing details you require. The only major variable in the exterior curtain wall retrofit is the choice of siding to be installed over the new wall.

Estimating the costs of the exterior retrofit is relatively simple. As the majority of the cost will be associated with the acquisition of the materials for the job, you should be able to gain a realistic idea of the total cost. Only a few items are required. First, the vapour barrier and insulation, followed by the lumber for the framing of the ledger plate and curtain wall. Next, the purchase of siding and, finally, the materials needed to upgrade the windows.

The cost of polyethylene will amount to between 2.5 to 3.5 cents per square foot of wall space. Insulation costs will vary considerably, but should range from between 28 to 32 cents per square foot for R-20 fibreglass batts, or slightly more for one layer of R-12 and a second layer of R-8.

The installation of extruded polystyrene below the ledger plate of the curtain wall will add to the total cost of the job. The polystyrene (styrofoam) will range in cost from 28 cents per square foot per inch of board to upwards of 35 cents. Installing R-20 (4 inches) would lead to a cost of between $1.15 to $1.40 for the material cost per square foot of installed wall. If the foundation wall is trenched to the footings by the homeowner, the total out of pocket expense for the average house would approach $1,100 — exclusive of the amount

of beer needed to keep your friends interested in the job. If the foundation is to be exposed using a back hoe, add another couple of hundred dollars. If a contractor is to be employed, you can double the expense.

Lumber costs will range from extremely low prices if you have an accessible supply of recycled lumber, to a maximum price if you purchase a construction grade lumber from your local building supply outlet. Assuming that people will endeavour to find cheap prices, we'll provide an estimate on store bought lumber. For the curtain wall you can use economy grade lumber. This wood (which is not dressed on all four sides) will usually result in a price of 40 to 50 per cent less than construction grade lumber.

On average the lumber requirements will range from 19 to 25 cents per square foot of exterior wall. This includes the lumber needed for the ledger plates, the curtain wall framing and the rough framing of the doors and windows. It is based on costs at the local building supply outlet.

In summary, the cost of the job which is directly attributable to the upgrading of the thermal envelope — the air-vapour barrier, framing and insulation — should amount to between 50 to 60 cents per square foot of exterior wall. An innovative purchase of materials or "deals" should reduce this figure considerably.

Over and above this aspect of the job the curtain wall will need to be sided. Here we encounter a major variable. Depending on the aesthetic and cost concerns of the homeowner, the price for re-siding will range from 50 cents to six dollars per square foot for a brick veneer. The decision is usually based on aesthetics and the amount of upkeep required. Aluminum siding has become increasingly popular because it is maintenance free and much less expensive than brick. Both of the above options require a considerable amount of energy to produce and will likely continue to escalate in price. Wood siding options are generally less expensive but will require a fair amount of maintenance over the years. The siding option that you choose will be the largest single component of the exterior retrofit, regardless of your choice. If you are not successful with your selection, re-use the existing siding of the building.

Only a few contractors have performed this job with enough frequency to quote a price. Most will provide estimates of between $3.00 and $5.00 per square foot with a reasonably priced siding. For the do-it-yourselfer, costs for the same job range from $1.10 to $2.00 per square foot of insulated wall. For the average size house this would amount to a total cost for the curtain wall of between $4,400 and $7,250 for the contracted job, and between $1,800 and $2,900 for the do-it-yourself version.

To determine the energy savings and projected payback of the job you will need to perform the calculations outlined in the technical appendix of the book. One must, however, recognize that when performed in conjunction with a thorough upgrading of the windows of the house, energy savings of between 75 to 80 per cent should result. On the average fuel bill this translates into a dollar savings of approximately $600 to $850 in 1981-82. One can only suppose that the savings will increase as fuel prices continue to rise.

As with most retrofit work, if renovations are already planned (i.e. new siding), the incremental cost of adding the curtain wall is easily justified. The payback period of the exterior retrofit will alter according to the existing condition of the thermal envelope. Adding R-20 to a house with little or no insulation can result in a saving of as much as 35 cents per square foot of wall in conductive heat transfer alone. Savings will be smaller if the house is already insulated.

Costs for a Typical House (1,500 square feet and basement)

Walls	Owner Built	Contracted
— Cheap siding	$1,600	approx. $3,200
— Aluminum siding	$2,900	$4,350
Basement (R-20)	$1,100	approx. $3,000
Total cost	$2,700 — $4,000	$6,200 — $7,350

Interior Retrofit

Super-insulating a house from the interior poses many difficult problems which call for innovative solutions. To attain a continuous air-vapour barrier and a thorough blanket of insulation is considerably more demanding on the interior. In spite of the difficulties this will be the preferred approach for many homeowners. Some people will be unwilling to cover the exterior facade of their homes, specifically those who live in brick or stone houses or those houses with historical value. The interior approach will make the most sense to those who are considering a major renovation.

Although the interior approach to the super-insulated retrofit will demand more time and attention to detail than is the case with the exterior work, a thorough job will result in equally significant energy savings. Similarly, the benefits of creating a quieter and more comfortable living environment will result from retrofit work performed on the building's interior. A conscientious effort to properly seal and re-insulate the house should result in energy savings of as much as 75 to 85 per cent.

The easiest manner of performing a super-insulated retrofit would involve a thorough gutting of the house interior and the removal of all interior partition walls which are adjacent to the exterior shell of the house. The job would be further simplified if the joists throughout the house were removed, but in most cases this would result in the walls and ceilings tumbling down around you. In most cases the homeowner will be working in less than the ideal situation. Much of the time will be spent working around the hidden spots of the house — between floors, around partition walls and in the attic.

One of the saddest elements of the interior super-insulated retrofit is that all of the work will be hidden away from sight when the job is complete. (In some cases this may be one of its redeeming features.) When your friends come to visit, few will notice the additional thickness of the walls or the newly recessed windows. No one will see the work performed to obtain a continuous seal between floors and around partition walls. Indeed, with the exception of the fuel company, people may question what you have been spending your time doing.

It is important to recognize the differences between the re-insulation of an existing house and the super-insulation of that same house. The main criteria required to attain the energy savings possible through the latter approach involves the correct installation of the air-vapour barrier. Whereas a re-insulation would involve the installation of a vapour barrier over newly constructed walls, the super-insulated approach calls for a vapour barrier that is continued throughout the house (between walls and floors) resulting in a completely air-tight shell. The super-insulated approach also requires the installation of higher insulation levels than would be considered necessary by the average contractor or homeowner.

Yet in most instances the super-insulated retrofit requires no greater construction experience or care. Most of the work can be easily performed by the homeowner, even if he/she has a minimal amount of experience with a hammer and saw. In many cases the non-trained conscientious homeowner will be capable of performing a better job than the carpenter or contracting firm who are set in their ways and haven't understood the requirements of the super-insulated retrofit.

As with all construction work, the entire job should be planned out in detail before hammering the first nail. There is little as depressing as being forced to tear down several hours of work as a result of a lack of planning or care. Such a thought is only surpassed by the prospect of spending several weeks and a substantial investment only to find that your fuel bill didn't decrease dramatically. If attention is not paid to all aspects of the job, this can indeed happen.

Assessing the House

Before drawing up plans or putting anything down on paper, take a slow walk around your house. Try to visualize the various aspects of the job: demolition (if it is required), construction of new wall and ceiling sections, installation of the vapour barrier and the potential means of ensuring its continuity and longevity, options for treating the existing windows (or the installation of new windows), means of shuttering the windows, and the finishing details of the job. Try to obtain a clear picture of the step-by-step process involved.

Let's take an imaginary walk through a typical house to determine some of the considerations which will come into play. Remember the general rules outlined in the *Primer* of the book to more easily perform the exercise.

Initially turn your attention to the various means of eliminating the uncontrolled movement of air into and out of the house. Ideally the interior of the house is totally enveloped in a layer of thick plastic. The house should be viewed as a huge receptacle: Once the air-vapour barrier is installed you should be able to turn the house upside down, and fill it full of water without any leaks occuring. By starting from that viewpoint, right away some of the problems become apparent.

The type of construction of the house will determine your plans. If the house is built

with frame wall sections on the exterior walls, you'll have to consider the merits of adding insulation to the cavities. Similarly, you'll need to determine whether a vapour barrier is present behind the existing walls so as to avoid a vapour lock situation. If, on the other hand, the wall has been finished with a lathe and plaster (as is typical in solid brick buildings), you'll want to determine whether to remove the wall before progressing with the construction of new walls.

In frame houses it will be worth your time to remove the existing interior wall board. In this manner you can easily upgrade the existing insulation if it has deteriorated over time. You may also discover that there is no insulation. The above mentioned concern about creating a vapour lock between the new air-vapour barrier and the outside surface has been discussed in the *Primer*. We mentioned that the rule of thumb suggests that two-thirds of the insulation should be on the outside of the vapour barrier and as much as one-third on the warm side. If a vapour barrier exists on the exterior wall, it will become located outside of the dew point when the new interior walls are installed. To alleviate any potential problems, the existing barrier should be removed or at least thoroughly scored before any new wall construction is performed.

In solid brick or masonry construction types, the lathe and plaster will generally encase no more than a $3/4$-inch air space. It would be hard to justify trying to fill this

cavity with any form of insulation. If the wall does not constitute a vapour barrier it can be left in place. If the wall has been painted with several layers of an enamel paint, it may become necessary to either bang holes in the walls or pull them down. If, on the other hand, the wall is adequately permeable, yet the extra $1^1/2$ inches will make a difference to the size of the room, demolition may also be justified. Although it is not a particularly difficult or time consuming job, tearing down a lathe and plaster wall is an exceptionally dusty and dirty process and should be avoided if possible.

Having thought this process through, turn to the individual rooms. Attempt to visualize how much of the room can be taken away for the new insulation, as this will determine the insulation levels to be allowed. If R-20 is the minimum amount of insulation to be installed, and you plan to use fibreglass batts, you will be taking away 6 inches from the exterior wall of the room. To attain an insulating value of R-32, the new interior wall will be more than 10 inches from the existing wall.

The basement of the house should also be toured to determine which of the options best suit your purpose. If you have recently upgraded your basement you may be reticent to demolish your work. At this point the option of an exterior insulation of the foundation walls in conjunction with proper sealing techniques may be preferable. In an unfinished basement you will want to visualize the construction of new interior walls and possibly the installation of a new insulated floor. Alternatively, you might even consider the option of turning your basement into an unheated area of the house by installing insulation between the joists of the first floor.

The ceilings and attic of your house will demand the same pre-planning. In order to properly seal these sections the air-vapour barrier will need to encase the entire area, stretching over or through partition walls. In analysing your house you should consider whether or not adequate insulation can be installed into the existing cavities. If not, you will need to frame out additional cavities.

If extensive wiring and plumbing alterations are to be performed at the same time as the retrofit, you should consider their implication on the work. Determine at what stage in the job this work should be performed, realizing that the integrity of the air-vapour barrier is your greatest concern.

If you can determine where the new walls are to be situated, you can also start to look at the work required to put the finishing details on to the now recessed windows. If new windows are to be installed, or if changes are to be incorporated into the existing windows, determine at which stage in the job this work should be performed. Similarly, measures for shuttering or shading the windows should be analysed and put into a work schedule.

No matter how serious you are about performing a thorough job, compromises may be forced on you in certain locations. Ideally all places in the building will be insulated. However, before you embark on this best-of-all-possible-worlds approach think carefully about dismantling kitchens, bathrooms and stairways which are located around the exterior perimeter of the house. You must realize the immensity of the task. This might not pose a concern to those undertaking a thorough gutting of the house, but if this is not your plan it is difficult to justify the additional work. If confronted with some of these problems, you can do little more than remedial work withoug adding a major component to the job.

By now you should have a better idea of the task ahead of you and what will be required. As this chapter progresses through the various means of upgrading the thermal efficiency of existing housing, you will be able to relate the options to your requirements.

Demolition

Although meticulous people fear the hazards of demolition it can be a rewarding task. Indeed, sometimes in the frenzy of the task it becomes necessary to restrain yourself from getting carried away. Demolition requirements will vary with each specific house and homeowner. If we assume that some demolition is already required in the house for renovation purposes, we can focus on the specific

demolition needs of the super-insulated retrofit. We have discussed the need, or lack thereof, for tearing down existing walls on the exterior shell of the house to allow access to the cavity sections, or to enlarge the size of the room before re-insulating. Over and above these requirements, several other areas will need to be considered: the space between floors, partition walls and ceilings on the top floor. To ease the job, consideration should also be given to the removal of exhaust vents, plumbing and wiring systems and even the heating system if major alterations to any of the above are forecast.

To create a continuous air-vapour barrier from floor to floor, you must expose the joist cavities at the perimeter of the exterior walls. In most cases this is accomplished by removing the floor covering and sub-flooring, as well as a section of the ceiling material below. You will need to expose a large enough cavity so that the job can be performed without causing the installer to contort his body while doing the required work. A safe distance to remove the flooring and ceiling is 12 inches, at least in those locations where the joists run perpendicular to the exterior wall. At the ends of the house where the joists are parallel to the walls as much as 2 feet will need to be removed. This accounts for the fact that when you get around to replacing the flooring and ceiling, you will need something to nail the wood or drywall to. In these cases the existing materials should be pulled off to the middle of the first joist.

If the thought of this demolition makes you queasy there is an easier, but less effective method of running insulation and the vapour barrier between floors. It involves exposing only the floor joists from below, but leaving the floor and sub-floor intact. The details are described later at the end of the "Insulation between floors" section of this chapter.

Most of the partition walls which butt against the exterior walls will need to be exposed in the same manner as the joist cavities. You will want to run the air barrier continuously through the walls from room to room. The wallboard on either side of the partition should be removed to the middle of the first stud inside the room (if the entire wall section is not being taken down as part of the renovations).

Where the cavities in flat roofs or cathedral ceilings are to be extended, the existing wallboard can be pulled down. If additional insulation is to be added above the ceiling, as would be the case in houses with attics, measures will need to be taken to allow for the installation of a new air-vapour barrier located below the joists. The areas at the top of partition walls will need to be removed to allow the barrier to pass over the top plate — not an easy feature of the job. The rest of the ceiling can be left in place as the air-vapour barrier and the new drywall can be installed over top of the existing ceiling.

If major alterations to the heating system, plumbing or wiring of the house are considered, removal of unnecessary ductwork, wiring and plumbing lines should be performed at this stage. By this time you should have consulted with your local contractors to determine what they can use and what can be discarded. Any exhaust vents which become redundant to the installation of an air-to-air heat exchanger should also be removed at this time, as well as recessed ceiling fixtures which protrude into the house attic. If unattended to, both of these items will bypass much of the work performed in tightening up the shell of the building.

If you plan to re-install the original trim around windows and doors after the retrofit is completed, it should be carefully removed and marked. This will enable you to store it in a safe place while working. If you're dealing with older trim, a great deal

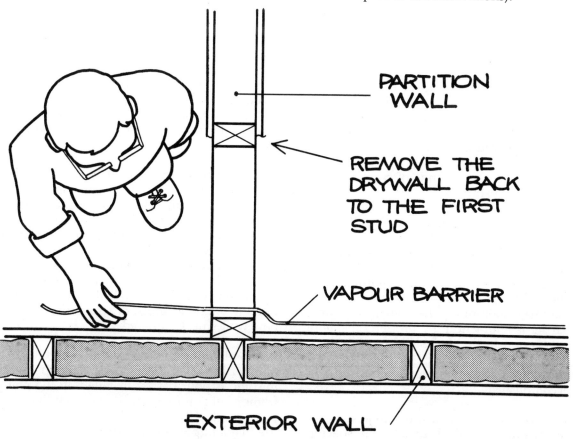

PARTITION WALL

REMOVE THE DRYWALL BACK TO THE FIRST STUD

VAPOUR BARRIER

EXTERIOR WALL

of care should be exhibited when removing the wood. Much of the older trim is extremely difficult to replace.

A Word of Caution

Perform all of the demolition work at the same time. It is difficult enough to live or work in a dust-filled house for a short period of time; even worse to force yourself through the ordeal more than once. It's psychologically beneficial to do all of the tearing down at the beginning of the job, so that from that point on you can concentrate on upgrading the structure. To be forced into a demolition job, no matter how small, at a later stage of the job makes you feel like you're going one step forward and two steps back.

Starting to Build

Insulating Between Floors

The most time consuming aspect of the super-insulated retrofit involves the installation of insulation and the air-vapour barrier continuously from floor to floor. It is important that this aspect of the job be performed before any work is started on the walls, both above and below. Be sure the details between floors and partition walls are completed before the new wall construction is begun. Simply speaking, without closing over the holes created between floors, there wouldn't be anywhere to place the newly framed walls. More importantly, by performing the between-floor joist job at an early stage,

greater flexibility is afforded.

Two options are available to install the vapour barrier and insulation between floors. You could take a sheet of plastic and extend it through the joist cavity so that it hangs down to the next floor. This would be the preferred choice on those walls of the house where the floor joists run parallel to the walls. However, to try the same approach on those walls where the joists span perpendicular to the walls is another story. It would require the plastic to be cut to fit over each individual joist which, of course, leads to all sorts of gaps in the barrier. To resolve this problem the plastic would need to be caulked and taped to each joist. At an estimated 10 minutes per joist it would take more than 10 hours to do the required job on each floor of an average sized house. This option can be discarded on the grounds of cruel and unusual punishment.

The more realistic option involves the use of extruded polystyrene in the joist cavities. It can serve as both an insulating material and a vapour barrier. This means that the requirement for the plastic sheeting can be eliminated. This is especially useful where the installation of a polyethylene vapour barrier is impractical. By properly installing sheets of extruded polystyrene or urethane between each of the joist cavities, a continuous vapour barrier can be accomplished.

To perform the job, each of the joist cavities must be filled. Ideally, the spacing

between each of the joists will be standard, but the reality of the situation may demand that each of the cavities be individually measured. The rigid insulation should be cut to the depth of the joists, then measured and cut to fit snugly between the joists. It is important that the insulating board be cut so that it fits flush to both the top and bottom of the joists. This allows for easier tie-in to the vapour barrier on the new walls to be constructed above and below the joists.

To ensure the effectiveness of the rigid insulation as both an air and vapour barrier, the boards should fit tight to the wood and seams between the insulation and the joists should be caulked with an acoustical caulk or taped with a vinyl duct tape.

Placement of the rigid insulation in relation to the joist header depends upon the insulating technique to be employed above and below the joist cavity. If you have already gone to these lengths, you probably also strive for super-insulated walls, which will sit a minimum of $5\frac{1}{2}$ inches inside the existing wall. This being the case, the rigid insulation should be installed between the existing wall and the spot where the new wall will be situated.

When planning this stage of the job the manner in which the rigid insulation is tied into the vapour barrier installed on the new frame wall is important. It is crucial that a piece of plastic be extended from the top of the insulating boards, placed between the floor joists, to the interior edge of the newly installed plate. Since the board is also your vapour barrier, it is important to make certain when installing the linking piece of plastic that at no point is it situated outside of the theoretical dew point.

Having determined where the walls above and below will eventually be situated, the rigid insulation can be installed. A chalk line should be drawn over the joists

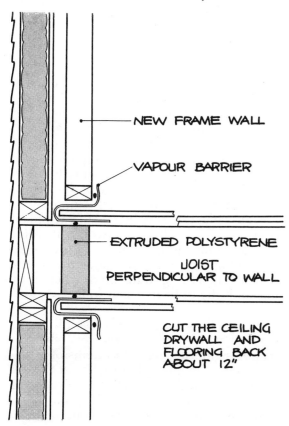

NEW FRAME WALL

VAPOUR BARRIER

EXTRUDED POLYSTYRENE

JOIST PERPENDICULAR TO WALL

CUT THE CEILING DRYWALL AND FLOORING BACK ABOUT 12"

extending the length of the room to make certain that the insulation installed is in the proper location. The insulation can then be cut and fitted into place between the joists. It is better to cut the rigid boards slightly larger than the actual cavity to ensure a tight fit. The boards are durable and can be wedged into their required location. Remember to cut the insulating material flush to the bottom and top of the joists. Once the boards are in place the cavity between the rigid insulation and the existing wall can be filled with fibreglass batting to increase the thermal resistance through the section.

Several types of insulating materials can be used for this aspect of the job. The main requirement is that it have low permeability to prevent the flow of water vapour to the outside. Several commercially available products have this characteristic, namely Styrofoam SM, rigid urethane materials and polyisocyanurate boards. Styrofoam is recommended because it is the least expensive option and it is an extremely easy material to work with.

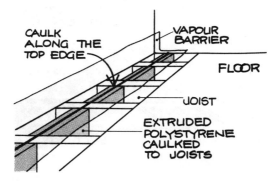

CAULK ALONG THE TOP EDGE

VAPOUR BARRIER

FLOOR

JOIST

EXTRUDED POLYSTYRENE CAULKED TO JOISTS

A 2-inch thick board of Styrofoam (blueboard) will provide a thermal resistance of R-10. By stuffing fibreglass batts on the outside of the rigid insulation you can probably attain an R value closer to 30. If even higher values are required, some additional fibreglass can be placed on the interior side of the rigid insulation, providing that it is placed inside the theoretical dew point.

Once all of the insulation has been installed, you can start thinking of how to join the rigid insulation to the walls above and below. For both the top and bottom sections, cut a 12-inch wide piece of 6 mil polyethylene, extending the length of the exposed joists. This sheet of poly will act as the bridge between the rigid insulation and the new vapour barrier to be installed on the walls. A thick bead of acoustical caulking should be placed on the top and bottom edge of the insulation, extending directly over the joists themselves. Once the bead is in place, one edge of the poly can be placed over the bead and compressed on to the caulk. The poly should be stapled through to the joist wherever necessary, making sure that the staple is immersed in the caulk. Make sure that their are no gaps between the poly and the rigid insulation or joists.

Once in place the 12-inch strip of poly sitting above the joist should be extended and temporarily taped to the existing exterior wall of the house. The strip sitting on the bottom edge will naturally hang down on its own.

Having dealt with the joist cavities that run perpendicular to the exterior walls of the house, turn your attention to the end walls of the building where the joists run parallel to the walls. Now that the flooring and ceiling have been removed back to the first interior joist, the rest of the job is quite simple. (Make sure that when you replace the flooring you have something to nail into.) If the last joist is hidden under the existing wall, you will need to nail another

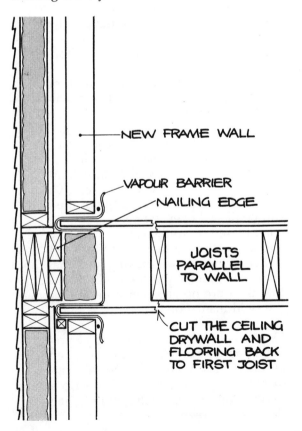

NEW FRAME WALL

VAPOUR BARRIER

NAILING EDGE

JOISTS PARALLEL TO WALL

CUT THE CEILING DRYWALL AND FLOORING BACK TO FIRST JOIST

stud to the edge of the joist so that a firm support for the flooring is provided.

A 2-foot strip of plastic should be cut to extend the width of the house. This strip can be laid in place so that several inches (8 inches) extend both above and below the joist. This will eventually be joined to the barrier installed on the new walls above and below. Fibreglass insulation can then be fitted into the cavity between the joists on the exterior side of the polyethylene. When the flooring and ceiling are replaced, the poly should be wrapped around the edge so that it is accessible. This allows it to be caulked to the air-vapour barrier that is installed on the new walls.

You can progress by replacing the subflooring and ceiling work which had to be ripped to allow access to the cavities. The first thing to remember at this stage is that you want the strips of polyethylene to reach back to where your new walls will be constructed. Secondly you want the poly to stay inside of the theoretical dewpoint.

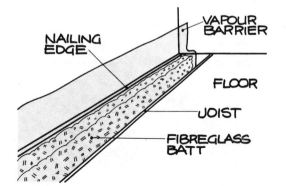

NAILING EDGE

VAPOUR BARRIER

FLOOR

JOIST

FIBREGLASS BATT

And finally, because the room in which you are working will soon be several inches more narrow, you don't necessarily have to replace all of the materials which were pulled down during the demolition.

Look at the cross section to see where you are at this point. You know where the new wall will sit. As no one will ever see what is behind the new wallboard (one of its greatest advantages), you need not be overly concerned with how much of the ripped out sections are replaced. Allow yourself to be guided by convenience and technical efficiency.

Start from above. You have ripped out a 12-inch section of subflooring to allow for easy access to the joist cavity. Some of the subflooring must be replaced to bear the weight of the new wall to be constructed above. But there is no need to go further than that. Replace the subflooring to the point where the exterior side of the new stud wall will sit. The 12-inch strip of polyethylene can now be folded back to sit over top of the subflooring so that it will lie under the new wall section. The process for the ceiling section below will be the same. Replace the ceiling to the point where it is inside of the to-be installed wall.

Although these suggestions result in somewhat slow and tedious work, there will be significant results in terms of improving the thermal efficiency of the home. The saddest aspect of the process is that no one will ever know that you've done anything different from a normal renovation. You can now move on to quicker sections of the job.

There is a short cut that will save on demolition work and installation time. It involves leaving the subflooring and flooring in place and sealing the vapour barrier onto the floor from above and below. Whereas this method is not as efficient, it may be appropriate where you have access to the joists below the floor, as is the case from an unfinished basement.

After installing the new frame wall on the first floor, bring the vapour barrier down to the floor level. Seal with acoustical sealant and staple to the floor/frame-wall junction.

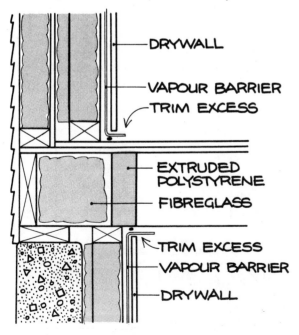

- DRYWALL
- VAPOUR BARRIER
- TRIM EXCESS
- EXTRUDED POLYSTYRENE
- FIBREGLASS
- TRIM EXCESS
- VAPOUR BARRIER
- DRYWALL

Insulate between the joists from below using a rigid insulation as described above. Caulk the insulation to the joists and to the subflooring above. The vapour barrier in the floor below is then caulked to the rigid insulation.

This technique gives a good job of providing a fairly continuous vapour barrier and insulation without having to demolish your flooring.

Interior Framing

First a few brief comments about interior framing options. Obviously it is desirable to minimize the amount of framing for newly installed insulation both on economic and technical grounds. Although you install a target amount of insulation between studs, you are left with the comparatively weak thermal resistance of the studs themselves. Take a standard wall section — say 10 feet long and 8 feet high — almost 10 per cent of the area is taken up by studs, plates and window and door framing. Even though the wall is insulated to R-20, the effective R value over the entire wall section may be only R-18 when the total thermal resistance of the wall assembly is taken into account.

Thermal bridging from the warm interior to the cold exterior (points where heat conducts directly to the outside) must also be considered. Ideally, houses would be built so that no component of the structure extends from the interior to the exterior. However, conventional houses are loaded with weak spots; foundation walls,

floor joists, window casings, etc. Some of these thermal bridges can be remedied through the proper installation of insulating materials, yet in most houses the bridges cannot be entirely eliminated. Different materials designed to reduce the impact of heat conducting from the interior to the exterior are usually referred to as thermal breaks.

The major problem you'll confront is installing the air-tight vapour barrier. Even though you should attempt to install a continuous vapour barrier throughout the house, many problems arise when working on partition walls and the floor joists. As the house is tightened up, the weak spots in the vapour barrier installation will be cause for greater and greater concern. Twenty-five pounds of water vapour per day is generated in the average house. This usually dissipates through the entire structure of the building. After the vapour barrier is installed the area through which all the water vapour can escape is minimized, thereby creating the potential for greater damage in those weak spots. Remember that even small holes in the vapour barrier can be cause for concern.

One other word of caution: If the house is relatively new, or if renovations have been performed over the last several years, a vapour barrier may exist on the exterior walls. This may pose the same problems associated with double vapour barriers. Since the new wall to be constructed will house insulation, the old vapour barrier may now be found outside of the theoretical dew point, causing a vapour lock in the cavity wall. If this is the case, the existing vapour barrier will need to be slashed or entirely removed. Do this during the demolition phase of the job.

Finally, plan the entire job with a view to minimizing your labours — an integral component of energy conservation. Plan so that most of the work can be performed at ground level, in prefabricated sections. Excessive work atop ladders leads not only to wasted time while running up and down to retrieve dropped tools, but also increases the potential for strained muscles and broken bones.

Framing New Walls

There are ways to bring walls to super-insulated status. Most simply, prefabricate frame wall sections, lift them into place, then nail through the plates into the joists below and above at the required distance from the existing wall. The second option, which is more technically efficient yet slightly more time consuming, involves building the same wall sections, nailing them into place and then, after installing a layer of insulation and vapour barrier, cross-strapping the new wall with 2 x 3's on edge. Both options, if carefully installed, with result in significant energy savings.

Framing

This is probably the easiest aspect of the super-insulated retrofit. Be aware that a touch of foresight will facilitate the finishing steps after the new frame is in place. Planning the job will eliminate needless time making up for errors committed at this early stage. As a rule, the majority of the job can be performed at floor level, providing that adequate space is available on a room by room basis.

Carefully measure the width and height of the exterior wall to be upgraded. Using 2 x 3's or 2 x 4's as the framing lumber, two plates extending the width of the room should be laid out on the floor in front of the wall. They act as the top and bottom of the wall sections to be constructed. Cut the studs to the height of the existing wall less $3^{1}/_{4}$ inches when measured from the floor to the ceiling. This length compensates for the top and bottom plates and allows room to raise the wall section into place.

Once the various pieces have been cut and laid out on the floor, the pre-fab process can begin. To minimize the required amount of wood, the studs can be spaced at 24 inches on centre. This also permits easy installation of fibreglass batts designed to friction fit between standard 24-inch on centre studding. In a room with a solid section of wall (no windows or doors) you can simply place the studs across the room at 24-inch centres. If there are windows or doors on the exterior wall, the first framing members should be put in place where the existing framing pieces are located. Depending on the type of finishing details planned for the window and door casings, the studs should line up to be either flush

to the existing casing or recessed the thickness of the wallboard to be installed. By this point you can no longer procrastinate about the finishing details without the risk of tearing down that which you have carefully constructed. The chapter detailing window treatment is useful for finishing work.

Having determined the correct positioning of the studs to be used as new framing for the windows and doors, the intermediate studs can be positioned to provide the required spacings for the wallboard to be installed. Once again think through to the wallboard stage of the job to minimize cutting and taping. You must also cut studs for the ends of the walls .

Having laid all of the studs in position, the entire wall assembly can be nailed into place. Ensure that it is square and that the individual studs are securely nailed to the

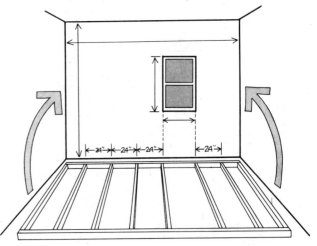

bottom and top plates. Once the entire assembly has been completed, it can be lifted directly into place against the exterior wall. Determine the positioning of the assembly by the amount of insulation required. Assuming you are adding an additional R-20 to the walls, the interior face of the wall assembly will sit 5½ inches from the existing wall.

At this point the 12-inch piece of polyethylene which was previously affixed to the joist cavities must be extended out from the existing wall so that the bottom plate sits over the plastic, and the plastic from the joist cavity above extends over the top plate and drops down the top couple of inches of the wall. To avoid destroying the integrity of the vapour barrier, the wall assembly should be carefully slid over the plastic both at the top and bottom. The plastic should extend out from the new wall by at least 3 inches.

Having fit the plastic over the new wall assembly, the bottom plate can be nailed into place. The plate should be squared to the existing wall at a distance of 5½ inches. The plate should be nailed directly to the joists below, using 3½-inch nails. Once the bottom plate has been fixed, the top plate can be nailed into the floor joists above. At this point place a level on the wall assembly to ensure it is vertical. In many older homes level surfaces are difficult to find. Having levelled the wall assembly it can be secured to the joists above. Shims may be needed. Now you have a new frame wall.

Insulating the wall section can be done by one of two methods. If you are after optimal performance and willing to abide a little more itching, two layers of insulation should be installed. In the cavity between the new wall assembly and the existing exterior wall, R-12 fibreglass batts should be laid horizontally. A second layer of R-8 insulation should then be fitted vertically between the wall studs. This provides an excellent means of insulation as any air gaps created between batts are virtually eliminated. If, however, it sounds like too much work, or the insulation is difficult to obtain at the required thicknesses, the easier option is to simply install R-20 batts vertically between the studs. The problem

with this option is that the insulation will not completely expand behind the studs to fill the void.

Before installing the vapour barrier electrical outlets need to be pulled out to the new wall assembly. These boxes can be accomodated in several ways. Many builders mount polypans on cross-strapping fitted between the studs. The electrical outlets are fitted in to a polyethylene pan which has a hole in the back to allow the wire to be passed through. The wire should be caulked to the box where it passes through with an acoustical caulk.

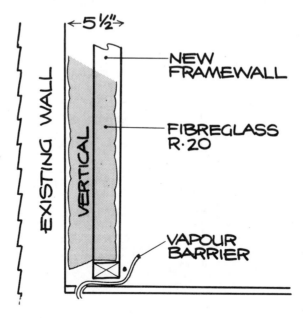

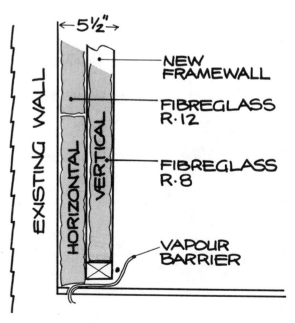

Two types of the polyethylene pans are available. The concept evolved out of Saskatchewan where a large PVC pan was installed between exterior studs to pieces of strapping placed horizontally between the studs. The electrical wire was passed through the hole in the pan and run into the electrical box placed inside the container. The vapour barrier was caulked to the flange of the box with an acoustical caulk.

Another similar product is marketed out of Montreal. The boxes are only slightly larger than the conventional electrical box. The electrical box is mounted in its normal manner by nailing through the sides of the plastic container to the vertical studs. Once

installed it is connected to the vapour barrier as described above.

In a recent publication detailing air-vapour barrier installation practices, reference is made to homemade polypans used by a Saskatchewan builder. A 2 x 4 shell is constructed to fit between the vertical studs. A piece of plastic is mounted on the back of the frame and extended around the edges to the front face of the box. The electrical wire is pulled through a pre-drilled hole in the 2 x 4 which is caulked to prevent any gaps. The electrical box itself is affixed to the edge of the newly constructed box and the whole frame is nailed into place between the studs. A relatively simple, easy-to-assemble option.

Sealing Outlets

Polypans are difficult to obtain in many regions of Canada and the United States. If accessibility is a problem for you, polyethylene can be used to perform the same function. Before nailing the outlet box to the stud, a 24-inch by 24-inch sheet of plastic should be cut. A hole punched into the center of the sheet allows the eletrical wire to pass through. The plastic housing is caulked and taped to the wire to prevent air or vapour passage. Extend the poly around the entire electrical box to totally encase it. The outlet box can now be nailed to the stud in the conventional manner.

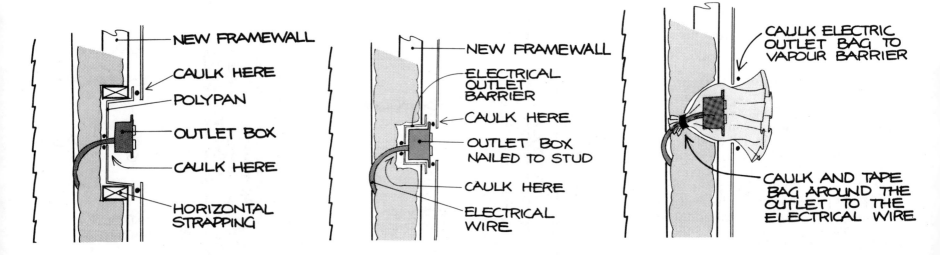

When the vapour barrier is hung over the new wall a hole can be cut directly in front of the outlet box. The plastic sheet encasing the box can be extended out through the hole and carefully caulked to the newly hung air-vapour barrier. As the plastic will probably have bunched up, caulking will need to be applied between the folds of the plastic.

This job is tedious and time consuming, but if performed carefully can have the same results as the use of polypans.

Having performed the preliminary requirements of extending the air-vapour barrier through the floor, and having sealed the electrical outlets, the vapour barrier can now be hung over the new wall. Initially the strip of poly extending from the joist cavities should be caulked to the plate and stapled to the bottom plate. Caulk the new sheet of poly and staple it over the flange to the top plate and extend it down the wall to the bottom plate where the same treatment is employed.

At the ends of the wall section where the vapour barrier is to protrude through partition walls, 6 inches of plastic should be overhung. Where the partition wall sections have been opened, covered with plastic and then re-closed, the poly can be caulked together using acoustical sealant.

The vapour barrier installed on the exterior walls of the top floor should overhang at the top of the wall section by 6 to 12 inches. This allows for easy tie-in to the new vapour barrier to be installed on the ceiling of that floor, preventing warm air and water vapour from escaping into the building's attic or roof sections. Similarly, if installing a new floor in the basement or on the bottom floor, excess poly should be left protruding at the base of the wall of the bottom floor. This will enable a tie-in to a new vapour barrier installed in this location.

Strapping

At this point in rebuilding the wall there is the option of strapping in front of the curtain wall and vapour barrier. This step can be taken instead of the previous steps presented on continuing the vapour barrier around electric outlets. Wrapping the outlets or polypans can be time consuming. The alternative, placing the outlets in front of the vapour barrier mounted on the strapping, is quickly accomplished.

Once the framing is in place the air-vapour barrier is installed without the problem of fitting around outlets, etc. At

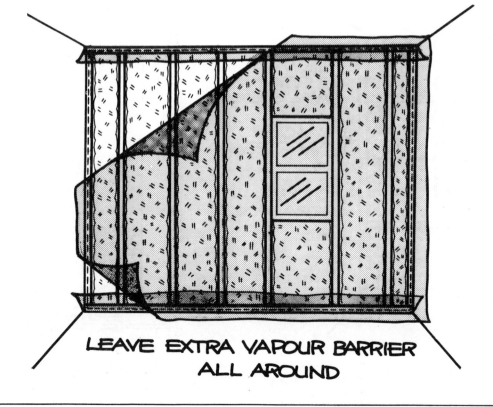

LEAVE EXTRA VAPOUR BARRIER ALL AROUND

this point 2 x 3 framing is nailed over the plastic to the studs behind. Nail the initial piece of strapping at floor level to provide a nailing bar for the bottom edge of the wallboard. The 2 x 3 should be laid flat on the ground, then nailed to the studs with 3½-inch nails. Additional strapping pieces are then installed moving up the wall at 24-inch centres, until a final piece of strapping is affixed at the top of the wall.

By installing the strapping on the inside of the vapour barrier, a channel now exists for the various electrical and plumbing runs. All of the necessary work can now be accomplished without destroying the integrity of the continuous air-vapour barrier. Electrical boxes can be fixed to the strapping in the desired locations. The cavity sections between the strapping can now be insulated with an R-8 friction fitting batt, further increasing the insulation levels of the wall assembly.

The brevity of this section should be compared with the lengthy description of the problems encountered when the vapour barrier is installed directly beneath the wallboard. The simplicity inherent in the addition of the strapping is matched by the improved performance of the vapour barrier which has been installed without any protrusions. Wherever possible we recommend this option.

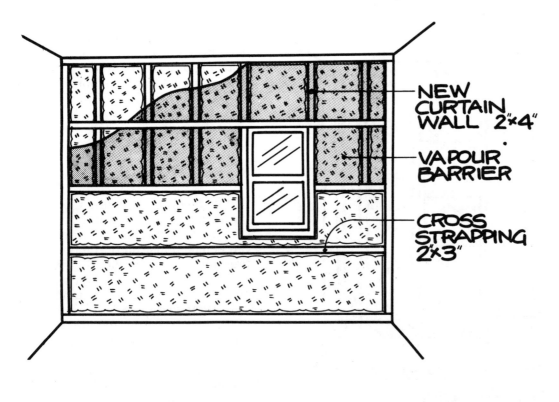

NEW CURTAIN WALL 2"×4"

VAPOUR BARRIER

CROSS STRAPPING 2"×3"

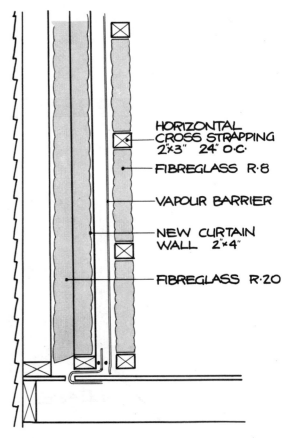

HORIZONTAL CROSS STRAPPING 2"×3" 24" O.C.

FIBREGLASS R·8

VAPOUR BARRIER

NEW CURTAIN WALL 2"×4"

FIBREGLASS R·20

Replacing the Wallboard

Once the framing, insulating and vapour barrier installation have been completed, a thorough check of the assembled wall structure should be performed. Make sure that all of the voids in the new cavities have been filled with insulation and that the vapour barrier has remained intact — free of punctures and well-sealed where seams meet.

The job of replacing the interior wallboard now takes place. You will quickly learn whether or not your stud spacing was well thought out. Ideally, you will have a minimal number of sheets of wallboard on each wall, eliminating the number of seams to be concerned with at a later stage. Similarly, if properly planned, the windows and doors can be easily integrated into the new room, using the same wallboard to encase the windows which are now recessed into the wall framing.

Drywall is usually used for interior walls. This material has several benefits. It is relatively inexpensive. It is relatively easy to work with and install, and finally, it provides additional thermal mass to the house interior. Sometimes designers specify two layers of drywall to further increase the mass of the building. This is worthwhile if you have concerns about overheating caused by a larger than normal amount of south-facing glass.

Drywall is readily available at all building supply locations. It is produced in 4-foot wide panels that come in standard heights of 8 feet or 10 feet. In large quantities the drywall can be ordered to other heights, but in most cases the 4 x 8 or 4 x 10 should suffice.

Working with the drywall is very easy. You need only a minimum number of tools and no construction expertise. A chalk line makes the job of drawing straight lines simple, cutting the boards can be accomplished with a utility knife, and a keyhole saw will speed the job of cutting holes in the drywall for electrical boxes.

To cut the drywall to the required shape, mark the distances, then join the measurements with the chalk line. It is usually easier to make the lines on the good side of the drywall — the side which will face inside the house. Run the blade of the utility knife along the chalk line making sure to score the covering layer of the board. This doesn't demand a great deal of pressure, only straight lines. Once the cut has been made in the board, turn it over and "break the back" of the drywall along the line. When the board has been bent, take the utility knife and score the paper on the back of the drywall at the seam. It's as easy as that.

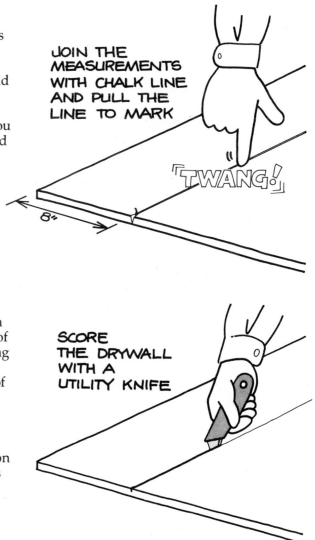

JOIN THE MEASUREMENTS WITH CHALK LINE AND PULL THE LINE TO MARK

「TWANG!」

8"

SCORE THE DRYWALL WITH A UTILITY KNIFE

BREAK THE BACK OF THE DRYWALL

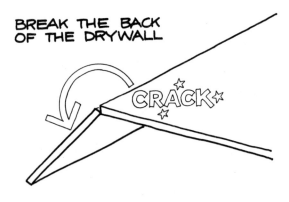

CRACK

CUT THE PAPER ON THE BACKING

If you're confident of your measuring abilities, holes for electrical outlets, switch plates, etc., can be performed while the board is on the ground. If not, the proper positioning of the openings can be obtained by putting the wallboard in place and pushing firmly against the outlet box. This should indent the outline of the box on to the back of the wallboard. The hole being marked, it can be cut out using either a utility knife or a keyhole saw.

The drywall can now be put up permanently. We recommend using drywall screws with a variable speed drill, rather than using blued gypsum nails. Although the nails are probably a bit easier to use and quicker, they have a tendency to pull out of the drywall over a period of time. Although this wouldn't pose major problems — aside from an aesthetic concern — it will lead to a hole in your perfectly installed air-vapour barrier. Screws, on the other hand, will seldom, if ever, pull out if they are properly installed.

There are protective measures for outside corners, which occur because of recessing windows and doors. Strips of metal corner beading should be screwed over the corners to ensure a superior product.

The next step is drywall taping and plastering. Either read about the subject or learn by trial and error to create a satisfactory product. There is a real art to this trade, so do your practicing in relatively inconspicuous areas of the house.

Once the drywall has been installed the finishing work required throughout the home can be performed. This involves casing work around windows and doors, re-installation of baseboards, cover places over electrical outlets, and ceiling light fixtures. Most of these jobs are simple to perform and require little more than attention to detail.

Basements

Basements and foundation walls can account for as much as 25 per cent of the heat loss (and the fuel bill) of the house. This major source of heat loss can be minimized several ways:
— the basement can be transformed into an unheated area,
— the basement can be insulated from the exterior,
— a thorough job of insulating the basement can be performed from the interior of the house.
If properly performed, each of these options should result in considerable energy and dollar savings. A brief analysis of the pros and cons of the various options will allow you to make your decision.

Reducing the Amount of Heated Area

Often basements are used for little more than storage and dust collecting. Large quantities of fuel are being consumed to keep garden tools, golf clubs and old rags warm throughout the winter months.

A practical approach to the problem of rising fuel costs involves isolating the main body of the house from the basement. This area could then be maintained at much cooler temperatures, possibly without requiring any conventional fuels. To accomplish this install a new air-vapour barrier on the floor of the first floor before installing the new flooring, then insulate the floor joists with friction fitting fibreglass batts installed from the basement. Heating ducts in the basement could then be closed off, as long as duct work or plumbing runs are adequately insulated to prevent excessive heat loss.

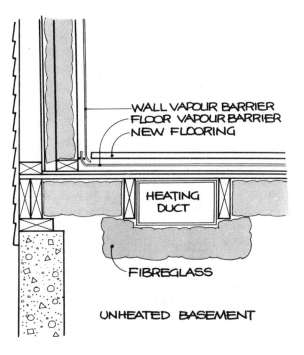

Exterior Insulation

Heat loss from the basement can be reduced by installing rigid board insulation on the exterior of the foundation walls. The main benefit is that the building interior needn't be altered, although damage to flower beds and ground cover surrounding the building will occur. Paving stones, asphalt and concrete close to the foundation wall pose a difficult problem. See the chapter on exterior retrofits.

The major disadvantage of this approach, at least when performed in conjunction with an interior retrofit, involves the weak spot in the thermal envelope which will occur where the interior and exterior insulation overlap. Not only will a thermal break be impossible to overcome, but equally important, a gap will exist in the air-vapour barrier of the house. The structural integrity of the gap may be in jeopardy over an extended period of time. It could act as a syphon for the water vapour in the house which is now prevented from dissipating throughout the rest of the building.

Interior Insulation

Although the interior approach to reducing heat loss through the foundation of the house involves a considerable amount of mess and work, if properly performed it can be the most effective. When installed in conjunction with the other interior insulation techniques outlined in this chapter, interior work on the basement can

be easily integrated into the thermal envelope of the home. Also, the floor of the basement can be upgraded if you want optimal results.

Tying in to the Air-Vapour Barrier Above

How to continue the air-vapour barrier from floor to floor has been explained in this chapter. Similar steps are required to allow a tight seal between the basement walls and the first floor. Rigid extruded polystyrene boards must be fitted tightly between the joists of the house and carefully calked to the joists with an acoustical caulking. A bead of caulking should be laid continuously across the top and bottom edge of the insulating boards and the joists themselves. A 12-inch strip of polyethylene should be laid over the bead of caulk with staples driven through the poly and caulking bead to the joists.

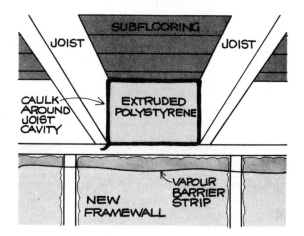

This strip of poly ties into the wall section on the first floor, and the strip extending from the bottom edge ties into the vapour barrier to be installed over the new basement walls.

Framing Basement Walls

Framing the basement is only slightly different than framing the walls.

First a word of caution: In a house with leaking foundation walls, remedial action should be taken before new walls are constructed. Several types of membranes can be installed on the exposed interior walls, although in extreme cases it is preferable to seal the wall from the exterior. Contact a local contractor for advice.

The easiest and least expensive way to frame the basement is to cross-strap it.The same steps used on the other floors are employed with only one additional step. To alleviate potential degradation of the bottom plate of the newly framed wall section, a 12-inch strip of polyethylene should be wrapped around the bottom plate before lifting the prefabricated sections into place. The strip of poly should extend around the plate and be stapled to the studs as a casing for the assembly.

The rest of the job is the same. Framing windows and doors will be required. Minimize the requirement for wood by placing the studs at 24 inches on centre.

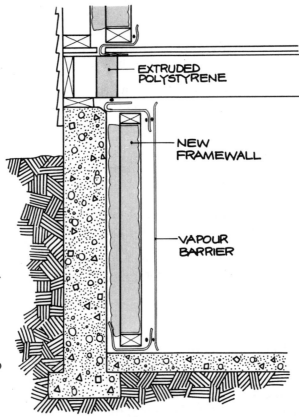

EXTRUDED POLYSTYRENE

NEW FRAMEWALL

VAPOUR BARRIER

There may be a significant number of plumbing stacks and other services in the basement so special care should be taken to ensure an air-tight seal around these potential holes. Similar problems may arise at the electrical service entrance to the building where it joins into the main service panel. All of these direct links from the interior to the exterior should be carefully caulked and sealed. You may confront vents or ducts which protrude

through the basement wall from either the heating system of the building or from appliances located in the basement. A more detailed look at some of the solutions follows.

Plumbing

In most houses tied into existing water and sewage services, plumbing to the city water and sewage system runs through the walls or the floor of the basement. To make the walls air-tight, the plumbing inlet and outlet should be properly sealed to the new air-vapour barrier. Where significant holes exist, the gap can be sealed with compressed oakum.

Electrical Services

The main electrical service panel of the house is probably mounted onto a plywood panel affixed directly to the foundation wall. If a newly insulated and air-vapour barriered wall is to be installed, there will be a gap in the thermal blanket of the house unless the panel is moved. To obtain optimal results an electrician should be called in to remove the service box and replace it on the new wall assembly. However, this may prove too drastic and expensive an option. The other approach to resolving this gap involves sealing, as best as possible, the new air-vapour barrier to the edges of the service panel, then trying to plug the holes in the panel with caulking. Not only should the areas around the conduit leading into the service panel be caulked, but you should also attempt to seal the area inside the conduit itself. Several caulking materials are approved for this purpose. Ensure that the material which you employ for this job is the proper and safe choice.

Vents

Air vents are required for clothes dryers, combustion air for solid-fuel-burning appliances, gas and oil furnaces, and air-to-air heat exchangers in extremely tight houses. Sealing the areas around these air vents is best accomplished by wrapping and caulking a strip of poly to the vents, then tying the strip into the new vapour barrier when it is installed.

Furnace Room

Many builders now construct rooms in the basement to house the furnace and hot water heater in a separate area, independent of the house air for their combustion. This can decrease infiltration since the heaters do not draw air from the house for their requirements. To ensure effectiveness, the furnace and water heater are surrounded by an air-tight insulated wall, isolating them from the rest of the basement. To further reduce infiltration losses, the floor drain for the basement can be located in the isolated room.

This is useful when undertaking a super-insulated retrofit since the existing furnace will need to be down-sized and replaced. While the mechanics of proper furnace sizing and installation will be detailed later in the book, consider the construction of the furnace room while performing the rest of the basement re-insulation. Simplistically, an exterior wall must be constructed on the interior of the furnace room. The same care exhibited throughout the house to obtain an air-tight seal should be shown when constructing the wall surrounding the new room. Once the new wall has been installed over the existing foundation wall, new stud walls must be constructed to enclose the furnace room. Not only should you be concerned with the seal needed on the walls around the room, but an air-tight seal is also required above the furnace room. A sheet of poly should be stapled to the joists situated above the area to be enclosed, then a sheet of drywall should be screwed into the joists, covering the plastic. Make sure that the plastic extends beyond the spot where the new stud walls are to be located, so that the poly can be joined to that covering the new walls. Similarly, the poly affixed to the ceiling should be tied into the vapour barrier installed over the foundation wall. When the framing has been constructed for the walls encasing the furnace room, a new vapour barrier can be installed on the exterior wall and caulked to the poly above. There is no need to insulate these wall sections, as the heat generated in the room by the furnace and water heater can be allowed to flow freely to the basement itself.

Caution should be heeded where heating ducts or pipes run from the furnace room to the rest of the house. Adequate clearance is needed between both the warm air ducts and the pipe runs and combustible materials. This requires the placement of metal sheeting around the ductwork where it passes through the new walls. To maintain the air-tight seal, a heat resistant caulk should be laid over the seam where the two metal materials meet. The poly can then be caulked to the metal stop directly. A metal firestop will also be required at the location where the chimney extends out of the furnace room.

Air-tight furnace rooms require a vent to provide outside combustion air for the furnace and water heater. The size of the vent will be determined by the size and type of furnace. Your serviceman can tell you the duct size your furnace requires. Generally this will range from a 5 inch vent to an 8 x 8 inch vent. Gas furnaces require less venting than oil furnaces.

Basement Floors

If you wish to obtain a total thermal blanket to the entire house, as well as optimum air-tightness, you may decide to insulate the basement floor. Vast quantities of insulation are not required since the differential temperature between the building interior and the exterior is somewhat tempered by the more constant temperature of the ground 5 or 6 feet below grade level. However, conduction does occur through the concrete slab of the basement and in a super-insulated home this can become a major source of heat loss. By installing even a small amount of insulation much of this thermal bridging can be alleviated.

The easiest means of re-insulating the floor is to alternate layers of strapping across the floor. The strapping (2 x 3 or 2 x 4's) placed over the concrete floor will need to be mechanically set into the concrete using a ''Ramset'' or other form of power-activated stud driver. The second set of strapping, if two layers are required, should lie perpendicular to the first layer and be shimmed, if it is necessary, to the proper level. Spacing for the strapping is determined by the loading to be placed on the area and the thickness of the subflooring to be installed. Once the strapping has been put in place, the insulation can be installed. An inexpensive, water resistant material should be used. The easiest material to install is a loose fill vermiculite which can be poured into the cavities. Alternatively, beadboard can be laid in sheets between the strapping. If you use beadboard put the insulation between the first layer of strapping before nailing the next strapping layer into place.

Neither of these materials will provide an adequate air seal for the house. To accomplish the total seal, a sheet of poly should be laid over the insulation and strapping before the subflooring is installed. This sheet of plastic should be caulked to the plastic extending down the walls of the basement for an air-tight seal.

In many cases the installation of insulation over an existing basement floor could lead to serious structural damage. In a poorly insulated basement enough heat conducts across the floor slab and through the foundation walls to prevent the freezing of the earth around the foundation wall. This eliminates concerns about frost heaving and the potential for structural damage. However, if the basement is totally wrapped in a thermal blanket, only a small amount of heat will escape to the exterior. In locations where the soil is not properly drained, or where the frost level extends to the footings of the building, you would be safer to allow for some heat loss from the building to maintain the above freezing temperatures of the soil adjacent to the footings of the house.

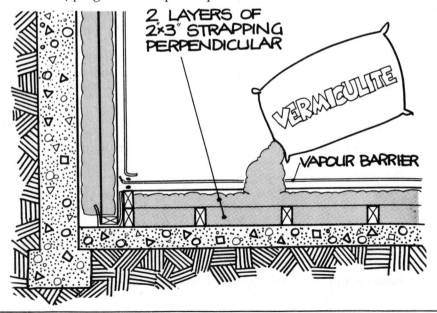

2 LAYERS OF 2×3" STRAPPING PERPENDICULAR

VERMICULITE

VAPOUR BARRIER

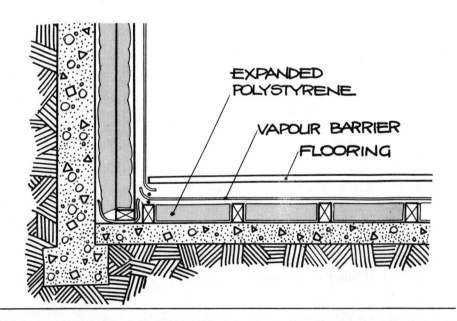

EXPANDED POLYSTYRENE

VAPOUR BARRIER

FLOORING

If this is a concern in your area, an intermediate solution involves the installation of the vapour barrier and subflooring without the installation of any additional insulation. This will allow for the required air seal without reducing the conduction losses across the slab of the basement floor.

Attics and Ceilings

The average house's heat loss through the attic or ceiling accounts for less than 20 per cent of the fuel bill. Heat loss through a square foot of the ceiling is greater than in any other area of the house. This is caused by the effects of several of the heat flow mechanisms at work within the house. The stack effect (warm, more buoyant air rises to the peak of the house) is the major cause of the problems. To alleviate heat loss through the attic three procedures should be followed. An extremely tight seal to the attic must be attained to prevent the penetration of air and water vapour to the insulation. The attic should be extremely well insulated to reduce conductive heat losses. And finally, the attic and ceiling sections should be well ventilated to remove any excess moisture and heat. If these three rules are followed, any variation of attic or ceiling design can be effectively super-insulated.

The simplest type of roof to retrofit is the attic in a pitched roof house. Access to the ceiling is easily achieved allowing for a relatively simple job. Problems will arise when upgrading cathedral ceilings and the ceilings of flat roof houses. In all cases we must stress the importance of a good job. The following sections outline the specific "how-to's".

Attics

This is one of the easiest areas of the entire retrofit. However, you must ensure that each of the three requirements of a good job are met. The first and most important phase of the work involves obtaining an air-tight seal from the ceiling located beneath the attic floor joists. Like the installation of the air-vapour barrier in all locations throughout the house, it is important to visualize completely wrapping the ceiling with no breaks or gaps in the finished product. Any imperfections will open channels for the flow of warm air and the accompanying water vapour.

While constructing the walls of the rooms below the ceiling a 6-inch strip of poly should be extended out from the wall. This strip allows for the new vapour barrier installed at the ceiling to be sealed to the vapour barrier extending throughout the rest of the house. If you are installing the attic insulation before the walls, the same strip of poly should be left extending from the ceiling to join the walls.

Installing the new vapour barrier on the ceiling of the house is simple, although sometimes awkward. There are two ways of performing this installation. One involves working around the existing ceiling, while the other means removing it.

Removing the Existing Ceiling

This causes a mess, but allows you to install the air-vapour barrier and the new drywall directly under the attic floor joists. You can easily determine the exact location of the joists above. In some cases uneven joist spacing may prevent the new ceiling from looking like a practice target for duck hunters with shotguns, because of nails missing the joists. It is relatively easy to pass the vapour barrier over partition walls which may exist on the floor situated below the attic.

If the Existing Ceiling is Removed

After swallowing copious amounts of dust and blistering your hands from pulling nails to remove the existing ceiling, you will now be able to see where the partition walls meet the attic floor joists. You should be able to visualize how to obtain a complete seal to the top of the house's interior. Different techniques will be required for those walls which run perpendicular to the joists and those which run parallel.

Where the partition walls run perpendicular to the attic floor joists, the vapour barrier, which is initially installed under the floor joists, can be linked using rigid insulation as the intermediate link over the top plate of the stud wall. The rigid insulation should be tightly fitted to the joists and sit flush to the bottom edge of the joists, extending at least several inches out from either side of the top plate of the wall. This technique allows the vapour barrier placed over the floor joists in the room to be caulked and sealed to the insulating board, providing a tight seal.

Where the partition wall runs parallel to the attic floor joists, blocking and a nailing strip will usually be installed to provide support for the ceiling materials. These additional pieces of lumber demand more work to obtain an air-tight seal, however, the same principles can be employed. Use the extruded polystyrene to bridge gaps that the continuous plastic cannot get by. Wherever practical, continue the plastic over the partitions, ensuring that the plastic stays close to the warm side of the insulation.

If the Existing Ceiling is Left in Place

The obvious benefit of installing the air-vapour barrier and the new ceiling directly over the existing ceiling is that of creating less mess and reducing the amount of labour required. This approach will, however, lead to problems when trying to obtain a complete seal through the partition walls of the home.

In this case the vapour barrier should be measured to extend from the exterior wall to the parallel partition wall. Cut the poly at least 12 inches longer than the measured distance to allow for the tie-in to the vapour barrier on the exterior wall. A bead of caulking (acoustical grade or equivalent) should then be placed around the perimeter of the room at the corners

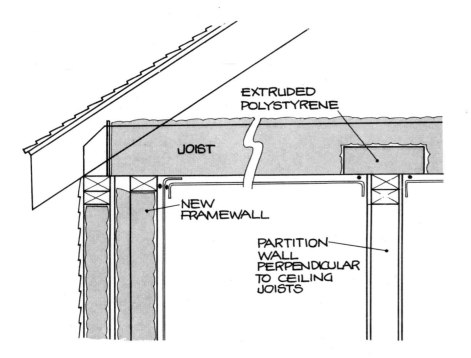

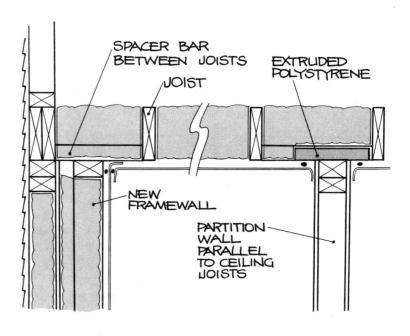

where partition walls meet the existing ceiling. Additional "gobs" of caulking should be placed over the existing ceiling to hold the vapour barrier in place when it is installed. Gravity pulls the plastic down, so staples are required to hold the air-vapour barrier in place until the drywall is installed over the plastic. Remember where the staples will be required, the acoustical caulk should be placed under the poly.

Once the caulking has been performed, the plastic can be extended across the ceiling. It is easiest to start from one side of the room and work slowly to the other side, rather than start from the exterior wall and work to the interior. Caulk and staple the vapour barrier to the strip of poly extending from the newly constructed exterior wall. Then slowly (to prevent tearing the plastic away from the staples) extend the plastic across the ceiling stapling over the "gobs" of caulking previously installed. When the opposite wall has been reached, staple the plastic to the bead of caulking at the corner of the wall. If the width of the room demands the installation of more than one sheet of plastic, the seam where the two sheets overlap should be caulked and sealed to prevent any air or water vapour passage. In this manner you can obtain a good seal on a room by room basis.

To reduce the amount of air and water vapour movement through the areas where the plastic does not extend, work will need to be performed from above the attic joists. Having squeezed up through the attic hatch, you now need to locate the partition walls below. Usually this requires an educated guess, then pull back whatever insulation exists so that you can see the plate of the stud wall. A bead of caulking should be placed at the spot where the original ceiling meets the header plate. This bead should reduce the amount of air flowing up around the stud wall. As a further measure, 12-inch long pieces of rigid insulation can be fitted between the attic floor joists directly over the partition wall top plate. Using a board of extruded polystyrene which has the required properties of an air-vapour barrier, much of the remaining air flow can be restricted. The boards should be tightly fitted between the joists and then caulked to the joists with an acoustical caulk. As the material is relatively costly when compared with other attic insulating options, only a 1-inch board is needed.

Rigid insulation should be installed between the joists above all the partition walls on the floor below. Once this aspect of the job has been completed, additional insulation can be put into place in the attic, remembering that the third requirement of allowing adequate ventilation of the attic must be met. In most houses, some form of ventilation already exists. The most common allows air which enters the attic directly from the soffits of the roof to be expelled through end vents, ridge caps or vents built directly into the roof itself.

It is extremely important when installing the new insulation to allow for the ongoing flow of air into the attic through the house's soffits. When installing insulation in the form of batts, this shouldn't pose a major problem as the batts can be installed far enough away from the roof line to permit the continued flow of air. If, on the other hand, you install loose fill or blown-in insulation, some precautionary measures should be taken to prevent the soffits from becoming blocked. Several options are available. Sheets of plywood can be nailed to the inside surface of the roof rafters, extending to the level where the new insulation will be blown. Alternatively, several commercial products are available which can be fitted between the roof rafters to ensure proper air flow from the outside.

To ensure that moisture and heat which build up in the attic are carried out, vents are required near the peak of the attic, either located on the end walls or situated on the roof rafters themselves. When a good vapour barrier is installed the amount of ventilation space required need not be as excessive as was previously required. However, the ventilation is still important. One square foot of vent openings will be required for every 300 square feet of ceiling area, with the vent area being evenly divided between the inlet and the outlet. Either one of the inlet or outlet vents are quite useless without their counterpart. If inadequate ventilation exists in the attic, (as indicated by excessive

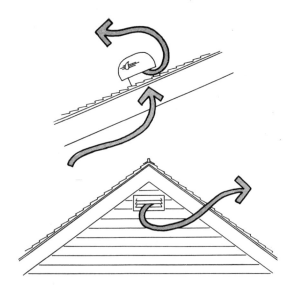

frosting), roof vents should be installed in conjunction with the required soffit vents.

Installing the New Insulation

New insulation can be added directly over any insulation which already is in place in the attic. The most economical options involve using fibreglass in either batts or blown in, or blown-in cellulose. Both of these options, if properly installed, will provide a long-lasting effective thermal blanket to the home.

If installing batt insulation, the job should be performed in stages. An initial layer of insulation should be installed between the floor joists. This layer of fibreglass should be at least thick enough to reach the top edge of the joists. Then the second layer of batts should be installed over the first, running perpendicular to the joists. This prevents any thermal bridging directly across the joists. Although the

super-insulated retrofit is defined as having attained a minimum R value of 40 in the attic (2 layers of 6-inch fibreglass batts), additional insulation can be easily laid over top to augment the thermal performance of the attic.

The second option, blowing either fibreglass or cellulose, can be even easier. Providing that access for ventilation air from the soffits has been guaranteed, the new insulation can be blown directly into the attic through the attic hatch. The insulation can be installed up to any thickness with a minimal amount of trouble. Ensure that an even covering is provided to the entire attic area, and that the density of the material meets the manufacturer's recommendations. A minimum of 12 inches of the material should be installed.

TOP LAYER PERPENDICULAR TO BOTTOM

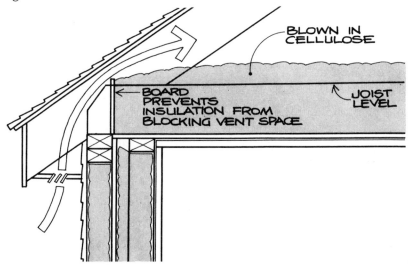

BLOWN IN CELLULOSE

BOARD PREVENTS INSULATION FROM BLOCKING VENT SPACE

JOIST LEVEL

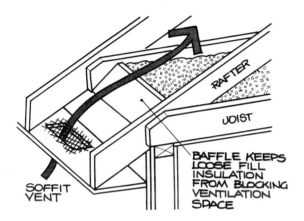

SOFFIT VENT

RAFTER

JOIST

BAFFLE KEEPS LOOSE FILL INSULATION FROM BLOCKING VENTILATION SPACE

Ensuring A Continuous Seal

Unless special efforts have been made, air leakage will occur through the various penetrations and perforations in the ceiling. Electrical fixtures, plumbing stacks and furnace chimneys were not built to be energy-efficient, consequently there are often great quantities of heated house air that escape into the attic. To ensure the continuity of the air-vapour barrier installed on the ceiling, several remedial measures are required:

Electrical Fixtures

Electrical ceiling fixtures should be dealt with in the same manner as the electrical boxes mounted in the wall cavities of the house. Although recessed ceiling fixtures have no place in energy-efficient buildings — building codes stipulate that such fixtures are not to be covered with either insulation or a vapour barrier to allow for cooling — some form of ceiling fixture will be required. Any surface-mounted electrical outlets should be removed and then re-installed on the inside of the newly installed 'polypan', or at least encased in a tightly sealed polyethylene sleeve. Joining the main air-vapour barrier of the room to the 'polypan' requires the application of a new bead of acoustical caulk and then a stapling job over the head.

Plumbing Stacks

As the vent stack for the various plumbing fixtures passes through the ceiling of the house, standard construction practices result in a significant gap between the stack and the top plate. The easiest means of reducing this source of air leakage involves

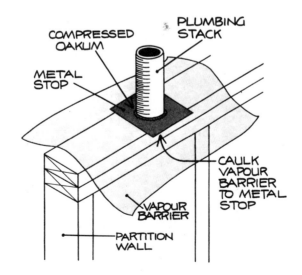

COMPRESSED OAKUM

PLUMBING STACK

METAL STOP

CAULK VAPOUR BARRIER TO METAL STOP

VAPOUR BARRIER

PARTITION WALL

packing the hole with compressed oakum to ensure that all of the gaps are properly sealed. The installation of a metal stop around the stack will adequately seal the air-vapour barrier to the stack.

Furnace Chimney

Building codes and common sense prevent the installation of any combustible material against the chimney. As a result, substantial air leakage into the attic may occur. To stop the flow of air around the chimney where it extends into the attic, a metal firestop should be installed. The gap between the firestop and the chimney should be well sealed with a heat resistant material such as muffler cement. The vapour barrier can then be caulked and sealed to the firestop to ensure a continuous seal.

Attic Hatches

The only remaining task involves insulating and sealing around the attic hatch. As there will be a break in the air-vapour barrier at this point, the means of sealing the hatch becomes extremely important. If poorly performed, the leaks around the hatch will promote a chimney effect, negating your painstaking re-sealing and re-insulating work. To alleviate this weak spot in the house, many builders are installing an access hatch to the attic through the gabled ends of the building. If possible this option should be seriously considered.

RIGID INSULATION

INSULATION

JOIST

HATCH LID

COMPRESSIBLE FOAM WEATHERSTRIPPING

If the attic hatch has to be left in the interior of the home, several considerations should be addressed. The hatch should be constructed so that a rigid insulating material can be laid on the top side of the ceiling board without fear of it ever being moved away. Several thicknesses of an extruded polystyrene can be laminated together using a foam mastic, then affixed to the hatch itself. A high quality weatherstripping should then be applied to the bottom edge of the frame of the hatch where it sits on the hatch framing. A sash clamp can be used to pull the hatch tightly down on to the frame of the hatch, resulting in a tight seal. The newly installed vapour barrier should be caulked and sealed to the underside of the hatch casing to further reduce the potential for air and vapour leakage.

Cathedral Ceilings and Flat Roofs

Both cathedral ceilings and flat roofed housing pose great problems to the retrofitting homeowner. These problems are caused primarily by the limited amount of space available between the ceiling and the roofing boards, and secondly by the venting requirements of the cavities. As a rule, these roofing variations will be constructed with 2 x 8's or 2 x 10's (even larger in older houses). This leaves little room for both the insulation and the ventilation, so these houses are usually faced with a relatively large heat loss through the roof.

It is easiest to view these roofing configurations in the same manner as the walls of the house. You can get by with a minimal amount of insulation in the existing cavities or, preferably, increase the amount of space for the insulation. As with the construction of new interior stud walls, the enlarging of the cavities in these roof types will take some space away from the living area by reducing the head room. In most areas of the house this will be hardly noticeable, however, it may prove restrictive in a few spots.

As with the work required to attain super-insulated status on walls and standard ceilings, you have the option of either removing the existing ceiling materials and whatever insulation lurks behind the ceiling, or adding framing and insulation to the existing ceiling. There are three reasons why it is worthwhile to

consider removing the ceiling. The existing insulation may be either non-existent or degraded. The insulation may have been installed in a manner which blocks the ventilation air from the soffits. Lastly, it will be easier to work with the exposed roof rafters.

When adding cavities to the existing rafters, several options are available. Cross-strapping can be installed over the existing rafters using 2 x 2's or 2 x 3's. To allow for the addition of adequate amounts of insulation, several layers of strapping, placed in perpendicular, will be needed. A second option involves the extension of the rafters with the use of plywood gussets and a new 2 x 4 forming a truss-like framing. Finally, and perhaps the most difficult option — yet at the same time the most effective — is the construction of a new framing section running perpendicular to the existing rafters, spaced out by as much as 8 inches. Each of these options has its advantages and disadvantages. A detailed description of each process might help you to decide which is the most appropriate for your situation.

Cross-Strapping

Strapping the ceiling or roof of the home offers you the option of leaving the ceiling intact. You should expose the rafters to check the details of the insulation and vapour barrier hidden behind the ceiling boards. In some cases this rather messy suggestion won't be pursued. In order to alleviate possible problems with double vapour barriers, existing barriers should be slashed to allow easier ventilation.

Whether the rafters are exposed or not, the job of cross-strapping the ceiling doesn't change significantly. If the rafters are exposed, re-install insulation between the rafters before progressing, remembering to leave adequate space behind the insulation for ventilation. In many jurisdictions building codes will require as much as 6 inches of air space between insulation and the roofing boards. These codes reflect the potential problems which can arise from shoddy construction habits which might not involve the installation of any vapour barrier, let alone an air-tight installation. Of course, you will install an impeccable air-vapour barrier and can probably justify as little as 2 inches of space between the insulation and the roofing boards.

Having installed the first layer of insulation between the rafters, or having simply decided to slash the existing vapour barrier, the strapping process can begin. The strapping (2 x 2's or 2 x 3's) should be installed perpendicular to the existing rafters. Starting at the bottom of the ceiling section, the strapping should be installed horizontally at 24 inches on centre all the way to the peak of the cathedral ceiling or to the other end of the flat roof section. If using 2 x 3's as the strapping option, nail them on their edge into the existing rafters using at least 3½-inch nails. This allows enough space

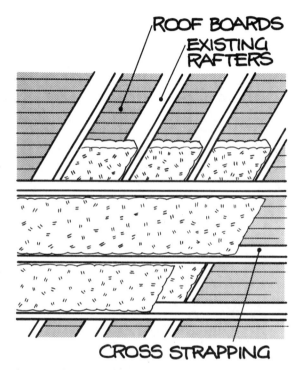

ROOF BOARDS
EXISTING RAFTERS
CROSS STRAPPING

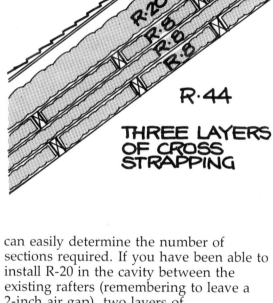

ORIGINAL RAFTER
R·20
R·8
R·8
R·8
R·44
THREE LAYERS OF CROSS STRAPPING

for R-8 batts to be installed. Make sure that the spacing between the strapping is properly measured, as the insulation will prove extremely frustrating to install if it doesn't fit tightly.

Once the framing is in place, the insulation can be installed. Remember to place the insulation in this layer before progressing to another level of strapping. The next and following strapping sections follow the same practices, extending down from the layer above until the required amount of insulation has been installed. Assuming that you are seeking a minimum R value of 40 in the ceiling, you

can easily determine the number of sections required. If you have been able to install R-20 in the cavity between the existing rafters (remembering to leave a 2-inch air gap), two layers of cross-strapping using 2 x 3's on edge would add another R-16. The addition of a third layer would lead to a total R value of 44 for the ceiling sections.

While not an extremely difficult job to perform, the disadvantage of this option relates to the number of steps required to achieve the desired insulating levels. One rather small concern relates to the direct thermal bridges which will occur where the different layers of strapping overlap. Although in total more than 12 inches of insulation may have been installed, heat is still permitted to conduct directly from the interior of the house to the exterior across these spots. The greatest advantage of the strapping option relates to the potential for the installation of an extremely effective air-vapour barrier. In the same manner in which strapping can be used to protect the integrity of the air vapour barrier in the walls of the house, so too can the vapour barrier be installed several inches away from the finished ceiling surface. The air-vapour barrier should be installed before the final layer of strapping is nailed into place, ensuring a sound linking to the barrier installed in the exterior walls of the building. Use the same care and attention detailed in the preceeding sections of the chapter. Once the air-vapour barrier is in place, the last layer of strapping and the insulation between can be fitted before the finishing wallboard is installed.

Extending the Existing Rafters

This option for re-insulating cathedral ceilings and flat roofs demands that the existing roof rafters be exposed. The end result will be a roof which is dropped from the rafters to the required depth. In a similar manner to that employed in the construction of prefabricated trusses, a new rafter is installed below the existing one, tied together with plywood gussets.

ORIGINAL RAFTERS
PLYWOOD GUSSET
NEW RAFTER

Each of the exposed rafters can be treated in the same manner. Having decided upon the amount of insulation to be installed, the new 2 x 4 should be dropped down accordingly. If you are again aiming for a minimum of R-40 using fibreglass batts, the 2 x 4's should be situated at least 14 inches below the roofing boards — 12 inches for the insulation and at least 2 inches for the ventilation air space. The spacing can be easily adjusted to allow for increased or decreased insulation levels.

To fix the 2 x 4 in its proper location, pieces of plywood should be nailed on either side of the 2 x 4 at 4 foot intervals.

The plywood should be at least 3/8 inch thick and cut into 6-inch wide strips. The strips can then be cut to the required lengths. Going back to the example where the 2 x 4 is to be located 14 inches from the roofing boards, strips should be 12 inches in length. This means that they will extend from the bottom of the new 2 x 4's up to within 2 inches of the boards. Less insulation would mean accordingly shorter gussets, etc.

The plywood gussets should then be nailed into the 2 x 4 while on the ground. On an 8-foot stud only 3 sets of gussets are needed. Each of the gussets should be nailed to the 2 x 4 with four 1 1/2-inch nails, making sure that the gussets are square to the edge of the new stud. When the gussets have been installed in pairs on to the 2 x 4, the assembly can be lifted into place. The gussets will form a sleeve that fits around the existing rafters.

The installation is completed by nailing through the plywood to the rafter, using the same 1 1/2-inch nails. Ensure that the 2 x 4's are parallel with the rafter, and that all of the new assemblies are at the same level. If the new ceiling to be installed requires that several pieces of wallboard butt together at the ends, an additional framing piece will be required as a nailing bar. Pieces of 2 x 4 cut to fit between the extended rafters can be nailed into place to perform this function.

After this process has been completed the insulation can be installed. In a very

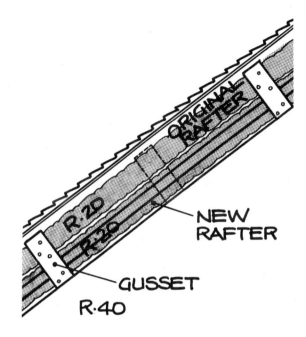

simple process the batts are installed to fill each of the sections between the rafters. To attain R-40, two 6-inch batts can be installed in each of the cavities. When pushing the first layer of insulation into place, make sure that the ventilation space between the insulation and the roofing boards is maintained. Don't push too far. As long as the insulation is properly fitted between the rafters, there should be no problem with its installation.

The vapour barrier can then be installed over the 2 x 4's before the new ceiling is put in place. If wiring runs through the ceiling sections, follow the same principles as in constructing the walls to eliminate

gaps in the air-vapour barrier. Similarly, plumbing stacks, chimneys, etc., should be carefully integrated into the air-vapour barrier (as previously outlined). When you get to installing the new ceiling, make sure that the screws (for drywall) or nails are lodged firmly into the 2 x 4's. It is usually wise to use a chalk line to mark the location of the rafters to eliminate needless holes in the vapour barrier.

The main advantage of this option of re-insulating cathedral ceilings or flat roof sections is the small amount of labour and materials required. Most of the work can be performed on the floor below, especially cutting and nailing the gussets to the 2 x 4's. If the new sections are "prefabbed" on the floor, only a small amount of work needs to be done on ladders. Also, installing the insulation can be done at the same time, so it involves little more effort than insulating stud walls with fibreglass batts.

The major disadvantage is the potential for inefficiencies in the thermal performance caused by air spaces which might exist between the original rafter and the new 2 x 4. Although the fibreglass batts will expand past the 2 x 4's, uninsulated gaps will probably occur leading to some convective losses through the sections. The other concern relates to the integrity of the vapour barrier which can be easily destroyed if adequate care is not taken when the new ceiling is installed. On the other hand, there is a likelihood that in older homes the

spacings between the rafters will be somewhat random.

The other disadvantage of this option results from the spacing of the original rafters. If they are located at 16-inch centres (or facimile) the new 2 x 4's will follow at the same spacings. Whereas the original rafters are bearing considerable weight, thus necessitating their close spacings, the new frame section has only to hold the new wall board or ceiling tiles.

Framing a New Cavity Section

The third option for dealing with cathedral and flat roof sections of the house is a hybrid of the two previously mentioned options. Some of the rafters are extended out in the same manner as mentioned above. These rafters are installed at 8-foot centres, then 2 x 4's spanning perpendicular to the original rafters are set in place between the trusses. This approach has the benefit of minimizing thermal bridging and allows for the insulation to be installed in only two steps.

Determining the location of the new framing section follows the same principles outlined above: R-40 requires extending the rafter 14 inches below the roofing boards. As was the case above, this level of insulation would involve the use of 12-inch plywood gussets on the trusses. If the rafter spacings are relatively centred, most of the framing can be prefabricated on the floor below the

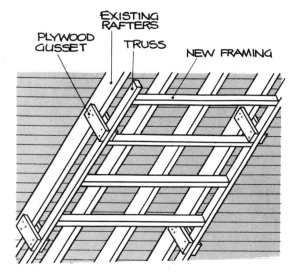

EXISTING RAFTERS
PLYWOOD GUSSET
TRUSS
NEW FRAMING

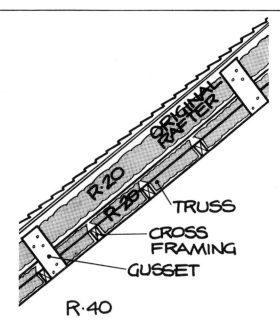

ORIGINAL RAFTER
R·20
R·20
TRUSS
CROSS FRAMING
GUSSET
R·40

lift into position. After making sure they are level, the gussets on the end sections can be nailed into place.

Spacer bars are used to hold the new frame to the existing rafters at the required depth. The new frame is nailed into place at 24-inch centres, running perpendicular to the existing rafters. This approach has the advantage of minimizing thermal bridging and gaps in the insulation, while allowing for the insulation to be installed in only two layers.

To determine the location of the new framing members follow the same principles outlined in the section above — R-40 means 14 inches from the roofing boards to the house edge of the new 2 x 4. Once again at this level of insulation the spacer bar should be 12 inches. The gusset system employed in the section above is used on two of the rafters spaced at 8-foot centres.

Two by fours are then nailed between the trusses spanning the 8-foot length. Place the first spanning 2 x 4 at the bottom of the cathedral ceiling or edge of the wall in a flat roof design. This will act as a nailing bar for the edge of the wallboard. Similarly, a 2 x 4 should span the trusses at the peak of the roof or at the other end of the wall in the flat roof design. Most of the new cavity section can be constructed on the floor below the ceiling, though make sure that the sections don't become too heavy to lift into place.

ceiling, then lifted into place. The 2 x 4's which are fitted with the gussets will act as the frame for the rest of the assembly. These should be laid out on the floor at the distance between two original rafters spaced 8 feet apart. Once the distance between the rafters has been measured, 2 x 4's can be cut to fit between the framing, running perpendicular to the original rafters. The first 2 x 4 should be nailed into place at the bottom of the framing section to act as a nailing bar for the edge of the wall board. Similarly, a 2 x 4 should be installed at the peak of the roof or at the opposite end of a flat roof configuration. Intermediate blocking may be required where the ends of the wallboard butt together. The sections can be constructed below, however, make sure that they don't become too heavy to

Once the framing grid has been installed to span the entire ceiling or roof, the insulation can be added in two steps. The first layer of insulation should be fitted between the original rafters. Ensure that space is maintained for soffit ventilation. The second layer of fibreglass is laid horizontally between the new framing sections. By using two sets of R-20 friction-fit fibreglass batts, a total R value in excess of R-40 will be attained. Because the insulation has been installed in an overlapping manner, thermal bridging and air gaps in the insulation should be maintained.

Once the insulation has been installed, the air-vapour barrier is applied in the manner outlined above. Remember to minimize the perforations in the plastic and to effectively seal all seams. Follow the prescribed procedures for dealing with plumbing stacks and chimneys.

Re-installation of wallboard over the newly insulated ceiling or roof is an extremely awkward procedure. The job is greatly facilitated with extra hands. (If you're performing the work by yourself, and you feel that there are a limited number of calls you can make to secure help from your friends — this is one of those times. Anyone who has been forced to nail a 40 pound, 4 foot by 8 foot sheet of drywall into ceiling rafters while it is balanced on your head will understand this advice.) If you can arrange for some help the job is simple. However, be careful to drop a chalk line onto the wallboard to mark the location of the studs so that unnecessary holes in the air-vapour barrier are minimized. Make certain that you use screws instead of nails to reduce the potential of nail pull-out.

While the above process may appear to be complicated, there is actually little difference between this approach and that employed for upgrading the existing walls of the home. In both cases a carefully prepared and installed job will result in significant energy savings.

Economic Considerations

In almost all cases the greatest contributing factor to the interior approach to the super-insulated retrofit is your time. As a general rule, the cost of the materials

involved will not be overly restrictive. Polyethylene, insulation, framing lumber and new drywall are relatively inexpensive. Yet in order to attain an air-tight seal to the existing structure, the amount of labour and the extreme measures required can greatly add to the cost of the job — especially when performed by a contractor.

Some aspects of the super-insulated retrofit are easy to estimate. The specific visible components of the interior retrofit can be readily identified. Re-insulating attics, constructing new frame interior walls and upgrading the thermal characteristics of the basement walls are all tasks which can be accurately estimated in terms of materials and time. However, the hidden parts of the job such as tieing the air-vapour barrier between floors and over and through partition walls will force most contractors to 'load' their bids because of the unknown aspects of the work.

Costs of Upgrading Walls, Attics and Basements

As mentioned above, it is relatively easy to make an accurate estimate of the material requirements for the walls and attic of the house. As long as the job has been planned in advance you will have an understanding of the amount of polyethylene, insulation, framing lumber and drywall needed to complete the task.

Re-insulating the attic of the house (if one exists) will be the easiest part of the job. The material cost of the work can be estimated by multiplying the area of the

attic space by the cost of the insulation required per square foot. Costs of the fibreglass batts will average between 1.5¢ and 1.6¢ per R per square foot. If you are installing R-40 into the existing attic the cost will range from 60¢ to 64¢ per square foot if you're the installer. The addition of R-20 would involve a capital cost of 30¢ to 32¢ per square foot. The only additional cost is the purchase of commercial soffit ventilators. The expanded polystyrene moulds ensure that the newly installed insulation does not block the movement of ventilation air into the attic space. These items may not be necessary if installing fibreglass, but they are a necessity if a blown-in material is to be used.

Contracted costs for upgrading attic insulation range from 45¢ to 60¢ for the installation of R-20 into an attic to give a total of R-40.

An incremental cost of re-insulating the attic is determined by the manner in which air leakage is prevented from entering the insulated space. As outlined, in the ideal circumstance a new 6 mil polyethylene vapour barrier is installed over the existing ceiling and then a new layer of ³/₈-inch drywall is installed. The cost of this job involves the purchase of the poly, the drywall, the tape and plaster, and the finishing paint. The total cost for these materials per square foot should average 25¢ to 30¢.

The material costs for framing and insulating new walls for the house can be used for estimating both walls above grade and the basement walls. For each section of wall space you will require poly, framing lumber, insulation, new drywall and the various finishing materials (tape, plaster, paint). For each square foot of insulated wall the costs will range according to the R value sought. Assuming the installation of R-20 on all of the newly framed walls, the square foot cost for the acquisition of the materials will range from 58¢ to 65¢ for standard materials bought in your local building supply outlet.

The only potential variability in this cost figure relates to the different finished work which the homeowner might desire. The above mentioned price assumes that the original moulding, trim and baseboards are removed and then returned to their respective locations on the new wall. Any other costs such as re-wiring, re-plumbing, or waterproofing the foundation wall will be viewed separately from the retrofit measures.

Flat roofed sections and cathedral ceilings are estimated in the same manner as the addition of new walls. Costs for the framing lumber, polyethylene and the finished wallboard will correspond to those outlined above. An additional cost for the extra insulation should be added and a small additional cost per square foot will be needed for the addition of the framing gussets. The cost of adding R-40 to a flat roof or cathedral ceiling will range from 88¢ to 95¢ for the acquisition of materials, per square foot of roof space.

Estimating the Hidden Jobs (Material Cost)

The materials required to join the air-vapour barrier from floor to floor will cost between 43¢ and 55¢ per joist cavity, using 2-inch (R-10) Styrofoam. If higher insulation values are required, either a 4-inch slab of Styrofoam can be installed at a cost of between 85¢ and $1.10 per joist cavity, or an extra layer of fibreglass can be installed behind the 2-inch Styrofoam at a total cost of 55¢ to 70¢ for the R-20.

Cost of Materials

We can estimate the materials cost for an average sized house using the above mentioned cost calculations. Assuming that the house has 1,500 square feet of living space, exclusive of the basement, we survey the following areas to determine the cost of upgrading.

Walls (1,440 square feet)	
add R-20	avg. $ 900
Basement (880 square feet)	
add R-20	avg. $ 550
Attic (750 square feet)	
add R-32	avg. $ 360
Between floors	
add R-20	avg. $ 100
	$1,910

Another 10 per cent should be added to this figure to accommodate miscellaneous expenses and to cover any unforseen costs.

Dealing With Contractors

Most contractors try and stay within their field of expertise. Having performed a job several times it becomes harder to 'get burned' when providing the homeowner with an estimated price of the job. When they start to venture into work which they haven't performed before, you can expect the cost estimates to be high. In order to protect themselves from the unknown, the contractor will boost his estimated cost.

When we are dealing with the super-insulated retrofits, we enter the realm of the unknown for the average contractor. Although the majority of the job is very straight forward, the demands placed on the contractor to ensure an air-tight seal will be a new situation. Rather than attempt to provide a range of contracted prices for the work specified in this chapter, we will only suggest that you understand what is required and what the materials cost will be. You should then contact several contractors for an estimated price. The more knowledgeable you appear when talking to the contractor, the more likely he is to offer a reasonable quote. As a general rule you might expect that the quote will be double the materials cost for the contracted job.

Concluding Thoughts

There is no doubt that performing a thorough super-insulated retrofit on the interior of a house is a monumental task. To suggest that everyone on the block will find the techniques outlined are appropriate to their situation would be a slight exaggeration. Indeed, the complexity of the entire job limits its application primarily to those houses which are in need of major renovations. It is difficult to justify tearing apart and rebuilding a house which is in excellent repair. However, once you've made the plunge into renovation work, the super-insulation techniques outlined in this chapter can be easily integrated into the job with minimal difficulty and expense.

It is important to realize that the super-insulated retrofit should be part of the total package. Every aspect of the job links together, without its various components you can experience greater problems than a high fuel bill. The addition of mounds of insulation without proper attention to the installation of a vapour barrier can lead to serious structural damage over a period of time. In many types of housing, limiting the retrofit to the accessible areas of the house (walls, basements and attics) while leaving the cavities between floors unattended to, can lead to a dangerous situation. An ever increasing movement of water vapour through these regions is potentially very damaging.

The super-insulated retrofit will demand strict attention to detail on the part of the homeowner and contractor.

A good job will take a considerable amount of time to perform. If necessary, take the time to convince a contractor of the value of the super-insulated approach.

Discuss the continuous air-vapour barrier between floors and partition walls, the air-to-air heat exchanger and the other details that are important to your job. A thorough understanding of the concepts involved and the techniques recommended will be important in ensuring a good job.

The energy savings which will result from all of this work will be considerable, especially for the poorly insulated section of the housing stock. In most cases you will only have one shot at a major retrofit. To perform the job without placing energy conservation as a top priority is to miss a golden opportunity.

We can surmise that fuel prices will continue to rise. Having performed a major renovation, it would be unfortunate to realize five years later that the insulation levels added were inadequate and that further remedial work was needed. Do the job correctly the first time and your foresight will pay for itself in dollar and energy savings.

Windows

In a typical Canadian home as much as 25 per cent of the total heat loss from the building occurs around and through the windows. This figure indicates the extent of the attention that windows should demand in an energy-efficient home. When considering the super-insulated retrofit, the factor of the heat loss through windows is of primary importance. As a house is made super-insulated and air-tight, windows become the largest single source of heat loss.

You can not simply view windows as heat losers. Windows provide natural light and passive solar gains to the house interior. They are also a major cause of overheating during the warmer months when solar gains are not required. Proper orientation, installation and operation of windows can result in greater comfort during the summer and winter months.

Retrofitting windows is an essential component of the super-insulated approach in existing houses. Some homeowners perform more radical surgery on their homes than others. The operation can entail the purchase and installation of new, higher efficiency windows, the re-orientation of existing windows, and the incorporation of shuttering devices to reduce night-time heat losses. On the other hand, significant fuel savings can result from the judicious use of caulking, weatherstripping and affordable movable insulation techniques in conjunction with the addition of extra layers of glass to the existing windows.

The different approaches will be examined. You should base your decision on a thorough understanding of how windows both lose and gain heat. Once you have successfully tackled the problem you will have achieved a more secure position, both at home and at the bank.

Heat Loss Mechanisms Through Windows

Windows lose heat due to three specific heat flow mechanisms. First, leaks and cracks around the window casing and movable joints result in the infiltration of cold air and the exfiltration of warm house air. These drafts not only create a burden on your wallet, but are also uncomfortable to live with. Second, windows conduct a significant amount of heat from the house interior to the exterior. These conductive losses are related to the very poor insulating characterisitics of glass. The third way windows transfer heat is through radiation. As a layer of glass is warmed by the absorbtion of long wave energy, heat will be radiated to the exterior or colder surfaces. These three heat loss mechanisms can be greatly reduced through a variety of measures, once they are more thoroughly understood.

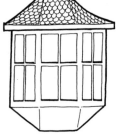

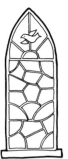
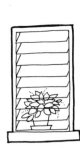

Convection

The means by which air is pulled into the cracks and leaks in the lower regions of the home and then expelled through similar holes in the upper regions has already been discussed. The stack effect, that is the tendency of warmer, more buoyant air to rise, will be greatly influenced by the severity of the gaps in the home's exterior shell. Similarly, the differential pressures exerted on a building by winds will result in large volume air changes proportional to the openings in the shell. Having tightened-up most of the other weak spots in the building with the installation of an air-tight vapour barrier, the windows now become the major source of air leakage into and out of the building.

Air leakage around windows occurs in two distinct areas. Because of past construction practices, a large gap will usually exist between the window casing and the wall framing, allowing air to pass from the interior to the exterior and vice versa in a relatively unobstructed manner. This is not only the case with older, double-hung windows which are equipped with cavities for counterweights, but also with newer, well constructed windows. At best, bits of insulating materials may have been squeezed into the gap between the casing and the wall frame. However, this does little more than slow (and filter) the incoming or outgoing air. A more comprehensive approach involves at least filling the gap with an air-tight insulating foam, or preferably, affixing the vapour

barrier directly to the casing of the window to prevent any air movement.

The other area of air infiltration results from leaks and cracks within the window itself. Leaks, often quite substantial, can occur around the parts of the window sash which can be operated either by lifting (as in the case of a single or double-hung window) or opening as a door (as in the case of casement and awning-type windows). If the windows are loose fitting or leaks have occurred over time due to the deterioration of the weatherstripping or frame, air will enjoy easy access to the living space. The proper installation of weatherstripping can dramatically reduce infiltration losses through these weak spots.

Conduction

Glass, by itself, is an exceptionally good conductor of heat. Holding a hot drink in a glass will vividly demonstrate this fact. Conversely, still air is a very poor conductor and a good insulator. In the same manner in which materials can be aligned to encapsulate small pockets of still air to become good insulating materials (e.g. fibreglass, cellulose and foam insulations), so too can glass be used to create still pockets of air. It is actually the air between and on either side of a window which restricts the flow of heat from one side to the other, not the glass itself.

The resistance value of a pane of glass is only a little better than nothing at all, R-0.01. However, the film of air on either side of the pane increases the R value of a single-pane window to 0.86. The film of air on the inside surface of a window accounts for R-0.68, which is much higher than the value for the outside film of air which is influenced by the buffeting effects of the winds. By encasing a still pocket of air between two panes of glass, the R value of a window can be increased to approximately R-1.8. The values of the interior and exterior air films remain constant at R-0.68 and R-0.17 respectively, but an R-0.96 is provided by the air trapped between the two panes of glass. By adding yet a third pane of glass to the window assembly the resistance value can be increased to as high as 2.6.

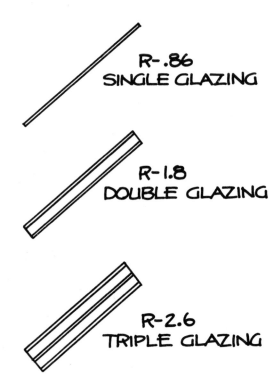

R-.86
SINGLE GLAZING

R-1.8
DOUBLE GLAZING

R-2.6
TRIPLE GLAZING

These figures fluctuate according to several criteria. If the air between two panes of glass is allowed to flow freely, its insulating values are greatly decreased. If the seals of glass are not tight, air leaks into and out of the cavity. This often happens when adding storm windows. Also the R value will change dependent upon the size of the air space between the panes of glass. Whereas a $1/4$ inch air space will give an R value of slightly less than R-0.6, a gap of $3/4$

inches will provide R-0.86. Between 1 inch and 4 inches the air gap remains relatively constant. With more than 4 inches the convections which would be established would result in decreasing efficiency. The optimum spacing will not only be determined by the thermal performance of a given air gap, but also by the restrictions placed by the size of the window casing. Ideally, the panes of glass should encase an air space of at least $5/8$ inch and be tightly sealed.

Conduction across windows does not simply occur through the glassed area. The casing and sash construction of windows has a significant effect on the heat loss characteristics of any given window. Historically, the casing and sash were constructed with wood. More recently, aluminium has been extensively used, both for the exterior and storms. Wood conducts heat almost 2,000 times more slowly than does aluminium — witness the use of aluminium as an absorber plate in some active solar collectors. As a general rule, wooden windows are more efficient at reducing the conductive flow of heat from a window, but some aluminium window manufacturers are using a thermal break to prevent the direct conduction of heat across the metal framing. The thermal break should be viewed as a prerequisite if using these windows. Don't think only in terms of the heat escaping through the glass; the sash and casing can account for as much as 20 per cent of the entire opening in a building wall.

Radiation

A warmer body radiates heat to a colder surface. The radiant energy of the sun passing through properly oriented windows can balance the heat losses through glass. But the sun is the warmest body only during the day. Windows have the advantage of allowing long wave energy (solar radiation) to pass through the material while at the same time preventing the flow of shorter wave radiation (heat energy) back through the glass to the exterior. However, if heat is radiated from warmed surfaces in the home (thermal mass, people, etc.) to the window, the heat can be absorbed by the glass, conducted to the exterior surface of the window and then radiated to the outside of the house.

You feel cold when sitting beside a window on a winter evening because, being a warm body, you are radiating heat to the colder window surface. Many people curtain windows at night, and more recently use insulating shutters and shades for energy-efficient housing. Often these insulating devices include a reflective surface in their design (aluminium foil, mylar, etc.) which can reflect radiant energy back into the living area of the home. Solar control films also reduce the amount of solar radiation entering the interior of a building.

Heat losses through infiltration , conduction and radiation can be significantly reduced while still leaving the existing windows in place. If for other reasons you remove the existing window, consider the heat flow mechanisms when purchasing a new window.

Heat Gain Mechanisms

Heat losses through air leakage, conduction and radiation can be significantly reduced while leaving your existing windows in place. In general, dealing with your existing windows will be less expensive than the purchase of new factory-built units. However, there are many reasons for remoiing the existing window including deterioration of the frame, casing or sash, to enlarge the glazed area or to entirely remove a north-facing window.

The Primer discusses the importance of proper orientation. This issue is extremely critical to the super-insulated retrofit, as the reduction of excessive heat loss and heat gain is of prime importance.

Average net heat loss/gain in million BTU during the heating season from a 12 square foot window in Thunder Bay, Ontario oriented in different directions:

South	East/West	North
+ 0.4	− 0.5	− 1.5

The above chart emphasizes the net heat gain of the south-facing window in relation to those facing in other orientations. The chart dramatically portrays the net drain that results from north-facing windows. At an early stage in the retrofit, the home-owner should consider the reorientation of some of the windows in the house. It is especially important that this work be done before the vapour barrier is installed to ensure a proper sealing of the building's envelope.

Removing A Window Opening

When performed at an early stage, any window in the house can be easily removed and replaced by an insulated section of wall. Once the window has been taken out of its rough stud frame, the opening will need to have an intermediate stud placed into the frame. This will act as an additional bracing for the new wallboard and/or exterior siding.

If the window is being removed as part of an exterior retrofit, the cavity should be insulated before the interior finishing work is performed. Once the face trim has been removed, you will want to hide the traces of the opening. The frame of the window may need to be shimmed out to allow new wallboard to sit flush with the existing wall. If this is not the case, simply install the new wallboard to the framing, tape, plaster, sand and paint the wall section to hide the evidence. The exterior of the house will be re-sided with the curtain wall insulation to hide the outside. If the job is to be part of an interior retrofit, the exterior work will need to hide the evidence of a window. In both cases you'll have replaced an R-9 window with a R-32 insulated core.

Additional South-Facing Glazing

Additional south-facing windows can enhance your solar gains during the winter months. The inclination to add vast quantities of glass to the south face should be tempered by concerns about over-heating, not only during the warmer months but throughout the year.

In a newly constructed super-insulated house, experience has suggested that south-facing glass be limited to between 6 to 7 per cent of the heated floor space of the building. Whereas some leeway will be available in the case of the super-insulated retrofit, the addition of more than 10 to 15 per cent of south-facing windows in relation to the floor area will demand that additional thermal mass be incorporated into the building's interior to reduce excess heat build-up.

The removal, enlarging or addition of new windows should be performed at an early stage in the retrofit. In frame houses the job is relatively simple. Having determined the location of the new window, the studs should be exposed on both sides. If the window to be installed is larger than the cavity section, the intermediate stud should be cut to allow for the top and bottom header to span the width of the opening. Similarly, if the opening between the studs is too wide an additional vertical stud will need to be installed to frame the window casing. Once the rough stud framing has been installed, follow the procedures outlined later in the chapter for installing a new window. After the new insulated wall has been constructed, finishing trim will be needed on both the interior and exterior.

Dealing With Excess Heat Gains

If proper control mechanisms are not installed in a super-insulated house, overheating may occur caused by excessive solar gain in the summer months. We have already discussed the importance of properly oriented windows.

However, in a super-insulated house, an over abundance of south-facing glass can lead to problems of excessive heat on sunny days throughout the year. Rule of thumb suggests that only between 6 to 7 per cent of the area of the heated floor space should be installed as south-facing glass. Whereas in a leaky house or a passive solar house equipped with additional heat storing materials, larger amounts of glass assist the heating performance of the building, the greatly reduced heating requirements of the super-insulated home causes most of the heat gain to be dumped to the exterior.

During the summer months you can use various window shading devices to prevent the warm sun from directly entering the house. Design overhangs or seasonal shadings such as awnings or shutters are time-honoured solutions. An exterior retrofit will provide the house with new overhangs on each window, as the glass will be recessed from the outside wall by as much as 8 to 12 inches.

When you consider re-orienting windows or changing their status of operation, remember the role which operable windows can play in providing natural ventilation during the warmer months. By ensuring that some operable windows exist on the windward and leeward side of the house, prevailing summer breezes (a natural cooling mechanism) can be assured. In your haste to beat the ravages of northern winters, remember that for up to five months of the year the outside temperatures can become oppressive and any air movement within the house is appreciated. In most parts of Canada the prevailing winds during the summer months originate from the west, shifting around to the northwest and north during the winter. Operable windows or vents on the east and west face of the house will promote cooling convections in the house interior.

Dealing With Existing Windows

Retain the existing windows wherever possible. Although in some cases the windows may have become useless through the rotting or warping of the frames, in most cases it can be considerably cheaper and often equally efficient to upgrade your existing windows and add sealing and glazing to that which is already in place. Not all of the windows in the home need to be left in their current locations. You may decide to replace some of the excess windows in the home with an insulated wall section.

Plan well in advance for these events so that the work can be performed at the same time as the rest of the wall re-insulation. Similarly, if you decide to increase the amount of glazed area on the south face of the house, the new framing should be installed during the early stages of the job.

Upgrading the thermal performance of existing windows will involve at least three distinct tasks: tying the new vapour barrier to the casing of the window, sealing air leaks around the movable sash of the unit, and adding glazing layers to the existing window.

Tying in to the New Vapour Barrier

One of the major sources of infiltration in older houses occurs between the window casing and the wall framing. To alleviate this weak spot in the building's shell, the window casing should be directly linked to the new vapour barrier which has been installed. It is easiest to perform this job at the same time as you re-insulate the walls.

When working from the exterior of the house, the installation of the air-vapour barrier is one of the first stages of the job. You must wrap the existing house with a thick sheet of polyethylene. The vapour barrier should be cut at the window openings diagonally from corner to corner in an X pattern. Proceeding from here, a bead of acoustical caulking should be laid on the front edge of the window casing. If the casing extends flush to the exterior of the house, the plastic can be sealed directly

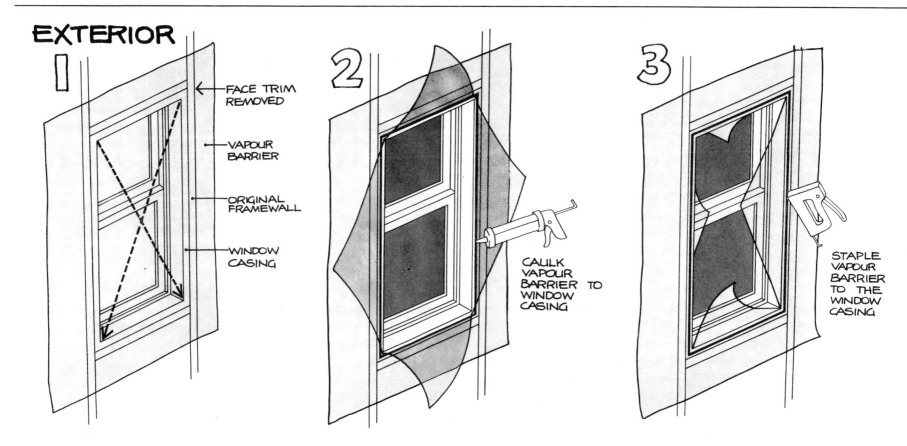

EXTERIOR

1

FACE TRIM REMOVED

VAPOUR BARRIER

ORIGINAL FRAMEWALL

WINDOW CASING

2

CAULK VAPOUR BARRIER TO WINDOW CASING

3

STAPLE VAPOUR BARRIER TO THE WINDOW CASING

to the casing by stapling through the caulking bead to the wood. If, on the other hand, the window casing is recessed in the wall casing, the plastic will need to be extended from the house exterior to where the casing is located in the recess. Then seal the plastic to the casing in the same manner. You will notice that gaps in the plastic will exist at the corners where it extends around the corner and where it ties in with the casing. In these locations you

will need to cut out smaller pieces of plastic and cover over the gaps. This plastic should be properly caulked to the main sheet of the air-vapour barrier so that no gaps for potential air and water vapour leakage exist. By extending the plastic directly to the window casing any leaks which had previously existed are now totally closed off. In a sense the window casing becomes part of the air-vapour barrier.

Sealing the windows when retrofitting from the interior is generally the same. When performing interior work you may need to remove the existing face trim so that access to the gap between the wall framing and the window casing is exposed. If this is the case, consider installing some insulation into the gap before attaching the air-vapour barrier to the casing. The poly will need to be extended from the interior surface of the new frame wall towards the exterior where

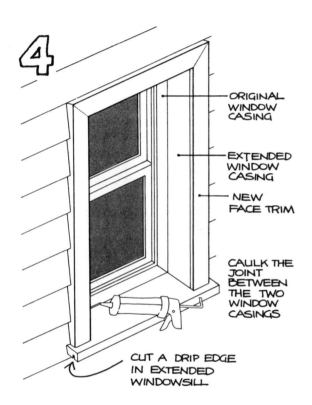

4

ORIGINAL WINDOW CASING

EXTENDED WINDOW CASING

NEW FACE TRIM

CAULK THE JOINT BETWEEN THE TWO WINDOW CASINGS

CUT A DRIP EDGE IN EXTENDED WINDOWSILL

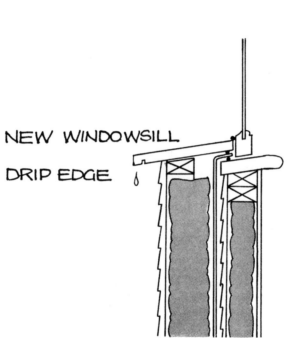

NEW WINDOWSILL

DRIP EDGE

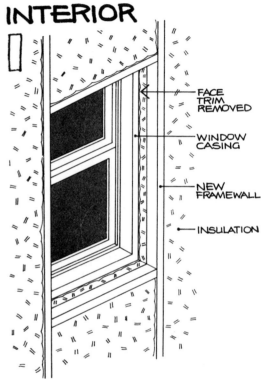

INTERIOR

FACE TRIM REMOVED

WINDOW CASING

NEW FRAMEWALL

INSULATION

it can be properly sealed to the window casing. Every window will demand attention to the gaps in the plastic at the various corners. Make sure that no air leakage can occur anywhere within the recessed area.

Allow for a degree of flexibility in the poly. If the plastic is stretched tightly at all of the corners allowing for no movement, problems might arise when the new casing or wallboard is installed. If the plastic is too tight it might be pulled away from the

staples and the caulking, resulting in large gaps which can't be seen.

Once the vapour barrier and insulation are properly in place, the similarity between the exterior and interior work ends. On the exterior, the finished product still has to be weather-strong. The best insulated section of wall will be of little help if it is constantly exposed to rivulets running through it each time it rains, snows, or melts. Ideally, when performing the re-siding of the house after the new

framing and insulation has been installed, one board should extend from the original casing to the exterior face. In this manner only one potential weak spot exists — the joint between the old casing and the new finished opening. Place a solid bead of a high-grade caulk at this joint to prevent water from running in between. Then there's the water running off of the sill of the window. Unless a drip edge is cut into the sill extention, capillary action might lead to water moving up and behind the siding into the insulated cavities. By cutting

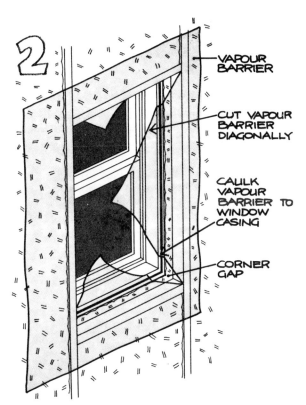

VAPOUR BARRIER

CUT VAPOUR BARRIER DIAGONALLY

CAULK VAPOUR BARRIER TO WINDOW CASING

CORNER GAP

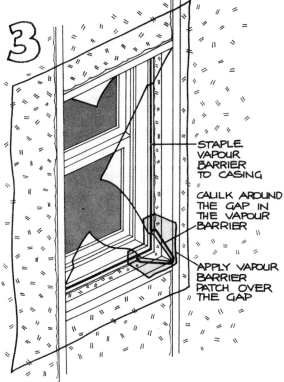

STAPLE VAPOUR BARRIER TO CASING

CAULK AROUND THE GAP IN THE VAPOUR BARRIER

APPLY VAPOUR BARRIER PATCH OVER THE GAP

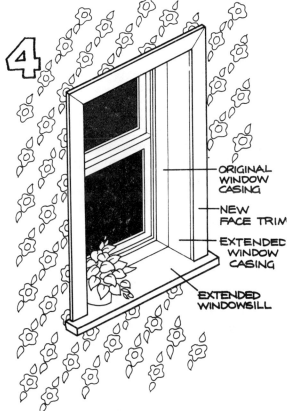

ORIGINAL WINDOW CASING

NEW FACE TRIM

EXTENDED WINDOW CASING

EXTENDED WINDOWSILL

a kerf into the bottom of the sill extension, this problem can be resolved as the water will drop from the kerf to the ground below.

Finishing work on the inside of the house presents no such problems. The finishing details depend on your tastes. If the window is to be totally framed in wood, wide boards will be required, but these are easily installed. Alternatively, the recessed window space can be more economically drywalled with trim placed directly against

the edges of the window casing. In either case the recessed window sill creates an ideal location for setting plants.

Sealing the Windows

A vast number of options are available to reduce the drafty areas around the movable sash of older windows. Determine whether it is necessary for all the windows within the home to be operable. In many instances a large room will be equipped with three or four windows, all of which

are never opened at once. Take a serious look at the windows within the house and see if you can manage without opening some of them. A good indicator is finding out how many of the windows have been opened since the house was last painted. Any of the windows which aren't needed can be sealed around the edges with a clear silicone caulking material. This provides a good, long-term seal to the window sash, without detracting from the aesthetics of the finished window. The more windows that can be sealed, the less air leakage into the house. Bear in mind that sealing too many of the operable windows can result in a lack of natural ventilation during the summer months, although doors can assist in providing ventilation.

Having resolved which of the windows can be sealed permanently, focus in on the movable joints of the remaining windows. As mentioned before, any movable joint in the window sash should be weather-stripped to prevent air leakage. Specific window types will require different approaches:

Double-Hung Windows: This is the worst violator in terms of infiltration. Seal the upper half of the window with silicone; the lower half of the window should be weatherstripped around its perimeter. A vinyl spring weatherstripping is easy to install once the window has been lifted out of its track and is relatively inexpensive. The material comes with an adhesive backing, but should be stapled or screwed to the casing to ensure it doesn't move. The weatherstripping should also be installed on the sill of the window and affixed to the outside edge of the top plate. If the counterweights are to be removed and the cavity housing them is filled with an insulating material (polyurethane foam), the window will require a wedge to keep it open. A better solution involves the installation of a tight-fitting weather-stripping which creates a friction fit between the window and the sash channels. This approach allows the window to stay open at the required height, though

SEAL THE UPPER HALF OF THE WINDOW WITH SILICONE CAULK

- STAPLE COMPRESSIBLE WEATHERSTRIPPING TO THE INSIDE TOP EDGE OF THE WINDOW
- REMOVE THE WINDOW STOP
- TAKE OUT THE WINDOW
- STAPLE SPRING VINYL WEATHERSTRIPPING TO THE CASING

WINDOW STOP

- STAPLE COMPRESSIBLE WEATHERSTRIPPING TO THE INSIDE EDGE OF THE WINDOWSILL

it may demand a bit more muscle to open and close the unit. To encourage a tight seal to the bottom piece of weather-stripping when the window is shut, a sash lock should be used.

Casement and Awning Windows: Casement windows, which operate like a door, and awning windows will generally provide a better seal than other windows. Their cranking mechanism and locking devices allow for a good positive seal to the sash when it is in the closed position. Nevertheless, leaks may have appeared in the original weatherstripping over the years. These windows are easy to upgrade

as you don't need to remove any of the components of the sash, unlike the double-hung windows. In their open position, clear access is gained to all of the areas in need of weatherstripping. The same holds true for some of the older hopper windows located below larger fixed panes of glass. A spring vinyl material will decrease leaks.

Horizontal Sliding Windows: Not entirely dissimilar from the vertical double-hung windows, horizontal sliding glass windows and doors need to be dismantled before an effective seal can be realized. As with the double-hung windows, one of the units can be sealed directly into place using a clear silicone caulk. Besides re-installing a good weatherstripping to the operable sash of these windows, a means of positively pushing the sash against the weather-stripping should be ensured when the sash is closed.

Reducing Conductive Losses

To reduce the conductive losses across existing windows add layers of glazing. Storm windows can be installed either on the exterior or interior of the window, or new glazing can be added directly to the window sash. Consider the aesthetics of the various options, and the ease of operation after the new glazing is added.

To prevent the build up of condensation between the new glazing and the existing window, ensure that the interior surface is tighter than the exterior surface. Vapour which leaks out through the interior window or glazing will be allowed to pass through to the exterior, preventing the vapour from condensing on the pane of glass which restricts visibility through the window. If you don't mind not being able to see outside, you might consider filling the gap with an insulated section of wall.

Storm Windows

Wood sash, and more recent aluminium frame windows, have been installed on the outside of the existing windows, usually on a seasonal basis. Now, new types of interior storm windows have been developed which are receiving great interest.

Storm windows, be they exterior or interior, prohibit the operation of hinged windows such as casement or awning windows. Although some of the newly developed interior storms can be easily removed and re-installed to allow access to the main window of the house, as a rule the use of storms makes the operation of these windows difficult. Storms can be more easily integrated with the use of vertical and horizontal sliding windows.

Some of the more expensive storms have an operable element. They incorporate a screened sliding window on the outside, or use tight-fitting magnetic tapes on the inside to allow ventilation. They need to be custom made and installed, and will be priced accordingly.

When adding storms ensure that the space between the new glazing and the storm is less than 4 inches for maximum benefits. If caulking or weatherstripping an exterior storm, make sure that the interior window is extremely well sealed.

Additional Glazing Inside the Sash

The number of glazing layers in existing windows, be they fixed panes or operable sashes, can be increased without changing the interior or exterior appearance of the house. While this approach can result in significant energy savings, it should only be done in conjunction with the already mentioned sealing techniques.

Fixed Panes:

Additional layers of glazing can be easily installed in conjunction with all of the fixed panes of glass in the home, be they small or large. New panes of glass can be ordered to fit the existing sash of the window and installed with a tight seal to the interior surface. Allow for the venting of any vapour which might find its way between the two glazing units.

Triple-glazing should be incorporated into windows oriented to the east, west and north. In most older houses, the existing windows will be only single-glazed. To reap the benefits of triple-glazing, a hermetically sealed, double-glazed unit can be installed on the interior of the existing pane. This process is very simple. The opening to be re-glazed should be carefully measured. Leave a small amount of room around the frame ($1/8$ inch around the edges). If the existing pane is set into a sash, the wood sash can be used as the stop for the new sealed unit, remembering that a still air gap of close to an inch is the ideal distance between the layers of glazing. Alternatively, a new stop can be installed against which the double-glazed unit can be sealed. When sealing the new window unit to the stop or sash, a layer of glazing tape should be used as the adhesive seal. This tape is widely available and provides both a tight seal and a strong joint between wood and glass.

If the existing glass is housed in a wooden sash, a new unit can be installed within the sash. This is a rather time consuming task, but it results in an unobtrusive addition to the extra glazing. The frame of the sash needs to be routed out or levelled off with a saw and chisel. In most cases the sash of the window will be a bevelled surface which renders the addition of any other glazing extremely difficult. By cutting out a square edge, the installation becomes simplified. When routing or cutting out the bevelled edge, set the depth of the router or saw to allow for at least a $1/2$-inch stop between the existing glass and the new unit. The glazing tape can be applied onto the stop to provide the required seal. In some cases, the sash will not be wide enough to allow for the installation of a double-pane unit with the optimum air gap between the panes ($3/4$ to 1 inch). If you want optimum thermal efficiency the sash of the window can be extended to the interior by installing additional pieces of wood around the window casing.

Before installing the new sealed unit, small holes for ventilation should be incorporated into the sash between the inside and outside glazing. Using a small diameter wood bit ($1/16$ inch or $1/8$ inch), a hole should be drilled vertically down through the sash about $1/2$ inch. This hole should then be joined to a hole drilled horizontally from the exterior of the sash. This channel allows for any moisture found between the two glazing layers to exhaust to the outside without allowing for a great deal of convections in the cavity. In large windows, you need to install more than one of these channels. To prevent insects from crawling through the holes into the cavity, a small piece of screening can be used to plug the hole from the exterior.

If a double-pane window already exists, or if you need to install only a single pane of glass, the same procedure can be followed. Interior finishing can be easily performed by covering the inside edge of the newly installed glass with either a piece of moulding (half round, etc.) or by enlarging the existing sash and nailing a new facing piece over the interior surface.

Operable Sashes

The same installation procedures outlined above for installing glazing inside the sash of the window can be followed for operable windows, except where the addition of extra facing or moulding will restrict the operation of sliding windows. However, it is important to remember that additional layers of glazing will add significantly to the weight of the window. Whereas a single-glazed window is generally very light, the addition of two more glazing layers may make the window more difficult to operate. This is especially true with vertically hung windows which have been properly sealed. Once the counterweights have been removed and weatherstripping installed, the tight-fitting sash will be harder to lift even if there is only one pane of glass. The addition of another sealed unit to the sash may bring about a grunt when trying to lift it.

Similarly, too much additional weight added to a casement or awning window could lead to problems with the hinging and cranking mechanisms as they strain under the added weight. If this is a concern, install only one additional layer of glazing or a lighter glazing material.

By upgrading the various elements of your existing windows, considerable savings can be realized. The other option of removing the existing window and purchasing new, more efficient units has an application in many homes. It does, however, involve a substantial capital outlay. By attempting to attain similar performance from the existing window, savings are already realized as at least one pane of glass is already in place. Similarly, the existing frame and sash can be used to house new layers of glazing.

You must perform a sound, conscientious job. If you seal the window around the casing and at the sash and add glazing to the upgraded window, you can achieve savings in the order of 60 per cent for each window. Some of the upgraded glazing systems should be viewed in conjunction with plans to incorporate movable insulation systems into the window design.

New Windows

When shopping for new windows to install in the place of those windows which were removed or to fill new openings built into the south face, consider several points. First, you want to install as many fixed panes of glass as possible, reducing the amount of potential air leakage through movable sashes. Many innovative builders are installing fixed panes of glass where the visual link to the exterior is required. Then they install small "door-like" vents just below the glazed area. This greatly diminishes the number of heat-draining joints in the building's shell. If purchasing a new operable window, try to find the window with the best possible seal. Most manufacturers can provide technical details outlining the air leakage characteristics of their windows. Admittedly a compromise often needs to be struck between the efficiency of the window and the money available. Finally, consider the number of glazing layers. In most northern locations (above 7,000 degree days) triple-glazing will prove to be a sound investment. If you plan to install, and use some form of movable insulation, double-glazing will usually suffice. On the south face of a house the optimum number of glazing layers is two. This accounts for the additional solar radiation which comes through these windows into the house interior. Again, colder regions should have triple-glazing on the south side, especially if there is a large glazed area.

Installing New Fixed Panes

Newly ordered fixed panes can be easily installed in the original window opening. Once the original window has been removed, a rough opening is exposed. A new sill plate and casing for the sides and top need to be installed over the rough stud framing. Ensure that the tie into the vapour barrier is effectively accomplished. The poly should be caulked and stapled to the new casing.

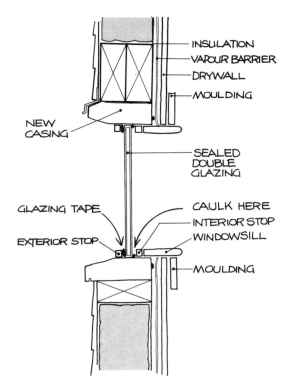

The next step involves installation of an exterior stop around the window casing. The stop should be nailed through to the casing using a galvanized finishing nail, making sure that the stop is nailed in at a level. Glass doesn't bend or warp very easily.

The glass should have been ordered to fit the new measurements. Ordering the glass to allow for an element of error is a wise decision. Take off $1/4$-inch on each measurement when making the order.

To install the glass to the stop, lay a strip of glazing tape on to the inside face of the stop. The glass is then pushed into place against the glazing tape. An inside stop is then nailed into place so that the new sealed unit of glass is sandwiched between the two stops. The interior stop can be caulked with silicone to ensure no potential problems with air leakage. Similarly, a bead of caulking should be laid on the exterior stop to prevent drainage problems. As long as the interior seal is tight, no problems with deterioration of the wood will occur.

If you decide that ventilation is needed through a specific window, a cheaper and more efficient approach to purchasing a new casement window involves installing a smaller fixed pane of glass then constructing an insulated vent below the glass.

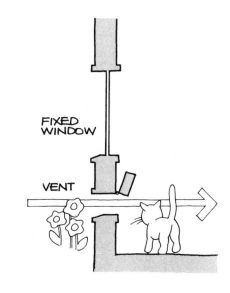

The benefits resulting from this approach are broader than the obvious savings in capital. From an efficiency perspective, the length of the cracks around the window have been reduced. Rather than having 12 lineal feet of cracks, as appear in the average casement window, the fixed pane-vent approach can reduce the cracks to 8 feet or less with the corresponding shrinkage in heat loss. Secondly, it is easier to gain a better seal with a small vent than with the larger window, and that seal will be easier to maintain over an extended period of time.

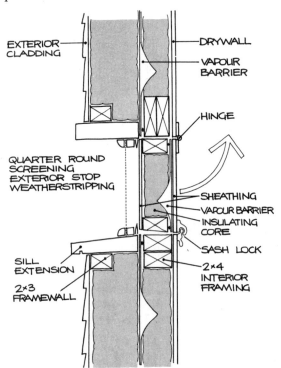

To construct the fixed pane-vent option, follow the steps detailed above for the fixed pane installation. You will, of course, need to add a new framing stud at the desired height of the vent. When nailing the new piece of wood between the vertical wall framing, make sure it is square to the sides. If the vent doesn't need to fill the entire width of the rough opening, vertical studs can be cut and nailed into place to frame the vent.

To install the vent use the same techniques that you would when installing a door, with the exception that the vent runs horizontally. Hinge the vent at the top and install a sash lock to close it tightly to the weatherstripping laid on to the stop of the vent.

Ideally the vent would be constructed of two sheeting layers on a 2 x 4 or 2 x 6 frame with an insulating core. It is, however, easier to use a solid core wood door section for this sash. The vent should be properly weatherstripped around its edges. Door threshold hardware can be used on the bottom edge of the vent to ensure both proper drainage and an effective seal.

Installing New Windows

Regardless of the type of new window you've decided to install, there are several procedures to ensure an effective seal between the new window casing and the house's vapour barrier. As a rule, this procedure should be performed before the new walls have been constructed.

Before placing the new window into the rough stud opening, a sheet of polyethylene should be caulked and stapled to the inside edge of the casing. The 12-inch strip of poly can be wrapped around the frame of the casing and pressed onto a bead of acoustical sealant, then stapled to secure the bond. When the window is placed into the opening, care should be taken so as not to rip or puncture the plastic. The plastic will then extend into the room by at least 9 inches.

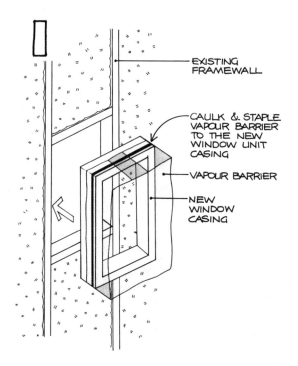

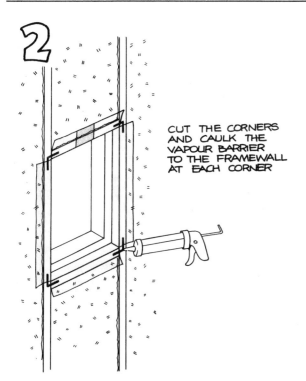

CUT THE CORNERS
AND CAULK THE
VAPOUR BARRIER
TO THE FRAMEWALL
AT EACH CORNER

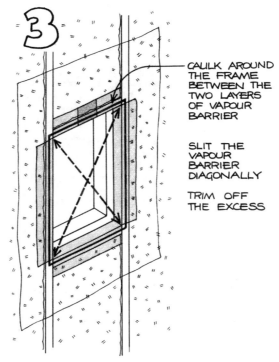

CAULK AROUND
THE FRAME
BETWEEN THE
TWO LAYERS
OF VAPOUR
BARRIER

SLIT THE
VAPOUR
BARRIER
DIAGONALLY

TRIM OFF
THE EXCESS

Before joining the poly around the window to the newly installed air-vapour barrier on the walls, the gap between the window casing and the rough stud opening should be filled with insulation — not to serve as an air barrier, but as a means of reducing conductive losses. When all of the gaps have been properly insulated, the two separate sheets of poly can be sealed.

This requires a bit of finicky work to ensure no gaps exist between the seams. Extend the poly from the window through to the interior of the house if performing an

interior retrofit. The poly can then be sealed to the new stud framing of the window which will be recessed several inches to the interior. When it has been caulked and stapled, the new vapour barrier on the walls can be cut to meet the window opening and sealed over the vapour barrier extending from the window. As the new vapour barrier will be cut in an X extending from the corners, gaps may appear at each of the corners. Smaller pieces of poly can be laid over the gaps and caulked and stapled into place.

The exterior retrofit approach is similar, although reversed. The poly wrapped around the window should be caulked and stapled to the outside edge of the casing. It will then extend to the original outside wall where it can be sealed to the new vapour barrier wrapping the house.

Locating the New Window in the Frame

Some flexibility is allowed when installing a new window in relation to its location in the new wall section, whether you have installed the newly insulated frame wall on the interior or the exterior. Conventionally, windows are located near the exterior face of the building. In Saskatchewan major retrofits have been performed from the exterior with new windows placed over the new curtain wall. This creates a large sill on the house interior which becomes an ideal location for plants, etc., but which causes problems when considering the use of insulating shutters or shades.

Alternatively, and preferably, the window can be recessed from the exterior into the opening. This improves the thermal efficiency of the window by reducing the convective losses associated with cold winds blowing over the glass. It also helps integrate both interior and exterior shuttering devices.

Economic Considerations

As a general rule it will be less expensive to upgrade the existing windows than to install new, higher efficiency models. Exceptions to this rule will, of course, exist. Those windows in bad repair, or multi-paned French windows will be extremely difficult to upgrade. However, anyone who has looked at the prices of new 'energy-efficient' windows will realize that a lot can be done to improve existing windows without incurring great expense.

Upgrading the existing window will require the purchase of materials to attain a better seal and the addition of panes of glass to reduce convective losses. Both caulking and high quality weatherstripping can be readily obtained at a low cost. Both represent an investment with a quick pay-back. The cost of a clear silicone caulk ranges from $7 to $10. One tube should be all that is needed in an average house. Weatherstripping with a high quality material will cost between 25¢ to 35¢ per lineal foot.

Installing additional panes will require the glazing itself and some means of affixing the glass to the window sash. The cost of glass will range from $1.25 to $2.40 per square foot for a single pane of glass, to between $3.25 and $4.50 for a double-glazed, sealed unit. The cost of glazing tape and caulking should be less than $2.00 per window.

An on-going battle rages over the economics of triple glazing. The installation of a sealed, double-pane unit over an existing single pane can be performed by the homeowner in a short time for less than $3.50 per square foot. The same task will result in a saving of more than three-quarters of a gallon of fuel oil per year. At an average Canadian price of $1.25 per gallon this represents a pay-back of less than four years.

The price of new triple-glazed windows will range from $7.50 to $12.00 per square foot, representing a slower pay-back period. The contracted price of performing any of the work outlined in this chapter will fluctuate wildly from job to job. As in all cases, we recommend taking some time to search for best value for your money.

Doors

Conductive and infiltration losses through doors account for significant quantities of heat loss. Poorly insulated and sealed exterior doors become increasingly problematic as the rest of the thermal envelope of the structure is upgraded.

Remedial measures can be employed to improve the thermal performance of existing doors. Improved weatherstripping, the addition of an air-lock entry and the upgrading of the insulating characteristics of the existing door will all result in decreased losses. Alternatively, the option remains to purchase some of the newer, energy-efficient doors which have recently been introduced to the marketplace. When properly installed, these new doors can result in savings amounting to as much as 75 per cent.

Upgrading Existing Doors

Initially you should direct your attention to the seal around the edges of the door frame. In the same manner in which infiltration is reduced around windows by affixing the air-vapour barrier to the window casing, drafts around door frames can be minimized. Remove the interior face trim of the door for the interior retrofit, or the exterior trim for an exterior retrofit. In both cases once the trim has been removed the polyethylene should be caulked and stapled directly to the door casing. The trim can then be re-installed. You have now

achieved a large reduction of air leakage.

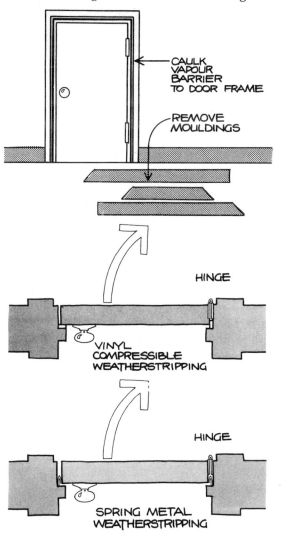

CAULK VAPOUR BARRIER TO DOOR FRAME

REMOVE MOULDINGS

HINGE

VINYL COMPRESSIBLE WEATHERSTRIPPING

HINGE

SPRING METAL WEATHERSTRIPPING

An equally large source of infiltration occurs when the door does not have a snug fit to its opening. In many houses you can see daylight through the cracks at the bottom, sides, or top of the door. If the door has not been adequately weatherstripped, the old material should be removed and replaced with a more durable and air-tight system. Several excellent possibilities are available in hardware stores and building supply outlets. We recommend the use of either spring metal or vinyl materials, or the purchase of more durable sets that can be installed over the existing door stop.

While attention is usually directed to the edges of the door frame, a large amount of air leakage can occur directly through the frame. An obvious source of air leakage is the mail slot found in many older homes. It should be replaced with a mail box located on the exterior of the house. The slot can then be tightly sealed and insulated from the interior before a plate is installed over the interior hole.

The threshold of the door should be upgraded if it has been subjected to excessive wear and deterioration. Several manufacturers make attractive threshold weatherstripping sets in which a vinyl or rubber bulb is used as a seal. The door may have to be trimmed slightly to ensure ease of operation. Be aware that too tight a fit will lead to a tearing of the bulb. The sets

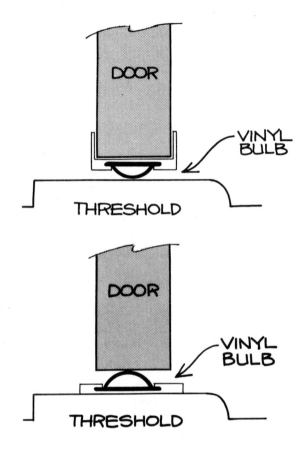

are easily installed by screwing them directly into the door sill.

Many front doors are equipped with windows to allow a visual tie from the interior to the exterior. Over the years the glass can become loose in the frame. A bead of silicone installed around the perimeter of the glass can stop this source

of air leakage without detracting from the look of the door. Similarly, over time cracks may have developed in the wood core of the door. If more major upgrading of the door is not planned, the cracks should be caulked. If your door is riddled with holes, it is probably wise to replace it.

Improving the thermal resistance of an existing door can pose more significant problems. Any glass within the door can be easily upgraded using the techniques outlined in the chapter on Windows. This will not result in any alterations to the aesthetics or functioning of the door. However, improving the core of the existing door may result in changes to both of the above characteristics.

If you wish to increase the insulating characteristics of the existing door, you may have to alter the appearance of one side of the assembly. This might lead to some operational difficulties. Insulation can be added in several ways. We suggest that the work be performed on the re-insulated side of the house. This enables the homeowner to alter the appearance of the door so that it is more compatible with new paneling or siding. In addition this allows the door to be placed into the recess created by the addition of new walls.

A door should be viewed in the same manner as a section of wall. To improve the thermal performance of the door a small cavity section filled with fibreglass or a slab of rigid insulation should be installed. As with an upgrading, the

installation of an air-vapour barrier should be considered. The insulation can be affixed to the door using the curtain wall concept, or by directly nailing the rigid insulation to the core of the door. In most cases the latter option will be the easiest to perform. The door then is covered with new siding or any other material that meets the homeowners requirements. Duplicating the original door covering may prove difficult, but it can generally be done by an experienced carpenter.

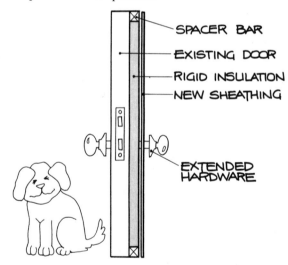

The major problem posed by the addition of extra insulation is the potential interference with the operability of the door. Any increased thickness will demand alterations to the door knob and latching assembly. This might make it difficult to open the door. The problems relating to the latching mechansim can be overcome with the use of extended door hardware sets (available from specialty hardware suppliers). Sets made for doors ranging in thickness from 3 1/2 to 4 inches can be obtained, but you may have to wait several weeks. Anything thicker than 4 inches **requires custom-made** hardware or the use of a dead-bolt latching mechanism. To resolve the operation problems, the door can be relocated on either the interior or exterior of the casing. There is now an allowance for the extra bulk. Both of these jobs will demand a great deal of attention to ensure that the door is tight.

one of the doors needs to be open at any time. This reduces the direct flow of exterior air to the house. Many people incorporate this feature into their house. It is sometimes labeled the "mud room" — the space where boots and coats can be removed and put away.

Because you want to minimize the cold air that enters the house when the inner door is opened, you want the air-lock space to be small. However, it should be large enough to accommodate two or more people when both doors are closed. Forty-eight inches between doors is usually a good compromise.

If you have a long and narrow hallway, the air-lock can be installed on the inside. Frame another door four feet back from the outside door, taking into account the arcs of both doors. For fire exit reasons, it is better if both doors open out.

Alternatively, a four foot structure can be built out from the door to form the air-lock. It is not necessary to insulate the walls, but you should weatherstrip the door.

Installing an Air-Lock

To reduce the direct access of cold outside air to the house interior each time the door is opened and to reduce infiltration losses through the edge seal of the door, an additional door can be installed in the hallway or outside of the house. This creates an air-lock. The addition or segregation of this space means that only

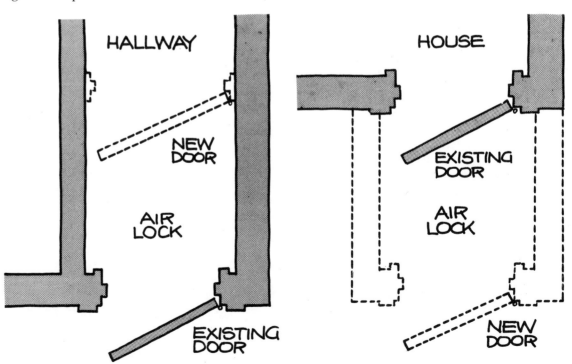

Installing New Doors

In many cases the existing doors of the building will be beyond repair when viewed from a thermal perspective. If this is true in your case, keep in mind that companies are now marketing an energy-efficient line of doors, most notably Pease and Stanley. The doors consist of well-insulated cores sandwiched between either steel or wood casing. The use of steel in these doors guarantees a long-lasting and efficient seal as no deterioration will occur. The better doors will provide an R value of between R-8 and R-12, a substantial improvement over a conventional door of R-3.

Most doors can be purchased in pre-hung frames, allowing for quick and easy installation. The existing casing of the door will need to be removed to allow for the new installation. The rough stud opening will then need to be altered to accommodate the new door framing. This may involve widening the rough stud opening or adding shims to narrow the gap. When the door is ready to be installed the same techniques that apply to the installation of a new window should be applied; ensure a continuous seal to the house air-vapour barrier.

Conclusion

While the relative size of the doors in an average house is quite small — roughly 36 square feet — their importance in relation to the rest of the super-insulated house is not to be underestimated. To leave the doors unattended to would be like buying an entire new wardrobe while forgetting that your shoes were filled with holes.

Window Insulation

No matter how much work you have done to improve the seal around your windows, and regardless of the number of glazing layers, the windows of your house will constitute a major drain on the building's heating system. Whereas during the day windows can be enjoyed for both the view they provide and their solar gains, at night there is generally little to see, and we have yet to observe anything that qualifies as 'lunar gains'.

When we compare the heat losses of even a triple-glazed window in relation to a well-insulated wall section the relative imbalance is greatly accentuated. In Ottawa (8000 degree-days) a 12 square foot window loses the equivalent of slightly less than 9 gallons of oil during the average winter. The equivalent space in a relatively well-insulated wall section (R-25) would only lose heat to the equivalent of 4/5 of a gallon of fuel oil. As solar gains will occur throughout the day, and the differential temperature will be greater during the evenings, the larger portion of these heat losses will occur at night.

By incorporating some form of moveable insulation — something which increases the thermal resistance of the window at night, but which can be put out of the way during the day — heat losses from windows can be significantly diminished. Similarly, by reversing the mode of operation during the warmer months, excessive heat gains during the summer can be reduced.

Moveable insulating systems cover a vast number of options. They include shutters, shades and curtains. They can be located on the interior or the exterior of the house, and can be operated diurnally or even seasonally. They may be integrated into the design of individual rooms or they can be stored in a specific area removed from the window. They can be owner built at a very low cost or purchased from commercial manufacturers — sometimes at an extremely high price. Finally, they can be very effective in reducing the heat loss characteristics of a window or, in the extreme case, they can actually increase the heat losses through that same window.

Any effective moveable insulation system will meet the following criteria: It will have as high an R value as is practical; it will restrict the flow of air and water vapour through the insulating core; it will consist of a reflective surface to re-radiate energy back into the living space; and, of greatest importance, it will have effective seals around the edges of the window to restrict the flow of air and water vapour. The above criteria will apply in one way or another to all effective moveable insulation systems. A more detailed explanation of each requirement will assist the home-owner when purchasing or constructing moveable insulation systems.

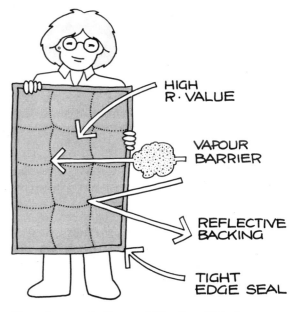

Requirements for an Effective Window Insulating Device

High R Value: To justify the time and expense of purchasing or constructing an effective window insulation system, conductive losses must be reduced to as low a level as possible. Any window treatment option should consist of an insulating core. The R value of the device should range from R-5 to R-10 to achieve significant fuel savings. For devices with rigid cores, such as shutters, this will pose no problem. Similarly, with insulating curtains additional insulation should not restrict movement or alter the aesthetics.

Attaining high R values with thermal shades will likely be more difficult, as storage on a roller mechanism may prove to be too bulky.

Incorporating an Impermeable Surface: To prevent vapour-laden warm air from reaching the window, a layer of polyethylene or aluminum foil should be built into most moveable insulating devices. Unless you're using a rigid insulation with a low permeability, the poly or foil should be installed with a minimum of perforations. This surface will prevent water vapour from condensing on the inner layer of glazing, thereby avoiding the staining and deterioration of the casing.

Ensuring a Tight Seal: Warm house air must be prevented from circulating behind the insulating device, either around the edges or through any seams. The sides of the device — be it a shutter, shade or curtain — should be well-sealed to the edge of the window casing. This can be accomplished with the use of weatherstripping in rigid shutters, tracking devices for an operable shades, or permanently sealed edges with curtains. A compressible seal at the bottom of the moveable insulation can prevent warm air from entering below the insulated core. A valance constructed above shades and curtains can reduce the flow of house air behind the curtain from the top. A tight seal will not only restrict heat loss through the window, but will reduce the problems caused by excessive condensate build-up. It is possible that without the seal, heat loss through the window can actually be greater than it would be without any insulating device.

Re-radiating Heat to the Interior: As we've already mentioned, one of the significant causes of discomfort in the home results from the radiant losses to windows. As we sit near a window heat is radiated from our bodies to the cold surface of the glazing. By incorporating a reflective material into the construction of an insulating system for windows, heat radiating towards the window will be reflected back to the interior of the house. This can be accomplished with the use of a reflective foil (builder's foil) or by Mylar or another aluminized material.

Types of Moveable Insulation Systems

A brief glossary of terms might prove useful before venturing too far.

Shutters

Shutters can be located either on the inside or outside of the house. In general they consist of a rigid core of insulation which is placed over the window opening at night. Shutters can be hinged at the sides or top of the window, or more simply they can be fit into the window at night using either a mechanical fastening device (such as Velcro or magnetic tape), or be fitted snugly to the window casing. As a rule shutters are more stable than any of the other options and allow for higher amounts of insulation. If properly designed they can be aesthetically integrated into the house.

Shades

Insulating shades are made up of several thicknesses of various materials. They are usually operated from a roller mechanism situated above the window. When in its extended position the shade should completely cover the window opening and should be tightly sealed to the edges of the window casing. It is generally more difficult to attain the high insulating values that are realized with shutters as the various materials must be rolled up during the day in a limited amount of space. The greatest benefit afforded by the insulating shade is its relative ease of operation. They require only a small amount of space directly in front of the existing window.

Insulating Curtains

Insulating curtains appear to be similar to other curtains. The major difference between the insulating curtain and its inefficient partner stems from the manner in which it prevents heat loss. The curtain must have a seal at the bottom, top and sides of the window to prevent any circulation of warm air over the cold glass surface. It must contain an impermeable surface to prevent water vapour from flowing through the material, and the curtain should be fabricated of materials which allow for a high thermal resistance. The major benefit arising from the use of thermal curtains results from the ease with which they can be integrated into standard design practices. With a little bit of work, existing curtains can also be upgraded.

Diurnal vs. Seasonal

Any moveable insulation system can be operated in several ways. Typically, the device is lowered or shut in the evening and then opened once again in the morning. This diurnal operation can result in significant savings but, as often happens, if the device is not always used the savings diminish. Another approach to insulating windows involves the installation of an insulating device in the late fall. With the advent of the warmer weather it is removed. This doesn't necessarily mean that the entire window must be blocked off, though in many cases this is the wisest option. An intermediary solution calls for the installation of an 'insulated storm window' in which the glazed area of the existing widow is decreased and surrounded by an insulated frame. In such cases the window is still in place, albeit somewhat smaller.

Exterior vs. Interior

Historically shutters have been installed on the exterior of a building to shelter fragile glass from buffeting storms. This still remains true in the tropical storm belt of the southern United States. In the same manner, exterior insulating devices can be fitted to the outside of the house and closed during the cooler evenings. However, certain problems need to be taken into consideration. One has to remember that it is often cold outside. If the exterior shutters are not manually operated from the exterior, some form of mechanical operating device will be needed within the house. Right away, whether you open the window to close the shutter, or pierce the vapour barrier with a cranking device, the gains you might have realized start to trade off with the higher infiltration levels. In addition, whereas it might be simple to manually close shutters located on the ground level of the house, any device on the second or third floor of the building will pose more significant problems. The benefits of any external insulating device result primarily from the fact that condensation problems — a 'bugaboo' of interior systems — are not a concern and that the problems of storage and allowing space for the operation of the device are alleviated.

Interior insulating devices are generally easier to operate and service. You do not need to be overly concerned with opening and closing shutters during howling blizzards. As previously mentioned, attaining a tight seal to the edges of an interior shutter, shade or curtain is of great importance if condensation build-up on the windows is to be minimized. Unless carefully designed, the storage of any rigid insulating device can pose problems. Similarly, the use of interior devices can restrict the use of the space adjacent to the window as the daily ritual of opening and closing demands some free access and clearance.

The most important factor relating to moveable insulation systems for windows has little to do with the actual design and construction of the device. The most efficient system in the world, when constantly left in an open position, becomes a useless addition to the home. If the homeowner is conscientious and uses the insulating systems nightly throughout the heating season, substantial energy savings will result. If it's not used the purchase of the system represents a total waste of time and money.

Pop-In Options

Pop-in shutters are the easiest to construct of all of the moveable insulation options. Hundreds of different designs can be formulated to suit any given location within the house. The simplest option involves taking a piece of rigid styrofoam, urethane or Thermax, cutting it to the dimensions of the window opening and pushing it against the window frame. When we consider the

design requirements several improvements will be needed, the least of which is some means of pulling the rigid board away from the glass. Pop-in shutters can be located either directly against the glass or they're set back from the window by a slight margin. The major problem encountered with the use of pop-in shutters relates to the storage of the device when it's not in use. If you're designing the shutter to fit tightly into the window opening, several considerations should be borne in mind.

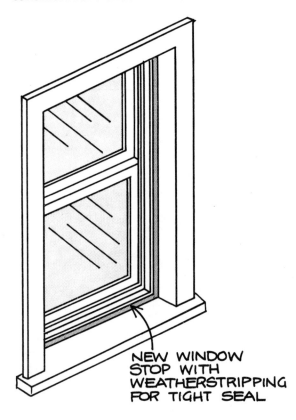

NEW WINDOW STOP WITH WEATHERSTRIPPING FOR TIGHT SEAL

Extended use of the shutter will result in some deterioration of the edges, resulting in air movement around the device. This can be resolved in several manners. By building a wood frame to encase the insulation, durability is increased. Alternatively, if vying for a less expensive and time-consuming option, the edges of a rigid insulating board can be covered with a vinyl duct tape. Another option involves the installation of an additional stop inside the window casing, onto which the shutter can be placed. If the stop is properly weatherstripped and a means of applying pressure from the interior is provided, a tight seal can be achieved.

If installing a shutter to fill the window cavity, make sure it fits within an inch of the window glazing. This prevents air flow behind the insulated core. If, on the other hand, the pop-in shutter is designed to fit directly on to the glass it should be placed as close to the glazing as possible. These glass-hugging shutters, if properly constructed, have the benefit of preventing air from circulating behind the insulated core. This eliminates much of the concern relating to edge seals. If the shutters are fixed in place within 1/8 inch from the glazing, enough resistance is provided between the shutter and the glass to prevent air from flowing through the cavity. Magnetic strips can be attached to the glazing and the shutter to hold the material in place. Alternatively, Velcro can be employed, although it is more difficult to fit tightly to the glass.

Once the insulating material has been cut to fit into the window opening or against the glass, the required fastening devices and weatherstripping should be attached. Finishing the shutter to make it look appealing can be done by many different means. Although an insulating core with exposed foil on either side will technically perform better, few people want to look at foil all evening long. The easiest approach to improve the looks of the shutter requires applying a covering material on the interior face. Wallpaper, posters, decorative fabrics or objets d'art can be applied using either an adhesive (glue or paste), or by mechanically affixing the covering to the frame of the shutter.

When it's not in use the pop-in shutter causes the greatest problem. To ensure that the shutter is used throughout the colder months, it should be relatively accessible and easy to install. Some of the more innovative answers to this problem call for also using the shutter as a picture or wall hanging. Alternatively, the shutter can be stored directly below the window or in a nearby cupboard.

SECRET UNOBTRUSIVE HIDING PLACE FOR SHUTTER

Pop-in shutters, whether designed to friction fit inside the window casing, hug the glass or fit over the entire window opening, can be easily and cheaply constructed. They seldom demand any construction expertise — only a bit of care. The pop-in shutters are free of expensive and unwieldy pieces of hardware, yet can result in as significant a reduction in the fuel bill as any of the more expensive options. They can be used in any situation ranging from small fixed panes through operable windows, sliding glass doors and greenhouse glazing systems. Their simplicity is their greatest attribute.

Hinged Shutters

Shutters located on both the interior and exterior of houses have been employed for many centuries. Generally these shuttering options have been hinged at the edges of the window casing to allow for easy operation and to resolve any problems of storage when not in use. In more recent years hinged shutters have been constructed with insulating materials and weatherstripping to be used as a means of preventing night-time heat loss.

Whereas the pop-in variety is primarily limited to interior applications, hinged shutters can be located and operated from either the inside or outside. Interior shuttering options are usually easier to operate but will demand greater attention to edge sealing details. Exterior shutters, hinged either at the sides or the top of the window opening, are more difficult to

operate but will generally result in greater energy-efficiency as convective heat transfer from the house interior to the glass is significantly reduced. In most cases the construction of a hinged shutter will demand more time and materials than is the case with the pop-in variety.

Interior shutters present the benefit of being accessible. They can be constructed to hinge from one side of the window to cover the window opening, or be put in place with two separate shutters hinged on either side of the window. When the latter is closed, it forms a tight seal at the edges and in the centre of the window. A third option involves the hinging of the shutter at the top of the device so that in its open position it sits above the window suspended from the ceiling above.

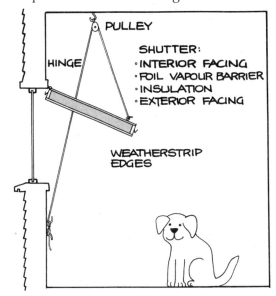

As the shutters need additional support a wooden frame will need to be constructed. The hinging mechanism is affixed to this frame. The insulating core can be composed of any insulating material, provided that the major criteria are met. The easier materials to work with include extruded polystyrene and foil-faced urethane or polyiscocyanurate. If employing a less permeable material such as beadboard or fibreglass, the shutter should be fitted with a reflective foil or at least a sheet of polyethylene. If using a rigid type of insulation a tight fit to the frame may be difficult to attain. A layer of vinyl duct tape overlapping the seam will prevent any air from circulating behind the shutter. A further construction detail is required to ensure that the shutter maintains its original shape if a flexible insulation is used or if the rigid insulation is poorly fitted. Diagonal bracing or a layer of sheathing will ensure that the shutter doesn't warp or rack over time.

Some innovative approaches have been developed to deal with the shutters when they are not in use. The same decorative ideas as mentioned in the section on pop-in shutters can be employed. However, with the hinged shutter you must remember that both sides will be exposed to the interior — one during the day, the other at night. One of the cleaner approaches involves recessing the shutter into the adjoining wall. This option must be thought out well in advance as it will involve a different framing detail at the sides of the window.

If the homeowner plans to install hinged interior shutters, the adjoining section of wall should be recessed to the planned thickness of the shutter. Thus, if the shutter is constructed to house 1 inch of insulation and is sheathed on each side with a $1/2$ inch material, the wallboard adjacent to the window should be recessed by 2 inches. This will allow the open shutter to lie flush with the existing wall. While it does improve the aesthetics of the room, this option requires that a small section of the wall have less insulation than the surrounding areas.

Other interior hinging details can be employed to deal with larger areas of glass. Bifolding shutters can be used to insulate sliding glass doors or larger fixed panes of glass. These shutters can be stored in a smaller area than that required for larger single-hinged units. It should be recognized, however, that the additional seams in the bifolding shutter present a greater likelihood for air leakage to the glazing.

Exterior shuttering options are devoid of the condensation problems, as the warm vapour-laden air cannot pass through a well-sealed window. If reasonably well fitted to the window frame, exterior shutters will also result in diminished convective losses from the house interior to the exterior as the differential temperature from the glass to the shutter is greatly reduced. The other major benefit of exterior shutters is that your furnishings do not have to be kept away from the window

Although the exterior shuttering approach is generally more efficient, significant problems must be addressed. The exterior shutter must be more durable than its interior counterpart, able to withstand the effects of sun, wind, rain, sleet, and snow. Unless you have easy access to the shutter from the exterior (as may be the case with a bungalow or one storey house), the shutter will need to be operated from the interior. If you have to open a window to gain access to the shutter you will probably lose more heat than is saved. Alternatively, some cranking device will be needed, creating a hole in your newly installed vapour barrier. We've even seen some top-hinged shutters which are operated from the interior by raising and lowering a rope. Probably the best approach will involve dealing with inaccessible areas from the interior of the house. You'll also want to consider whether you will mind closing all of the exterior shutters in the midst of a blizzard.

The shutter should be strong enough to withstand the buffeting of winds (when closed and open) and the materials employed in its construction should be able to weather the various elements. Warpage and shrinkage will lead to poor fitting and performance. Side-hinged shutters are the most conventional and can be easily integrated into the design of the exterior facade of the house. Top-hinged shutters have the advantage of doubling as a summer overhang, thereby reducing the amount of sunshine on the glazing. While shutters which are hinged from the bottom

have been used as a means of reflecting more winter sunshine into the living space, in severe northern climates their operation will be severely limited by snow and ice. These shutters are most commonly designed for greenhouse glazings.

Sliding Shutters

Shutters situated on tracking devices can be constructed on the interior, exterior and even between layers of glass. These shutters are all easily operated and can be readily integrated into the house design. While the efficiency of the shutters will depend upon the actual design of the tracking system and edge seals, good performance is easily attained. The major disadvantage of sliding shutters relates to the relative complexity of the installation, as the tracking systems can be difficult to purchase and install.

Interior sliding shutters can be located directly over the window sill, which can be extended to allow for the tracking mechanisms. A similar extension will be required of the top face trim of the window to allow for the header tracking device. When in the open position the sliders will be located adjacent to the window on either side of the opening. Close attention should be shown to the sealing detail at the top and bottom of the shutter. If the shutter is designed to operate too easily it will be difficult to maintain a good seal. For the same reasons that sliding glass doors have a high rate of infiltration, a sliding shutter on the house interior should be carefully designed. A combination of weather-stripping and insulation should allow for satisfactory performance. Tracking devices such as louvered door and barndoor hardware will be extremely difficult to seal.

Several new houses have been designed to allow the shuttering device to be hidden inside the walls of the house when they're not in use. This requires that a cavity be installed adjacent to the window so that the shutter becomes part of the wall insulation during the day. While this means a reduced thermal resistance in a section of the wall when the shutter is covering the window, it counters many of the arguments concerning the problems of storing shutters during the day. These 'pocket shutters' can be easily incorporated into the retrofit by having the shutter slide into the cavity between the original and the newly constructed walls.

Sliding shutters can be easily integrated into the exterior design of the house, especially when alterations to the facade have been made during an exterior retrofit. As the super-tight seal required for the interior shutter is not as important, the exterior shutter can be operated on several commercially available tracking systems. Sliding barndoor hardware can be easily altered to accommodate an insulating shutter.

Thermal Shades

Many commercial shades are currently on the market as well as several how-to design kits. The commercial systems can be evaluated according to their insulating values and the efficiency of the edge seals. Most of the systems are relatively expensive, ranging from $5.00 to $8.00 per square foot. Any flaws in the design of these systems becomes quite evident at these prices. The plans available on the construction of these shades call for a significant capital outlay for materials and a considerable investment of time.

The problem with shades usually relates to the varied number of layers required to provide effective insulation. The goal is to reduce conductive heat loss by trapping still air, either in between layers of foil or in the insulating core of the various shades. This would not be difficult if the shade were stationary, but most of the available devices are stored above the window on a roller mechanism. This places restrictions on the thickness of the shade as the entire

assembly must neatly roll up above the window.

An alternative to the roller mechanism, such as the Roman shade, offers a much greater flexibility in the design of the insulating shade, but will experience significant problems with the edge seal. To achieve a tight seal, magnetic strips or Velcro can be employed or, alternatively, a wooden clamping bar at either edge of the window can be installed on a spring-loaded hinge.

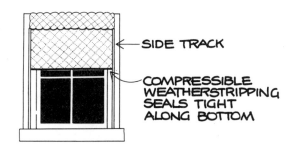

If you are making your own shade, several available fabrics can be used to provide the required thermal resistance. Thinsulate, Hollofill and PolarGuard are all materials which are used in the fabrication of cold weather garments. They can be found in specialty fabric stores. The shade should also house a reflective foil to prevent vapour passage and radiant heat losses. Builder's foil, Mylar or aluminized nylon can all be used in this role. An attempt should be made when fabricating the shade to maintain the integrity of the foil. Any

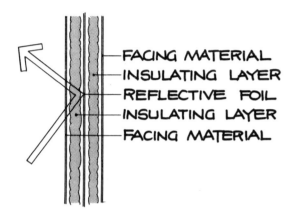

- FACING MATERIAL
- INSULATING LAYER
- REFLECTIVE FOIL
- INSULATING LAYER
- FACING MATERIAL

stitching should be restricted to the edges of the material to prevent holes in the shade.

Thermal Curtains

From an aesthetic perspective, the use of thermal curtains will be the easiest of the window insulation options for the homeowner to accept. Yet at the same time thermal curtains are the most difficult of the window insulation systems to properly fabricate and install. For years we have been led to believe that any curtain with a thicker than usual liner constituted a thermally efficient curtain. However, with very few exceptions the curtains being sold in the local department stores do little to reduce heat loss through windows. To significantly reduce heat losses the curtain requires good edge seals and a reflective surface in addition to insulating fabrics.

The curtain should be heavily weighted at its bottom to prevent any air from circulating behind the material, and the edges should be tightly sealed to the window casing or the adjacent wall. The seal at the edges of the curtain should be permanent to minimize air movement. This means that the only real problem area occurs at the seam of the curtains when they are closed. Strips of Velcro allow for a relatively tight seal to the curtain. To prevent warm air from dropping behind the insulating core at the top, a wooden valance should be constructed over the top of both the curtain and the shade. The valance can most easily be made from several pieces of wood mounted on the wall above the curtain rod or roller mechansim.

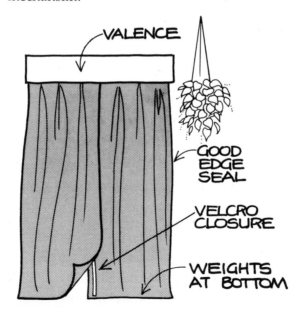

- VALENCE
- GOOD EDGE SEAL
- VELCRO CLOSURE
- WEIGHTS AT BOTTOM

A list of many of the commercially available window insulation systems is included in the *Materials* chapter of the book. The entire field of window treatment has received a considerable amount of interest over the last several years. It is expected that the relative efficiency will increase and cost of the commercial systems will decrease over time as new materials and designs reach the marketplace. At this point it is the authors' contention that the handy homeowner can construct or fabricate efficient and cost-effective shutters or shades using readily available materials.

Economics

A shutter which is equipped with a good edge seal and an impressive insulating value should save the homeowner in a climate with more than 7,000 DD, more than the equivalent of 5 gallons of heating oil per year. This estimation assumes, of course, that the shutter is used throughout the heating season for an average of 14 hours daily. The above calculations refer to the use of an R-5 shutter over a double-glazed window. Even greater savings will result from the use of the same shutter on single-glazed windows, but the increased heat loss through the window during the day will result in a larger total loss through the shuttered single-glazed window.

The calculations required to determine the savings achieved by adding moveable window insulating systems are included in the technical section of the book. By determining the dollar savings which will result from the incorporation of these systems, the homeowner can then decide how much money to invest in their purchase and construction. The incorporation of insulating systems for windows can pay for themselves within a few years if owner-built. Most commercial systems will demand a longer term investment, usually between seven and fifteen years.

The importance of effective window insulation techniques must be stressed. If you have performed all of the other aspects of the job as outlined in the previous chapters, the heat losses through your windows will constitute the largest component of your fuel bill. With the proper design and use of effective window insulating techniques, the benefits of solar gain and natural lighting during the day can be realized without the expense of significant heat losses at night.

Heating Systems

If you have performed the majority of the work outlined in the previous chapters, you will have reduced the heat loss of your home by as much as 75 per cent. Further savings will result from upgrading or altering the existing heating system of your home. As fuel prices continue to escalate it remains critically important that you maximize the amount of heat provided to the house through each gallon of oil, cubic foot of gas, kilowatt hour of electricity or cord of wood.

Conventional furnaces in the average Canadian home operate at efficiencies ranging from 50 to 60 per cent. This means that when the furnace consumes a gallon of oil (containing 165,000 BTU), or a cubic foot of natural gas (containing 1,000 BTU), only 50 to 60 per cent of the heat is supplied to the home. The rest is exhausted up the chimney and does little more than warm the outside air. In part, these inefficiencies can be attributed to improper maintenance of the furnace, oversizing of the equipment, and the poor design of the distribution system.

Today's new furnaces are capable of running at efficiencies in excess of 90 per cent. This is primarily due to a series of design modifications to the heat exchange mechanisms within the fire chamber of the furnace. These new systems, if installed into a conventional house, could result in fuel savings of up to 35 per cent.

For the homeowner who has undertaken the super-insulated retrofit, several options are available. In many cases your existing furnace will have outlived its usefulness. Whereas before the retrofit your house may have required a furnace capable of delivering more than 100,000 BTU per hour on the coldest day of the year, your design heat load may now be reduced to less than 17,500 BTU per hour and, if one of the higher efficiency furnaces were installed, it would only need to consume 20,000 BTU per hour on the coldest day. The original furnace will now be grossly oversized, resulting in sporadic on-off cycling even on the coldest day of the year. It is important to realize that a furnace will operate at higher efficiencies when the burn cycles are prolonged, as a large amount of energy is wasted when the burner is fired or turned off.

If for some reason the homeowner decides to keep the existing furnace, several things can be done to improve its operating efficiency. (Be aware, however, that these changes will only marginally improve its performance if the oversizing is significant.) Proper servicing, the use of add-on devices, and a change of fuels can all result in a reduced operating cost to the homeowner. If the efficiency of the distribution system is upgraded, savings can result with a smaller capital outlay.

If a new heating system is to be installed, the homeowner must consider several criteria. From an efficiency perspective, the homeowner will seek a heating system which closely matches the requirements of the retrofitted house. This will automatically narrow the options as small sized furnaces are not readily available. Indeed, the homeowner with an extremely small design heat load may be required to look to some uncommon alternatives such as trailer heaters, small wood stoves or even oversized domestic hot water systems.

If several possibilities fit the bill, the homeowner must then consider the fuel source options. We have been confronted with extensive advertising campaigns on the part of both industry and government. They are trying to persuade us that one option is better than the rest. We hear a myriad scenarios describing the future prices of oil, natural gas and electricity. Each of the energy supply sectors confidently speaks about the reliability of supply of their respective fuel source. Of course, no one has any real idea of what their supply options will cost twenty years down the road, and in most cases there is no real insurance that the fuels we currently use will be in abundance at the end of that time period. All that we can really count on is that the prices of all of the supply options will continue to escalate and, if we don't curtail our appetite for energy, we are going to run out of choices in the foreseeable future. Each homeowner will want to evaluate their own options on the basis of cost, availability and security of supply.

The other criteria to be considered relates to the heat distribution system preferred by the homeowner. Many of the older homes in Canada have been equipped with water-based (hydronic) heat distribution through radiators. In the last several decades many of these systems have been replaced with forced-air distribution systems which allow for easier control of the air within the home. One of the major factors in favour of the forced-air system has been the need for increasing humidity in leaky houses. Humidity control is easily incorporated into the home's heating system. Radiant heat, on the other hand, can have a drying effect on the interior air of the house.

A major consideration when deciding upon the type of heating system to be installed into your newly retrofitted house should be the effect that system has on the air quality in the home. As most super-insulated retrofits will require an air-to-air heat exchanger to deal with excess humidity and environmental contaminants, some air-handling duct work will be necessary. In most cases the use of a forced-air system will represent the best option.

Houses which have a large passive solar heating component will also benefit from a forced-air system. Tight houses are draft-free and so less air circulation occurs. A forced-air system can be used to transfer solar gains from the south side and any high points within the house to the rest of the home.

Finally, a note about meeting the cooling requirements of the building in its finished state. As the increased insulation levels and the significantly diminished air change rate within the house will assist in easing the heating load, so too will the cooling load of the house be reduced. It would be extremely difficult to justify the purchase of any air conditioning machinery for the building. In these cases the use of a heat pump becomes questionable as only one-half of the operation of the heat pump would be required. When one considers the substantial capital outlay needed for the purchase of these systems, savings must be realized throughout the year in both the heating and cooling seasons to justify the investment. Although the heat pump may have some application for the homeowner of the typical leaky house, its application is unnecessary for the homeowner who has performed the super-insulated retrofit.

The decision to replace your existing heating system is a difficult, but important one. The homeowner will want to carefully analyse the various options. The following section will shed some light on what can become a very murky issue.

Improving the Performance of Your Existing System

The decision to keep your heating system should be made with substantial reservations. In some cases it may prove to be too expensive to replace the old system, so you'll be forced to live with the resulting inefficiencies. If this is the case, you should at least perform all the necesary tasks to minimize heat losses. If your heating system has seen better days the task of tearing it out won't be quite so painful.

The first order of business calls for some common sense. Make sure that the furnace is properly maintained so that it works to its maximum potential. Regular servicing of all heating appliances is a must, not only in the case of the super-retrofitted house, but for all furnaces. Oil-fired furnaces should be serviced at least once a year to ensure that soot build-up in the fire box and dirty air filters don't become a problem. To increase the efficiency of the furnace, the size of the fuel nozzle can be reduced to restrict the flow of oil into the combustion chamber. You can't downgrade the nozzle size too much, but it's a good first step. Optimum efficiency for oil furnaces can be identified by analysing the characteristics of the flue gases escaping up the chimney. By

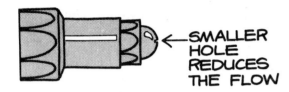

← SMALLER HOLE REDUCES THE FLOW

OIL BURNER FUEL NOZZLE

finding the optimum temperature of the gases and determining their CO_2 levels, modifications to the burner nozzle can be properly performed. Although it is frequently suggested that this work be done by a qualified furnace serviceman, kits are available which allow the homeowner to make the required changes.

Gas-fired furnaces do not require servicing as often as their oil counterparts. This is attributable to the relatively clean burning characteristics of the fuel. Nevertheless, the air filters should be regularly cleaned or replaced and an inspection of the furnace conducted every year or two by a qualified service mechanic. Burner adjustments (preferably by instruments) can result in improvements to the operation of the heating system. In both oil and gas-fired appliances alterations to the circulating fan of the furnace can improve its efficiency. If excess heat is being lost up the house chimney, the circulating fan can be sped up to improve the transfer of heat from the heat exchanger to the house air passing over the exchanger. Similarly, by elongating the operation of the fan, the furnace begins to cycle before it normally

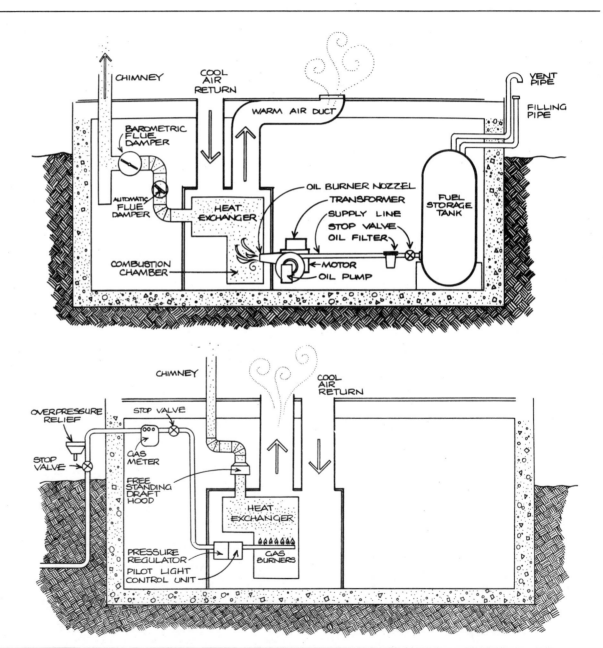

would. This causes it to run longer. To accomplish this, run the fan control mechanism so that it cuts in at a lower temperature and cuts off at a later time. These are alterations which should be done by your serviceman.

Several add-on devices are available as a means of improving the operation of existing furnaces. Because of the more stringent controls placed on the combustion of natural gas, most of the add-on devices have been approved only for oil burning appliances. Most of the following devices are now common items on the newer furnace models:

Flue Dampers: These devices are installed into the flue of the furnace. They automatically operate to reduce much of the heat lost up the chimney after the furnace burn cycle is over. When the furnace shuts off, the damper in the flue closes to retain the heat in the combustion chamber. This allows increased heat to the house interior. To prevent the potential ignition of the residual flue gases when the furnace turns back on, the flue damper is opened before the burner is ignited.

Delayed Action Solenoid Valve: These devices are installed between the fuel pump and the burner nozzle and assist in providing more complete combustion of the fuel in the combustion chamber. The solenoid valve allows for oil pressure to be built up during the first several seconds of operation of each cycle. The additional pressure in the fuel line ensures cleaner

burning during these initial few minutes. At the other end of the cycle the solenoid valve acts to stop the flow of fuel to the combustion chamber after the required amount of heat has satisfed the thermostat. This prevents furnace run-on. The valve can greatly reduce the inefficiencies which result at the beginning and end of each combustion cycle of the furnace.

Flame Retention Heads: These devices, which fit over the burner nozzle of an oil furnace, result in a more thorough combustion of the fuel supply by allowing for greater CO_2 levels within the combustion chamber.

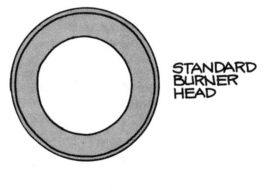

STANDARD BURNER HEAD

FLAME RETENTION HEAD

Electronic Pilot Ignition: These replace the old pilot lights that normally burn continuously. By igniting the flame only as it is required several percentage points can be gained in efficiencies.

The above devices should only be installed after receiving approval from your local serviceman or Fuel Safety Branch. The installation of some devices which have not gained approval can invalidate your furnace warranty and possibly your fire insurance in the event of trouble. It is usually wisest to allow your furnace serviceman to perform the installation.

Sizing The New Furnace

A properly sized furnace is an important element of energy-efficient design. Large fuel savings can be achieved by engineering the heating system so that the furnace burns almost continuously on the coldest day of the year. This factor relates to the relative inefficiences associated with sporadic on-off cycling, and attempts to take advantage of the maximum peak operating efficiencies of the different systems.

In determining the size of your furnace or heating system, you need to be able to calculate the design heat load of the house — the amount of heat required to keep the house at a comfortable temperature on the coldest day of the year. A simplified method of performing this calculation is presented in the technical appendix. To allow for any error most engineers will size the furnace to 110 per cent of the design heat load. If you have difficulty with the calculations, your local heating contractor will be able to perform the necessary procedures.

If you have done a good job of retrofitting the house, you should have a design heat load of between 15,000 and 35,000 BTU per hour. If you have achieved these results you will require a heating supply capable of delivering 17,000 BTU per hour for the super-efficient example and 40,000 BTU per hour in the latter case. It is important to stress the term "delivered heat". For conventional oil and gas furnaces only 60-70 per cent of the heat content of the fuel will end up as useful heat to the living area of the home. With some of the newer furnaces on the market as much as 90-95 per cent of the energy content of the fuel is delivered to the house. The only fuel which operates at higher efficiency in the home is electric resistance heating, either through a furnace or baseboard heaters. In these cases 100 per cent of the electricity is delivered to the home as usable heat. On the lower end of the scale, most solid fuel (wood, coal) burning appliances will deliver little more than 60 per cent of the energy content of the feedstock at best.

The homeowner, knowing the design heat load of the building, the peak operating efficiency of the heating system and the energy content of the fuel employed, should then be able to analyse the various options available.

NOW THAT YOUR HOME IS SUPER-INSULATED AND SUPER TIGHT, A SMALL FURNACE IS ALL YOU NEED!

Choosing a System

If you mention over the phone to your heating contractor that your design heat load is 15-25,000 BTU per hour, he'll probably scoff and assume you don't know what you're talking about. These contractors will have become so used to sizing and installing 80,000 — 150,000 BTU per hour furnaces that they assume anything smaller will result in frozen pipes.

But the contractor won't be your most difficult problem. Your search for a conventional heating system small enough to meet your needs will present the real challenge. At present the smallest gas and oil furnaces available are 50,000 and 68,000 BTU per hour respectively, considerably larger than you need. To meet your greatly reduced fuel requirements you will have to look at some not-so-conventional options; small propane trailer heaters, electric resistance duct heaters, resistance baseboard heating (for coil heaters which use your domestic hot water supply as the heat source) and solid fuel (wood, coal) burning appliances. Each of the systems has its advantages and disadvantages when cost factors (capital and operating) and the availability of the fuel required are considered. A summary of the pros and cons of each option is presented below with a more detailed explanation of installation requirements.

Small Propane Heaters

The same heaters used to keep the occupants of a mobile home adequately comfortable can provide the heating requirements of a house which has undergone a super-insulated retrofit. These heaters are available in sizes ranging from 10,000 to 40,000 BTU per hour.
With difficulty, they can be integrated into a forced-air heating system as a replacement for your conventional furnace. If the circulating fan was part of the furnace, a new fan and controls will be required to operate in conjunction with the heater.

Propane is a fairly common heating fuel in many rural areas. It is stored in pressurized containers which are located outside of the house. The containers can be either taken to a local propane dealer for recharging or they can be replaced on site. Propane is a very clean-burning fuel which will result in only minimal servicing requirements.

A propane heater will require combustion air and an exhaust flue. We suggest that if you're using this option the propane heater be located in a basement furnace room which is isolated from the rest of the house. (see Interior — basements). This will allow for exterior combustion air to be provided to the heater, reducing infiltration rates in the house. The chimney exhausting the flue gases will need to be a class A chimney (as listed through either CSA or ULC in Canada). The same chimney used by your old furnace, if it was oil or natural gas-fired, will possibly be adequate. It should be inspected by a qualified serviceman before re-using.

The use of a small propane heater is becoming a standard item in new, energy-efficient housing design. It's applicability to super-insulated retrofits should become accepted by local building authorities and heating contractors as the demand increases.

Advantages
— general availability of propane heaters and fuel
— relative ease of finding an appropriately sized unit

— clean burning characteristics
— ease of retrofitting.

Disadvantages
— potential difficulties with building authorities/mortgage institutions
— natural gas as feedstock

Electric Resistance Heating

In philosophical terms, it is extremely difficult for us, as authors of this book, to condone the use of electricity for home space heating. The relative inefficiencies of the entire thermal generating process, and the ensuing transmission and distribution losses must be considered in relation to the often-mentioned 100 per cent efficiency of electric resistance heating. In reality less than one third of the energy which is contained in the fuel consumed at the power plant reaches the household, resulting in less than a 30 per cent efficiency. The increased use of electricity also must be viewed in light of the issue of nuclear generation in several Canadian Provinces and American States. Any increase in the demand for electricity may lead to the legitimization of the utilities' desire to increase their generating capacity. To those people concerned with the expansion of our nuclear generating capacity, a reduction in electrical demand is the best manner of showing the folly of any need for expanded generating capacity.

Having explained some of our concerns, we find ourselves in a sticky situation. In many cases the installation of electric resistance

duct heaters or baseboard heating units may prove to be the most logical investment for the homeowner who has performed the super-insulated retrofit. The installation of these devices to replace an inefficient furnace will result in reduced capital costs (the purchase of the heating units) and a significant reduction in the amount of work needed to install the new system. One is only able to rationalize the contradictions if the demand for electricity is extremely small, as is the case in most super-insulated retrofits or new energy-efficient houses.

Installation of either a resistance duct heater or resistance baseboard heaters is a relatively simple procedure. They may, however, demand that the electrical service to the house be upgraded to accommodate the increased load. Generally, if you have a 100 amp service you can easily add 5 kilowatts to the load, more if it is controlled. This requirement should be confirmed with your local electrical utility before any plans are made. In most cases you will be looking at adding another 5 to 10 kilowatts to the peak demand.

Some initial work may be required before the heating units are installed. If a forced-air furnace has been removed, the duct work around the old furnace will need to be re-installed. Similarly, the installation of the air-to-air heat exchanger should be performed at this time. Ideally, you'll be able to schedule the job so that all of the work that requires a heating contractor can be done on the same day.

Electric baseboards which are installed in various locations around the home will need to be wired independently from the existing home wiring. This should be scheduled into the job so that no damage is created to the air-vapour barrier. If the new wallboard is to be installed directly over the studs, the wiring should be done at an early stage in the job. If the studs are to be cross-strapped, the wiring can be done after the vapour barrier has been installed and before the wallboard is put into place. Some baseboard units will allow for the wiring to run in conduits on the inside of the room, usually following the line of the wooden baseboards. In these cases the installation of the heating units and the necessary wiring can be performed at the very end of the job. Regardless of the timing of the installation of the new wiring, the homeowner should make sure that the electrician is totally aware of the importance of the barrier and that under no circumstances is he to ruin its integrity.

Fan coil resistance heaters can be easily installed into the main supply duct of the home in the basement. The duct heaters will range in price from $200 to $600 the average retrofitted house. This should end up being slightly more expensive than the equivalent amount of baseboard heating units when all the material and labour costs are added up.

High Efficiency Furnaces

In the last several years significant improvements to the design of oil and natural gas-fired furnaces have resulted in a 20 per cent improvement in the seasonal efficiency of new units. These improvements have been based on improved thermal transfer characteristics in the furnace heat exchangers, reduced losses through the flue of the furnace, and improvements to the ignition systems of the combustion fuels. When combined these improvements have resulted in a new generation of high efficiency furnaces, which by themselves will result in a 20 to 30 per cent reduction in the home's fuel consumption.

More recently attention has been focussed on providing fuel for the new generation of energy-efficient houses, with their small design heat load. At present the smallest oil and natural gas furnaces are in the 45,000 to 50,000 BTU/hour range. When operating at efficiencies of 90 to 95 per cent on a seasonal basis the losses associated with furnace oversizing are greatly reduced. However, with the increasing demand for smaller and smaller furnaces, the manufacturers are responding with prototype designs in the 20,000 to 30,000 BTU/hour range.

The capital cost of these new furnaces is significantly higher than that associated with the conventional models. Prices for the smallest units currently available range from $2,000 to $3,000. Economies of scale may result in some reduction in the cost, but they will probably always be more expensive than the conventional systems. Nevertheless, the fuel savings associated with these furnaces should result in a short payback period.

One of the major benefits resulting from the new, high efficiency furnaces is in the elimination of the standard chimney. Because of the increased efficiency in the heat exchange mode of the furnaces, flue gas temperatures are reduced to less than 140°F. At these temperatures there is not enough energy to power the gases up the conventional chimney. In its place the high efficiency condensing furnaces are equipped with a small PVC pipe which acts as the exhaust for the unit. The pipe can be

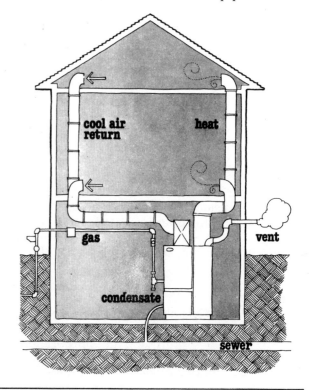

vented to the exterior through the wall of the room in which the furnace is located. To remove the liquid condensate from the furnace a small plastic pipe must be fed into the floor drain in the building's basement. The liquid effluent, which is slightly acidic (PH 4), is then directed into the sewage system.

Using the Domestic Hot Water System

In several cases where buildings have been constructed to extremely high and exacting standards, the domestic hot water system of the home has served as the main supplemental heating supply. If the heat load of the building is small enough and the hot water system is adequately sized, an independent space heating plant can be totally ignored. This system incorporates many benefits, the most significant being the reduced capital expenditure.

By installing a fan coil into the duct work of the house, hot water can be circulated through a heat exchanger in the forced-air supply duct. As the air is blown over the coil, heat is transferred from the water to the air circulating around the house. If the recovery time of the hot water tank is adequate, the water circulating from the tank through the heat exchange coil will be kept at the required temperature. The integration of this system into the home heating supply may require that the thermostat on the hot water heater be maintained at a higher than normal temperature.

If the homeowner intends to have continual circulation of the interior air, controls will be required for the heating loop from the hot water tank. A pump which is integrated with the main house thermostat will need to be installed onto the supply line of the heat exchange loop. When the house calls for heat the pump will turn on and the hot water will flow into the heat exchanger in the ductwork. When the house has received the required heat the pump stops.

Installed costs of the fan coil and the required controls should amount to $500 or more if the existing hot water tank can handle the increased load. If the hot water tank needs to be relocated in the basement of the house, more substantial costs result. The same system can be installed using a new water heating unit, but this may demand major alterations to the existing fuel supply system. If additional flues had to be installed in conjunction with new fuel lines, the investment might become less favourable.

Heating With Wood

Although most people associate wood heating with the increased trend towards energy-efficient housing, in many cases the opposite holds true. The inefficiency of the standard fireplace in our homes has become accepted by most people. Minor improvements can result from the use of glass doors, but even these will not overcome the heat draining characteristic of an open fireplace. Air-tight stoves can

operate at efficiencies of greater than 60 per cent if the stove is properly maintained and operated. They are a great improvement over the leaky heaters of yesteryear.

When a good air-tight stove is installed in a super-insulated house several problems can arise. First, to allow for good combustion the stove must have an adequate supply of fresh air. Immediately there is a contradiction with the aims of energy-efficient housing that strives for air-tight construction. Unless supplied with its own fresh air intake, the wood stove will either pull significant amounts of air into the house through the tiny perforations in the air seal of the house, or it will consume all of the oxygen in the building, resulting in dangerous living conditions for those people who enjoy breathing. It must be assumed, therefore, that a fresh air supply duct is installed for the wood burning appliance. The result is a large hole in the shell of the building which is almost impossible to seal, even if the ducting is equipped with a damper. A trade-off is obviously needed if wood is being considered as the main heat source for the super-insulated house.

The other problem relates back to our discussion about furnace sizing. Although it is similarly difficult to find an adequately small wood burning appliance, the problems resulting from the oversizing of the wood stove are more severe than the energy inefficiencies associated with the conventional furnaces. If the wood burning appliance is too large for the house, the homeowner will need to drastically reduce the amount of air reaching the combustion chamber to keep the heat output of the appliance within the comfort range. When the stove's air supply is choked down, combustion of the wood and gases is less than complete. As the warm gases escape up the flue, they will be cooled and condense on the walls of the chimney. The resulting build-up of creosote, if unattended, can present a serious fire hazard. To alleviate these problems, purchase the wood stove which most closely meets your design heat load. More than likely the stove will be oversized, as the market has yet to respond to the need for small (15,000 to 25,000 BTU/hour) stoves. This being the case, make sure that your installation procedures follow the required safety precautions; use dry hardwoods, and ensure that your chimney is cleaned regularly to remove any creosote build-up.

To ensure a more even distribution of the heat put out by a free-standing wood burning stove, a large return air duct should be located at the top of the room in which the appliance is located. If properly engineered, the heat can then be re-distributed throughout the house through the forced-air distribution network. This option will only apply to those people who are maintaining continuous air circulation within the home.

Conclusion

The system that makes the most sense for you will vary from house to house and region to region. It is critical to make the best choice so take your time and choose carefully. Don't forget that often keeping your old system will prove the best solution. Ensure it is well maintained and have it professionally downsized to the greatest extent possible. If you live in a region that permits it, incorporate an add-on automatic flue damper. It will reduce your oversizing losses for a relatively small investment.

Check on the availability of super-efficient furnaces. The extra expense may be worth it at the energy prices we'll be paying over the next fifteen years.

Check on the availability of other alternatives: wood stoves, trailer heaters, heating with a domestic hot water tank, etc.

When making the decision consider:
- availability of the fuel
- compatibility with your house
- capital costs of the equipment (including any changes that have to be made to your house or heating system)
- maintenance costs
- price of the fuel.

Your personal preferences, whether based on comfort, security or philosophy will dictate the final decision.

Air Quality

It is the ambition of every retrofitter to try to achieve as air-tight a house as possible. If, after super-insulating you develop indoor air quality problems, such as too much humidity, congratulations. You have been successful. Just how good a job you did making the house air-tight will determine what actions are required to maintain an acceptable air quality. The necessary steps range from venting your bathroom after a shower in semi-tight houses, to installing an air-to-air heat exchanger, if you did a really thorough job.

As in the *Primer,* excessive moisture on double-glazed windows is the first sign that you have a problem. If this cannot be controlled by reducing the moisture you generate, then you have to start to ventilate.

Although ventilating may seem like a step backward after taking such pains to make the house air-tight, a controlled ventilation rate is much better from an energy-efficient perspective.It is also good for the structure of your house. It is preferable that the moisture exit through a window or vent rather than through walls and ceilings where it can get "stuck".

Triple-glazed windows are less problematic than the double-glazed variety. If your windows are inset on the interior side of the house, they will develop less condensation since they are sheltered from

the wind, and inside air can circulate over the inner surface more easily.

An insulating strip (about 6 inches high) placed on the bottom of the outside window will help keep the inner window warm at the bottom. This works to prevent water from collecting on to the window sill.

Choose one of the following options if excessive moisture persists. The methods are given in increasing order of complexity.

Vent specific areas during high moisture-producing activities. If your moisture problem is not too great, it often can be resolved by opening bathroom windows a crack when taking showers or kitchen windows while cooking. This helps to exhaust these high moisture areas before a problem can arise.

Provide an outdoor air intake to the return air plenum of your house. The duct, from a screened louvered intake, should have a good working damper. It connects to the cold air return of the furnace. This ensures that the outdoor air is heated and filtered before it is distributed throughout the house. If the duct work has a U-shape bend in it, it will act as a cold trap and prevent heated air from escaping. The damper should be gradually closed over several days when it is cold outside. When condensation appears on the windows the damper can be opened slightly.

Use exhaust fans. Exhaust fans are commonly used to vent kitchens and bathrooms. Since these are high moisture areas the same system can be used to control hunidity. If the fans are vented to the outside, they should bend down instead of going straight through the roof. This helps reduce the continuous air-leakage which occurs around the usually poor-fitting damper and reduces condensation drip back.

A better arrangement, if you are renovating, is to install the exhaust fan on an interior wall and run the duct work down to the basement and out. This technique has several advantages. The cold air is less likely to leak in when the system is not is use. The condensation problem that many vents have should be eliminated, and it is generally easier to seal the vapour barrier to the duct when it is in the basement (rather than the ceiling). Another important benefit is the ease with which you can now install an air-to-air heat exchanger, should your house prove to be tight enough to warrant its use.

While exhaust vents are manually operated, and therefore not as reliable for humidity control, they can be connected to a humidistat which automatically vents the house wherever humidity exceeds a predetermined level.

Air-to-air Heat Exchangers

An air-to-air heat exchanger allows maximum air control. It permits even the tightest house to have a high air change rate, but without the associated heat loss.

The decision of whether or not to include an air exchanger in a retrofit is a difficult one. From an energy-efficiency point of view, it is a difficult task to tighten-up an old, leaky house to the point where an air exchanger is required. From an air quality perspective, an air exchanger bypasses the problems of too-tight houses. On balance, an air-to-air heat exchanger should be included as part of the super-retrofit house.

If you are conscientiously working your way through a retrofit job then your house should experience less than one-quarter air change rate per hour. The information now available indicates that this level of air change is not enough to ensure that moisture and indoor pollution levels are low enough to be harmless to both you and your house. Therefore the air-to-air heat exchanger should be built into your plans.

The air exchanging system will be expensive ($200 for the do-it-yourselfer, up to $1000 for a complete commercial system), but it should be seen as an integral part of your new energy-efficient house.

Usually the air-to-air heat exchanger sits in the basement or utility room. Often it stands upright and is comparable in size to

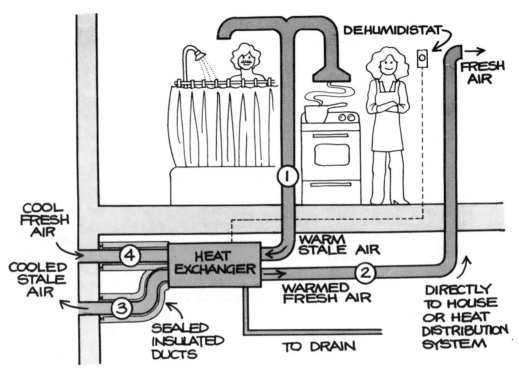

your hot water tank. Some models are built to fit between the floor joists on the ceiling of the basement.

There are four main ducts running to and from the air exchanger:

duct one: humid, stale indoor air (feeding into the air exchanger). The ducts come from vents on interior walls located in moisture and humidity generating areas: bathrooms, kitchens (with a grease filter) and clothes dryer (with a lint filter). Two or three points in most houses would be sufficient. Never connect a gas dryer to the system, but vent it to the outside directly.

duct two: warmed, fresh air (feeding into house). This pre-heated air can be dumped directly into the house, usually into the basement, or it can be fed into the return air duct going to the furnace. This method ensures that there will be no cold drafts.

duct three: cooled, stale air (exhausted from house). This duct from the air exchanger to the outside should be insulated and sealed with a continuous vapour barrier.

duct four: cool, fresh air (from outside). This duct, usually 5 or 6 inches in diameter and flexible, feeds fresh air to the air exchanger. It should be insulated with a continuous vapour barrier covering the insulation. This vapour barrier must be sealed at the wall and the heat exchanger ends.

Ducts three and four (the outlet and inlet vents) will be near each other where they exit through the basement wall, preferably through the floor joist header. These holes should be sealed just as you would any opening in the air-vapour barrier.

The outside vents should be far enough apart to prevent short circuiting of the air. Four to five feet should be sufficient. Use standard weather-proofing hoods with screens to finish the vent openings.

If you have equipped your house with exhaust fans and duct work to the basement, it is an easy task to connect the heat exchanger. If the bathroom or kitchen fans are located close to the heat exchanger, then you may not need an additional exhaust fan. Plan the ducts so that the length of runs, elbows and connections are minimized. If the total distance travelled is greater than 100 feet, then you probably require an extra fan system. All joints in the duct work should be taped.

Commercial units should come with instructions on hooking up both the electrical circuits (connections between fans, humidistat and power source), as well as the duct work.

Control of the heat exchanger can be

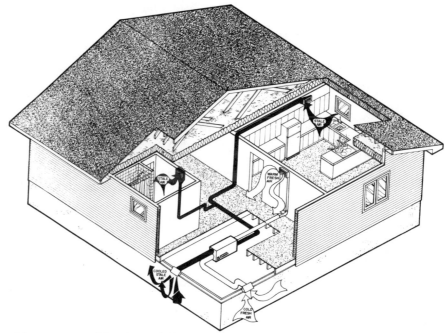

achieved by any combination of three modes:
— continuous run on low speed
— manually operated high speed
— automatic operating on high speed controlled by a dehumidistat.

It is recommended that you maintain the humidity at no higher than 35 to 40 per cent. This will probably correspond to an air-change rate of .4 to .5 air changes per hour.

The air exchanger also needs a defrosting mode, as the efficiency drops as frost forms on the core surfaces. Some models shut down until defrosting takes place. Others

leave only the exhaust fan running to quickly defrost the unit. Since much water will condense within the system, it should have a 1/2-inch flexible hose draining the water away.

Another advantage of the air-to-air heat exchanger is that it can be used in the summer to cool the house. Your air-tight, insulated house will naturally be much cooler in summer. The air-exchanger will help keep it that way.

The publication "An Air-To-Air Heat Exchanger for Residences" (listed in the bibliography) includes do-it-yourself plans for fabricating a unit.

The Born Again House

In the energy field most of our society's efforts have been directed towards finding cheaper sources of supply. In recent years many different options have been promoted as the panacea for the homeowner. Natural gas, propane, electricity, heat pumps, high efficiency furnaces and even exotic solar heating systems have been strongly promoted. Our embrace of the supply side of the issue has led most people to overlook the more significant energy and dollar savings which can result from the implementation of energy-conserving principles.

By altering our focus to the demand side of the picture, we don't have to dwell on a search for the heating system that provides the cheapest energy. As the old adage relates, 'When one is dealing with a leaky bucket it is easier to plug the holes in the bucket than to search for a cheaper supply of water'. The super-insulated retrofit will dramatically reduce the importance of the home's heating system.

We have not attempted to suggest that the super-insulated retrofit be taken lightly. In many cases the job is indeed monumental. In almost all cases the retrofit can be most easily performed from the exterior of the house, thereby reducing both the capital and time required for the job. An idealist would write a book that explained nothing but the exterior approach. However, reality suggests that many people are unwilling to perform this type of facial uplifting. To those of you in this position, but seeking to retrofit your house to super-insulated status, the more complicated and messy interior approach has been presented. Be prepared for a big job.

As realists we have been watching the impact of continually escalating fuel prices on the disposable income of the average family. Here in Canada we know that energy prices will at least double over the next four years. By that time the average Canadian family will have a heating bill in excess of $2,000 annually. We maintain that the energy conserving measures outlined in this book represent one of the homeowners best long-term investments. By the mid 1980's the super-insulated retrofit will be saving in the order of $1,500 annually for those with the foresight to perform the task.

In many cases only a lack of information can be cited as the logical reason for not upgrading the home. Thousands of homeowners are performing major renovation work on their home's interior while an equally large number of people are re-siding their houses. To ignore the chance to reduce your fuel bill at the same time as the rest of the work is being performed is to waste a once-presented golden opportunity.

As authors of this book we have elected to not use these pages to deliver an eloquent rational on our personal reasons for promoting the super-insulated retrofit. Indeed, we may have stressed the technical and economic benefits of the super-insulated retrofit at the expense of the broader societal benefits that will result from a reduced demand on our dwindling supplies of cheap, accessible, non-renewable energy options. Suffice it to say, for us these broader issues are, and should be to all, the prime rationale for the promotion of the conservation of energy. The super-insulated retrofit represents the greatest single potential for energy conservation in all sectors of society.

If our efforts and your work can negate the need for an extra power station (be it nuclear or coal) or any other of the proposed mega-projects (be they pipelines, frontier development, or solar power towers), we believe that society will be better served.

Survey

An interior retrofit
followed by an
outside curtain wall

Newmarket House

LOCATION:	Newmarket, Ontario
TYPE:	frame, interior and exterior retrofit
SIZE:	900 square feet
DEGREE DAYS:	7400 (°F)
YEAR CONSTRUCTED:	1946
RENOVATED:	1980

This was an old frame house built on posts. Typically, it was single-glazed, very leaky and had minimal insulation. The first phase of the retrofit involved interior renovations which allowed for increased insulation and an air-vapour barrier throughout most of the house. The second phase involved an exterior curtain wall, R-20 insulation, and new siding. The sole heating source for the house is a wood-burning Jotul 600, the smallest stove on the market at the time of the purchase.

OLD HOUSE

This 900-square-foot frame house rests on posts over a crawl space. The insulation consisted of mineral wool batts, R-8 in the walls, R-4 in the floor and R-12 in the attic. There was no vapour barrier other than the kraft backing of the insulation and no air barrier. The house was very leaky with no, or poor, weatherstripping around the windows. All windows were single-glazed. A centrally located oil space heater provided heat for the home.

NEW HOUSE

Interior Retrofit

The old inside finishing and mineral wool was removed. R-12 fibreglass batts were installed between the 2 x 4 wall studs. On the sloped ceiling 6 inches of fibreglass batts and 3 inches of white beadboard (expanded polystyrene) were installed for a combined total of R-32. Six-inch fibreglass batts were installed in the floor from below under the existing mineral wool to create a floor value of R-24. \

Wherever possible (all exterior walls and ceiling, with the exception of one wall), a 6 mil poly air-vapour barrier was installed on the inside of the insulation. The poly was overlapped and caulked with a bead of acoustical sealant. The poly was also wrapped around and sealed to the window and door frames.

Electrical Wiring: Much of the house was rewired and many of the outlets were relocated on interior walls. Those outlets remaining on the exterior walls were wrapped in poly and sealed to the new vapour barrier.

Chimney: A firestop was placed around the chimney and the vapour barrier was caulked to the sheet metal.

Exterior Retrofit: A curtain wall was hung over the old siding. This allowed a 6-inch fibreglass batt to surround all four walls.

This was the sequence followed to install the curtain wall:
- A vapour barrier (6 mil poly) was installed on the one wall which didn't have an interior vapour barrier. It was overlapped and caulked with acoustical sealant
- Next a ledger plate was fixed to the wall near the foundations. It consisted of a 2 x 4 fastened to the wall and a 2 x 6 on to the 2 x 4 (see diagram).
- The curtain wall was made of 2 x 3 members 24 inches on centre running vertically from the outside of the ledger plate and affixed to the soffit. For the most part the curtain wall sections were prefabricated on the ground, lifted into place and nailed down. The sections were framed for the windows and doors.
- R-20 batts of fibreglass were friction-fitted between the 2 x 3's.
- Horizontal strapping of 1 x 4 were nailed on to the 2 x 3's 24 inches on centre. This step was necessary to provide a membrane on which to fasten the vertical siding.
- Building paper was stapled horizontally starting from the bottom.
- The siding was nailed onto the horizontal 1 x 4's. It consists of pine roofing (1 x 12) boards with 1 x 3 battens. It was finished with stain.
- The windows and doors were framed with the same siding material with new sill plates extending from the original casing to the new exterior.

HEATING

A Jotul 600 has become the sole heating source for the house. This model was the smallest air-tight stove that was available at the time. It was set on bricks in a central location within the house and an insulated flue was installed. The Jotul is rated at 20,000 BTU output. Water is heated by a small 12 gallon electric water heater. It is placed next to the composting toilet chamber in an unheated, but insulated space below grade. The home's water supply enters through this space.

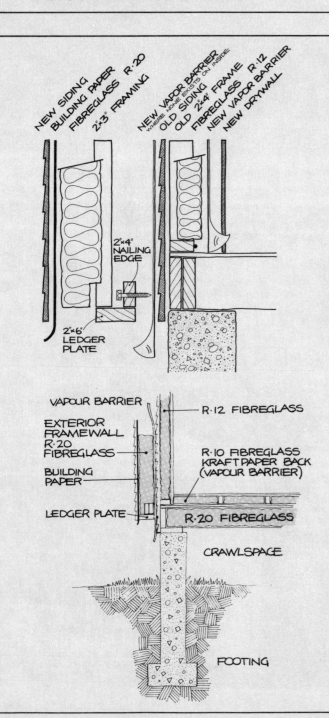

NEW SIDING
BUILDING PAPER
FIBREGLASS R-20
2"3" FRAMING

NEW VAPOR BARRIER WHERE NONE EXISTS ON INSIDE
OLD SIDING
OLD 2"×4" FRAME
FIBREGLASS R-12
NEW VAPOR BARRIER
NEW DRYWALL

2"×4" NAILING EDGE

2"×6" LEDGER PLATE

VAPOUR BARRIER

EXTERIOR FRAMEWALL R-20 FIBREGLASS

BUILDING PAPER

LEDGER PLATE

R-12 FIBREGLASS

R-10 FIBREGLASS KRAFT PAPER BACK (VAPOUR BARRIER)

R-20 FIBREGLASS

CRAWLSPACE

FOOTING

WINDOW TREATMENT

Triple glazing was achieved by adding thermopane units to the existing single-pane windows. The recycled units were sealed with glazing tape to the window opening. Ninety-two square feet of glass faces south-east. This is about 3/4 of the glazed area. Exterior shutters were made for the windows facing north-east and north-west. Shutters consist of a two-inch styrofoam core. Because they were accessible from the ground, they were mounted on the exterior. Generally they are used as seasonal shutters, remaining closed for most of the heating season. A two-foot overhang helps to prevent summer overheating, as does the south-east orientation of the house.

OTHER FEATURES

The house was outfitted with a Toa-Throne composting toilet. The house doesn't have a well but relies on roof run-off into a cistern. The composting toilet reduces by half the water demand.

PERFORMANCE

The house, due to its super-insulation, maintains its temperatures well. It went through a typical cold winter burning less than one cord of wood. No other back-up system was used. On a sunny, winter day it is not necessary to fire-up the stove.

All the labour was done by the owner and friends.

The cost for the materials was $1,600 for the interior work, half of which was for the insulation and vapour barrier. The materials cost for the exterior curtain wall, including insulation, lumber and siding was $1,200.

OBJECTIVES

The house was insulated from the interior.

The exterior work was done the following year to reduce the heat load and to experiment with the curtain wall system. The overall objective was to reduce the load to such an extent that the smallest stove on the market would be adequate for heating.

PROBLEMS

The space from the walls to the ceiling was a difficult area to apply an air-tight vapour barrier to.

The floor lacks a vapour barrier, but this is not considered a problem since the house is tight enough as it is.

A vapour barrier, or adequate insulation, could not be added on to one wall during the interior renovation because of cupboards. This problem was circumvented by installing an exterior vapour barrier and insulation. The roof, a cathedral ceiling, could not be super-insulated because of a lack of space. An exterior re-insulating and roofing job is planned for the future.

Ceepee House

A worlds' first;
a super-insulated
retrofit community

LOCATION: Ceepee house
TYPE: Exterior insulated bungalow
SIZE: 1050 square feet
DEGREE DAYS: 10,410
YEAR CONSTRUCTED: 1930's
RENOVATED: 1980

The house is a fifty-year old wood frame bungalow located on an exposed rural site in the village of Ceepee, Saskatchewan. Ceepee is the first 100 per cent retrofitted community in North America. Both houses have been converted with an exterior re-skinning job.

The goals of the retrofit were to reduce air-infiltration by upgrading the air-vapour barrier, increase insulation levels and improve the heating system. The first winter after the work was done the house required only 3 per cent of the pre-retrofit non-renewable fuel consumption.

OLD HOUSE:

This is a single storey frame house, sheathed inside and out with $3/4$-inch tongue and groove fir. It was originally built in the 1930's for the manager of a grain elevator. An addition was constructed in the 40's and a backroom added sometime in the 60's.

Ceepee House

HEAT LOSS IN THE HOUSE

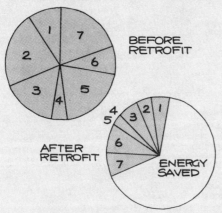

BEFORE RETROFIT

AFTER RETROFIT

ENERGY SAVED

1··· NON·SOUTH WINDOWS
2··· ROOF
3··· WALLS
4··· DOORS
5··· FOUNDATION
6··· BELOW GRADE
7··· INFILTRATION

The attic had a combination of rockwood and wood chips which provided insulation values that ranged from R-5 to R-11. The wood chips in the cavity walls provided R-10 insulation. The foundation, 8-inch concrete, had no insulation.

Air infiltration was estimated to be about ³/₄ of an air change each hour. The windows were primarily single-glazed double-hung windows. An old oil furnace and an uninsulated electric domestic hot water tank provided heat.

The interior was not in bad shape, though some partition walls were rearranged. The exterior siding, three-quarter-inch clapboard, had some dry rot. This contributed to the decision to insulate and re-side the exterior.

NEW HOUSE

INSULATION:
Fibreglass was added to the existing insulation in the attic. The 400 square feet insulated to R-5 had 2 R-20 batts added for a total of R-45. The 553 square feet with R-11 had either R-40 or R-20 added.

The uninsulated foundation walls were insulated with 4 inches (R-20) of extruded polystyrene on the exterior. R-12 was put in the floor.

The walls had R-20 added to provide a total of R-30. The studs (2 x 6) were nailed on to the old siding at 24 inches on centre. Some of the alternate studs were only 2 x 4's. The wall sections were pre-built in 14-foot sections so they could be put into place by 2 people. R-20 batts were installed, then a layer of tar paper, followed by ³/₄-inch utility cedar for siding.

VAPOUR BARRIER:
Before the 2 x 6 studs were nailed on, the old siding was covered with a 4 mil polyethylene vapour barrier. This was caulked on to the soffit and hung down. All joints were overlapped and caulked with acoustical sealant. The vapour barrier hung down 6 inches below the sill plate. The infiltration, because of the new air-vapour barrier and the new windows, is estimated to have decreased from .75 to .3 air changes per hour.

STORM PORCH:
A new storm porch was constructed on the east door. The door, insulated steel, insulates to R-15. In addition, the storm porch provides an air-lock entrance. It is insulated to R-17 on the ceiling and R-20 on the walls.

Ceepee House

PERFORMANCE

The owner, David Neufeld, has kept very good records of the cost and performance of the house and retrofit activities.

HEAT LOSS	Old House		New House	
	million BTU	% loss	million BTU	% loss
Windows	14.9	10.0	9.2	18.9
Storm Porch Roof	2.1	1.4	.4	.8
Walls	25	16.7	7.2	14.8
Doors	5	3.3	.3	.6
Ceiling	30.7	20.5	1.6	3.3
Foundation Wall	31.8	21.3	6.2	12.8
Basement	12.1	8.1	12.1	24.9
Air Infiltration	28.0	18.7	11.6	23.9
	149.6	100.0	48.6	100.0

HEAT GAIN	million BTU	% Required	million BTU	% Required
Utilities	7.7	5.1	7.7	15.9
Animal Gains	2.1	1.4	2.1	4.3
Passive Solar	1.6	1.1	5.1	10.6
	11.4	7.6	14.9	30.8

	Old House	New House
Supplemental Heat Required	138.2 MBTU	33.7 MBTU
Annual Heating Bill (if all oil)	$1245.42	$303.25
Savings:		$942.17

Actual Breakdown of Heating Supplied:

	Old House		New House	
	MBTU	% Required	MBTU	% Required
Utilities	7.7	5.1	7.7	15.9
Animal Gains	2.1	1.4	2.1	4.3
Passive Solar	1.6	1.1	5.1	10.6
Oil	138.2	92.4	3.8	7.9
Wood	—	—	29.8	61.3
Non Renewable	145.9	97.5	11.5	23.8
Renewable	3.7	2.5	37.0	76.2

Total Reduction in non-renewable use is 134.5 MBTU or 92.2%

WINDOW TREATMENT:

All windows were replaced with either double or triple windows. Many are fixed in place. The opening windows (ventilators) are generally the awning type.

The non-south facing windows were reduced in size so that the total window area (except south) went from 89.4 square feet to 66.5 square feet. The south window area was increased from 35.1 square feet to 54 square feet.

In addition, there is a 33 square foot thermosyphon collector on the south wall. It was originally framed for a large used thermopane unit that was to be obtained cheaply. It broke before arriving at the house and the cost of a specially ordered new unit was prohibitively expensive. The thermosyphon system is estimated to operate at about $^1/_3$ the efficiency of the windows.

There is a $3^1/_2$-inch thick insulated shutter that is used to seasonally insulate the east window.

HEATING SYSTEM:

The old oil furnace was upgraded. It was cleaned and tuned and the hot air ducts were carefully sealed. The hot water heater was moved from the unheated basement to the main floor. An air-tight wood stove was installed.

COST

The total cost of the materials for the retrofit was $3705.00. Labour was logged at 240 hours. At $12 per hour that would equal $2900. The total cost of materials and labour is $6605.

Wrapping the house from base to peak made an efficient and complete job

Fort Saskatchewan

LOCATION: Fort Saskatchewan, Alberta
TYPE: Exterior insulated bungalow
SIZE: 900 sq. ft.
DEGREE DAYS: 10,268 (°F)
YEAR CONSTRUCTED: 1945
RENOVATED: 1980

This 35-year-old wood frame bungalow is located on a farm north-east of Edmonton. The house was in poor shape in its pre-retrofit days. There were large cracks around the window rough openings and leaky doors, sill plates and plug outlets. The house was almost unlivable in winter.

The owners approached the retrofit from an energy conservation perspective. The job is unique in that the entire house, including the walls, soffits and roof, was wrapped in plastic and re-insulated on the exterior.

OLD HOUSE:

The house had little potential for passive solar heat and was protected from northerly winds by trees. The walls were filled with approximately R-10 of shavings. Insulation in the roof was R-7. The single-glazed windows were in poor condition. The house was extremely leaky, to the extent that you could see outdoors through many of the holes and cracks.

NEW HOUSE:

The interior was left much as it was. The majority of the retrofit entailed re-skinning the facade. The technique used was similar to the "Cadillac Version" discussed in the Exterior Insulation section of the Manual.

AIR-VAPOUR BARRIER:

The entire stucco house was wrapped in a 6 mil polyethylene air-vapour barrier. This went from the grade-line up, completely covering the walls, porch, windows, roof and dormer. The poly was caulked at all joints and tacked down under the eaves and soffits until a new frame was constructed.

A layer of 2 x 6 strapping was placed horizontally to hold the poly in place and provide a nailing surface for the new vertical studs.

INSULATION:

The walls were covered with 2 x 6's nailed vertically on edge at 16-inch centres. Altogether a 7-inch gap was created to allow R-25 fibreglass batts to be installed. Horizontal wood siding was nailed into the vertical studs.

More than two-thirds of the insulating value of the walls is now on the outside, exterior to the vapour barrier.

The new wall continues to the grade-line. Extruded polystyrene will be installed below grade sometime in the future.

Short support walls were constructed on the roof over the new vapour barrier. Two by six rafters were then placed on the support walls, creating a large cavity. This cavity was insulated with fibreglass batts to a value of R-63. Sheathing and cedar shakes completed the roof.

The job of creating a continuous air-vapour barrier and re-insulating the entire house was not difficult because there was virtually no overhang.

The front porch was closed in to create an air-lock entrance.

WINDOWS:

New wood frame double-glazed windows were installed throughout. They were placed on the exterior of the new wall assembly. This created a useful interior sill space.

The existing windows were then removed from the inside. The openings were finished to match the interior wall.

PERFORMANCE:

It was impossible to accurately determine the gas consumption of the pre-retrofit house. Another family house and a farming operation were all on the same gas meter.

The winter after the retrofit was completed, the gas-fired furnace only came on for a one week period when the family was away. One and a half cords of wood were the sole heating source over the winter.

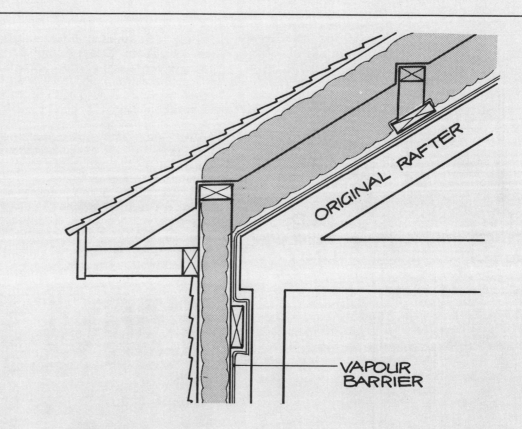

ORIGINAL RAFTER

VAPOUR BARRIER

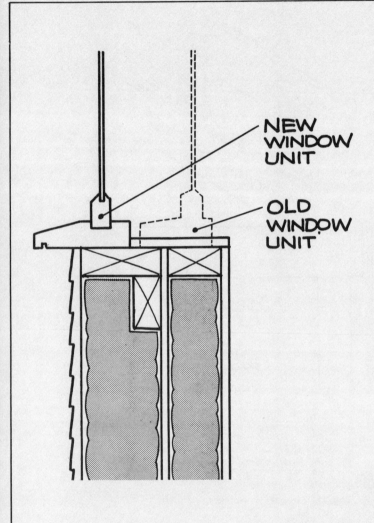

NEW
WINDOW
UNIT

OLD
WINDOW
UNIT

In July 1981, an air infiltration test was carried out. This indicated 2.8 air changes per hour under negative 50 pascals pressure. This translated to about .16 air changes per hour under normal conditions.

Smoke pencil tests showed existing leakage around the sill plate, through the unfinished cement block foundation. These areas are to be retrofitted in the future. Another area of leakage occured around the glass and wooden sash of the new windows. No infiltration was noted around window rough openings or plug boxes above grade.

The first winter the occupants noticed that the air became stuffy. They plan to install an air-to-air heat exchanger before the next heating season.

The total material cost for reframing, insulation and polyethylene was $3,300. The new windows cost an additional $2,500. A rough estimate for the labour (two men in their spare time) totalled 500 man-hours for the entire retrofit.

These volunteers
creatively demonstrate
urban conservation

Ecology House

LOCATION: Toronto
TYPE: brick, interior &
               exterior retrofit
SIZE: 5000 square feet
DEGREE DAYS: 6827 (F°)
YEAR CONSTRUCTED: 1891
     RENOVATED: 1980

Ecology house, in downtown Toronto,
is set up as a demonstration of urban
conservation techniques. A large,
solid-brick house has been
super-retrofitted by a group of
volunteers to demonstrate a wide
variety of energy conservation and
related environmental techniques. It
includes both interior and exterior
sealing and insulation, passive solar
features, a greenhouse, waste
management systems, organic
gardening and other energy-efficient
features. The house is open to the
public. It is located at 12 Madison
Avenue, Toronto.

OLD HOUSE

This house has 5000 square feet of
heated floor area. It was a double-brick
house with no insulation in the walls
or basement. The attic area had R-12 of
compressed mineral wool. Most
windows were single-glazed and double-
hung. The house was very leaky. An
old oil boiler heated the house. After
years of being a rooming house the
interior was run down so the house
required extensive renovation.

NEW HOUSE

Most of the re-insulation was done in the interior to save the brick front. The north wall, a featureless wall in an alley, was insulated on the exterior. Four inches of styrofoam (R-20) was nailed directly onto the wall using metal channel nailing strips. The ship-lapped styrofoam had channels cut to accept the metal channel. A hole was pre-drilled through the assembly into the brick and a concrete nail was tapped in. The wall was then covered with horizontal wood siding.

The basement was also insulated from the exterior. A 2-foot trench was dug with a backhoe around the perimeter which permitted the basement walls to be waterproofed. Two inches of styrofoam (R-10) were placed against the house, and extended out 2 feet at an angle. The trench was then backfilled.

Interior walls (east, west and third floor south) were generally insulated by building the wall out. With the brick exposed, a 2 x 4 wall was constructed on the floor and lifted into place, about two inches out from the brick. This cavity allowed 6 inches (R-20) of fibreglass batts to be fitted. A 6 mil poly vapour barrier was lapped and caulked, and the new drywall was nailed onto the 2 x 4 studs. In some areas space was at a premium as window frames and moldings were to be preserved. In these cases the frames were removed, the cavities sealed and insulated, and 2 inches of styrofoam (R-10) was installed. The flat attic sections were insulated to R-52 with fibreglass. The sloped ceiling sections of the third floor had the original 2 x 10's exposed. Then 2 x 4 stand-offs were nailed onto the rafters and a horizontal strapping was applied. This allowed two 6-inch fibreglass batts, one horizontal, the other vertical, to be installed for a total of R-40.

A 6 mil poly vapour barrier was installed throughout. It was overlapped and caulked with an acoustical sealant. In the few areas where a vapour barrier could not be installed, coats of a vapour barrier paint were applied.

WINDOW TREATMENT

The windows throughout the house were transformed from single-glazed to the equivalent of triple-glazed. Most of the windows also have movable insulation.

Since many of the frames were in good shape (and beautiful examples of Victorian detail), they were kept wherever possible. A notch was routed out on the inside of the frame in front of the existing glazing. Thermopane units were ordered to size and were held in place by glaziers tape. Small (1/8 inch) vent holes were drilled beforehand between the new and old glazing and the outside. Many of the windows were sealed with silicone. This technique worked well for windows of all sizes and shapes. The only problem was the added weight of the now triple-glazed units was considerably more substantial. Windows not worth saving were replaced with new triple-glazed units. One window was replaced with a Watershed honeycomb unit. This is double-glazed with about a 3-inch air gap that is threaded with horizontal transparent sheets of Llumar spaced about 3/4-inch apart. These inhibit convection losses and provide an insulation value better than triple-glazing, while still maintaining a high solar transmittance.

A variety of shuttering techniques are used throughout the house. Some are simple pop-in shutters made of rigid insulation and covered with an aesthetically pleasing material. Some are held in place by small strips of magnets or velcro and some commercial units are used.

PASSIVE SOLAR WALL

The south side, which has good southern exposure with the exception of the early morning sun, has been outfitted with a mass wall system. A double-glazing was erected over most of the south brick, for a gross area of 1325 square feet. An 18-inch gap was left between the wall and the glass to allow access for cleaning.

Foundation posts were poured and a platform erected about 4 feet off the ground and ledger plates affixed to the wall. The framing system, made of 2 x 6's and sized to fit the thermopane units (which were bought as seconds), was constructed on the ground, lifted into place, and tied to the ledger plates. The brick is stained a dark brown. Sunlight turns to heat on the bricks and is absorbed through the wall. Windows on the first and second floors can be opened causing a powerful convection current of heated air. Air returns down two stairwells on the north side of the house. Two large (24 inches) ducts are opened to allow the heat to escape during the summer. This draw helps to pull cooler air into the house from the basement.

GREENHOUSES

Ecology house is fitted with two greenhouses: one a ground floor attached, the other a third floor integrated greenhouse.

The ground floor greenhouse had to be attached to the west wall since the lot line would not allow a south-facing greenhouse. The greenhouse is 12 x 11 feet and is insulated to R-28 on the back, north wall and the ceiling and R-20 on the west wall. Two-hundred and fifty gallons of water (in recycled anti freeze containers) add to the thermal mass. The greenhouse connects to the house by a kitchen door.

The third floor greenhouse was made by removing a dormer and widening the hole. The area (168 square feet) was glazed with Acrylite SDP. Because of weight restrictions the greenhouse has a trickle-type hydroponic system.

Both greenhouses are ducted to a basement room containing 173 cubic feet of rock-bed storage. Both greenhouses also have a movable insulation system.

OTHER FEATURES

Three workshop-built solar collectors supply domestic hot water.

There is an owner-built grey water system that has a trickle-filter feed into the greenhouse soil beds.

A Toa Throne composting toilet handles human and kitchen wastes. Energy-efficient appliances, water-saving shower heads and recycling and composting systems are also demonstrated.

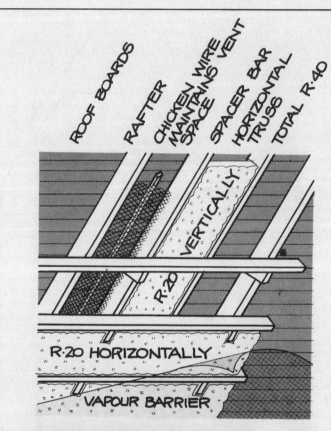

Ecology House

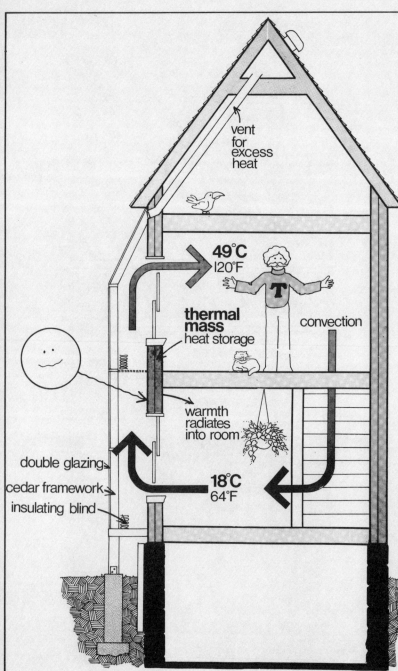

vent
for
excess
heat

49°C
120°F

**thermal
mass**
heat storage

convection

warmth
radiates
into room

18°C
64°F

double glazing

cedar framework

insulating blind

HEATING SYSTEM

The back-up heating is a new generation super-efficient gas furnace. The electronic ignition and condensing-gas heat exchanger means a seasonal operation efficiency of over 90 per cent, compared to 60 per cent for a standard gas furnace.

An air-tight wood stove feeds into one of the old fireplaces that has a new flue running through it.

PERFORMANCE

The total retrofit is estimated to have reduced the demand for auxiliary heating by 90 per cent. That is, a $3000 fuel bill (oil at 80¢ per gallon) has been reduced to $400. Before the heat load was 600-million BTU (MBTU). Now the mass wall supplies 75 MBTU, the greenhouses 29 MBTU and 70 MBTU is required for auxiliary heat.

The total cost of all the conservation features, excluding labour, is $7,500, plus another $9,000 for the passive solar aspects of the project. The three panel solar domestic hot water system costs $1400.

PROBLEMS

Because of the combination of exterior and interior approaches to re-insulation, there was a problem of tie-in between the two systems. Both the insulation and the vapour barrier could overlap, from inside and outside, but they could not meet. There was nothing to be done about these weak spots except to make the overlaps as wide as possible.

Because of zoning regulations, the first floor greenhouse could not be placed against the south wall, but had to be mounted on the west wall.

Going between floors with the air-vapour barrier was also difficult. Where the floor joists ran parallel with the wall, a line was cut with a circular saw and the vapour barrier was pulled through this cut to the floor below. Where the joists ran off of the wall the vapour barrier had to be caulked above and below to the joists.

An interior retrofit
gave this old house
a new lease on life

Ottawa House

LOCATION: Ottawa
TYPE: balloon frame,
              brick veneer,
              interior retrofit.
SIZE: 1900 square feet.
DEGREE DAYS: 8700 (°F)
YEAR CONSTRUCTED: 1890's
      RENOVATED: 1979

This is an old balloon frame house
with brick veneer. It is in downtown
Ottawa on an escarpment with a
magnificent north-west view. The
building is oriented 22° east of south.
Typically, for its style and vintage, the
house had no existing insulation. The
decision was made to totally retrofit it
from the interior, maintaining the
brick exterior.

OLD HOUSE

The original house had no insulation,
but relied instead on its bricks and
various air spaces to keep out the cold.
Thus it was a cold and drafty house.
The windows (single-glazed) and doors
were in poor shape. An old oil furnace
was the heat source. While the brick
exterior was in good shape, the
interior was unsalvagable and so a
complete gutting job was necessary.

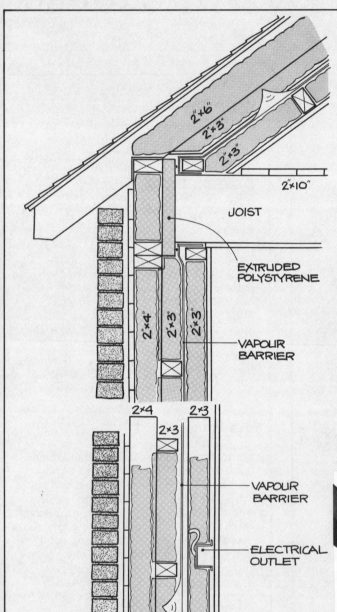

JOIST

EXTRUDED POLYSTYRENE

VAPOUR BARRIER

2"×6"

2"×3"

2"×3"

2"×10"

2"×4"

2"×3"

2"×3"

2×4

2×3

2×3

VAPOUR BARRIER

ELECTRICAL OUTLET

ORIGINAL

NEW HOUSE

The new house was fitted to be air-tight and with super levels of insulation. The walls were built up to R-36. The ceiling was built to R-36 to R-48 and the floor over the unheated basement contains R-28.

The typical wall section (from the outside in) contains:
— 4 inches of claybrick
— 1 inch air gap
— 1 inch plank sheathing
— 2 x 4's at 24 inches on centre, with R-12 friction fit fibreglass batts, 24 inches wide and $3^1/2$ inches thick laid in vertically
— 2 x 3 strapping, 24 inches on centre laid on edge perpendicular to the studs. These contain R-12 fibreglass batts laid horizontally
— 6 mil polyethylene vapour barrier stapled to the inner 2 x 3 stud wall. It was taped and caulked at all joists
— 2 x 3 studs, vertical, 24 inches on centre with R-8 fibreglass batts placed vertically
— $^5/8$ inch foil-backed gypsum wallboard.

The floor was insulated above the unheated basement. The basement had protruding rock that would have been difficult to seal and insulate. The new floor consisted of (from the bottom up):
— 2 inches galvanized chicken wire on the underside of the 2 x 10 joists (to hold the insulation in)
— 2 x 10 joists with R-28 fibreglass batts
— a new sub-floor
— a 6 mil poly vapour barrier in the floor
— $1^1/2$ inches grout and ceramic tile finish.

A typical roof or rafter section involved (from the outside in):
— asphalt shingles in 1 inch planks
— 2 x 6 rafters, 24 inches on centre. 2 x 3's were nailed to the underside of the rafters to expand them. This cavity was filled with R-28 fibreglass batts
— 6 mil poly vapour barrier, lapped and caulked at all joints
— 2 x 3 strapping nailed 24 inches on centre. An R-8 batt was placed horizontally
— $^5/8$ inch foil-backed gypsum board.

The vapour barrier was extended continuously through the wall between floors, through the wall to the ceiling and from the wall through the floor. In most cases it could be extended to the next section, lapped and caulked. Generally a piece of $1^1/_2$-inch styrofoam was placed at intersections to prevent thermal bridging and to provide a base upon which to seal the vapour barrier. Where the joist bears on the ledger (where the second floor meets the wall), $1^1/_2$-inch styrofoam was nailed to the firestop to extend 2 inches above and below the joists. Two-inch strips of styrofoam blocks were placed at the top and bottom of the joists to form a continuous seal. The 6 mil poly vapour barrier was sealed to the styrofoam.

An air-to-air heat exchanger was placed in the unheated basement. The duct work from kitchen and bathrooms was insulated. The heat exchanger is a variable speed air exchanger, ranging from 60 to 400 cubic feet per minute. It is in continuous operation at low volume with a manual high speed overide. The heat recovery is 60 to 80 per cent, depending on flow rate and temperature differential.

WINDOW TREATMENT

All windows were replaced with thermopane units. A major passive solar heating system was installed on the south side (22° east of south). A large portion of the south brick was removed (300 square feet). In its place was put 120 square feet of thermopane and 180 square feet of Acrylite SDP, a double-wall acrylic with good light transmittance characteristics.

The bricks removed from the south wall formed an inner wall, running perpendicular to the glazing (north to south) in the middle of the glazed area. The wall gets direct morning and afternoon sun and rises two floors. It also houses all the return and supply air ducts, as well as the flue for an air-tight wood stove. All windows are equipped with movable insulation. The "Window Quilt"™ was used throughout. They are also used as a shading unit in the summer.

HEATING

A 15 kilo watt electric, forced-air furnace was installed. It has continuous air circulation (through the masonry wall) with intakes at each floor. A "Vigilant"™ air-tight wood stove has its flue within the masonry wall as well.

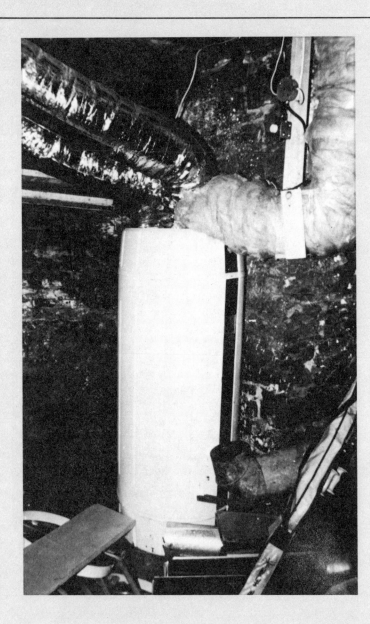

PERFORMANCE

The gross heat loss is calculated to be about 90-million BTU. Twenty per cent comes from internal gains, 57 per cent from solar heat gains and the additional 20 per cent is supplied by the auxiliary heat supply (the electric furnace).

The house is noticeably cooler in the summer and warmer and more comfortable in winter. The cost for the retrofit/renovation was comparable to similar total renovation costs.

OBJECTIVES

The house was worth saving and the owner wanted to maintain the brick exterior. He also was interested in making it as energy-efficient as possible. A passive solar and energy conservation consultant, Bruce Gough, was given a free hand to develop the insulation, air-tight and passive solar package.

PROBLEMS

Achieving the continuous vapour barrier required much planning and a lot of work, especially cutting out the styrofoam and placing it between the floor joists and caulking.

The basement would have been very difficult to seal and insulate because of the exposed foundation and floor rock. It was decided to have an unheated basement. The floor was sealed and insulated (R-28).

Adding an appropriate amount of mass to the house was accomplished by recycling the bricks from the south wall.

The commercial movable insulation was chosen, not for its insulating value (which is only R-3.4), but because the rolling blind system with side tracks made a fairly air-tight seal.

Air-tight construction
was combined with
interior renovation

Hamilton House

LOCATION: Hamilton, Ontario
TYPE: Double-brick interior retrofit
SIZE: 2,058 sq. ft. (duplex)
DEGREE DAYS: 6,800 (°F)
YEAR CONSTRUCTED: 1906
RENOVATED: 1981

This solid brick duplex was totally renovated on the inside. It is a good example of an interior job in which space was at a premium. Although the levels of insulation are not substantial (R-20 walls and ceiling), careful consideration was given to create an air-tight house with passive solar features.

The house is on the south side of an east-west street.

OLD HOUSE:

This was a typical turn-of-the-century brick house. There was no insulation in the walls and basement. The ceiling contained compacted cellulose to a value of R-6. The windows (single-glazed) with aluminum storms and doors were in poor shape, and in general the house was very leaky.

No preservation was possible as the interior was in terrible shape. The outside brick was in fair condition.

NEW HOUSE:

The house was entirely gutted from the inside. A new 2 x 4 frame wall, sheathed with tar-impregnated fibreboard was erected. R-12 batts of fibreglass were applied. A 6 mil poly vapour barrier was then installed, caulked and sealed with acoustical sealant. Two by two strapping was nailed horizontally over the 2 x 4's on top of the vapour barrier. An R-8 batt was put in this cavity. This left enough room for the electric wiring to be moved through the cavity, thus leaving the vapour barrier intact.

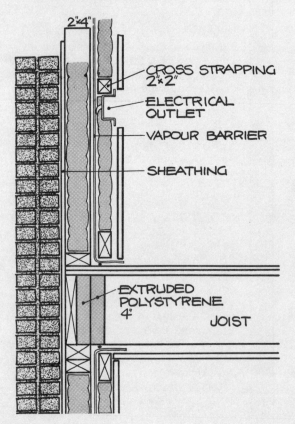

The ceiling over the 3rd floor loft area sloped. It was insulated with R-20 fibreglass. Since the building code required a 6-inch air gap behind the insulation (the code doesn't recognize properly installed air-vapour barriers), they had to either: 1) lose headroom, which was already at a premium; 2) lose insulation; 3) not open up the third floor. A compromise between one and two was chosen.

A 6 mil poly vapour barrier was used throughout. It was lapped and caulked at all seams. When it couldn't run continuously through floors, slabs of 4-inch styrofoam were caulked between each joist and the vapour barrier was caulked to the styrofoam. This technique maintained both the air-vapour barrier as well as R-20 between floors. Because the vapour barrier was behind the 2 x 3 strapping, it was not pierced by the electrician.

The basement walls were covered with R-14 of white beadboard, then a vapour barrier, strapping and gypsum board were added.

WINDOW TREATMENT:

The old windows that were in the worst condition were replaced with double-glazed units with a 1-inch air gap.

A new "solar bay" was added to collect the south-west light.

There are 85 square feet of south-facing glass on the two floors. In addition there will be a large south-facing greenhouse. It will have 225 square feet of double-glazing and be connected to the house with sliding glass doors. A three course thick brick wall common to the house and greenhouse acts as thermal storage.

HEATING SYSTEM:

The smaller north unit of the duplex is heated with electric baseboards. The south unit is heated with a natural gas furnace.

The north unit has an efficient wood burner fed by an outside supply of combustion air.

An air-to-air heat exchanger was installed to service the south unit. This is an Air Changer model which was developed by the same Toronto firm which designed the renovation, Allen-Drerup-White Ltd. It is estimated that the infiltration rate has been reduced to only 10 per cent of the pre-retrofit level.

There is a high air return located at the top of the stairwell on the south unit. Continuous air circulation ensures the automatic circulation of hot stratified air. In the summer the high air return, in conjunction with openable attic windows, eliminates the need for air conditioning.

PERFORMANCE:

The total cost, including the original purchase and all energy-related additions, was about $45 per square foot. About $35 of that represents renovation work. The pay-back on the energy measures is hard to determine because of the difficulty in separating the energy-related components from the rest of the functions. The incremental capital cost of energy-related improvements is estimated at 7 per cent of the total renovation work, or $2.45 per square foot. Annual heating loads are calculated to be 7.4 kilowatt hours per square foot.

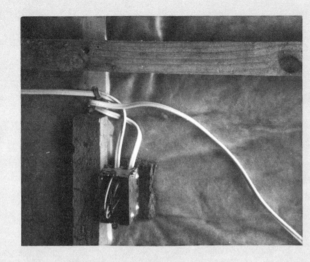

OBJECTIVES:

The house was bought specifically because of its southern exposure and the poor condition of the interior. At the same time the exterior brick work was in good shape. The owner wished to create a comfortable, efficient house, but did not want to sacrifice too much interior space, especially the head room on the 3rd floor.

Fire codes for the duplex stipulated that fire dampers be added between units. This prevented the integration of the air-handling system, the air-to-air heat exchanger and the solar heated air movement.

The contractor did a good job applying the insulation and air-vapour barrier (under supervision). However, some of the sub-trades were a little careless and consequently tears in the vapour barrier had to be patched.

The stairwell was moved. This allowed the wall behind it to be insulated and sealed. At the same time it created a space that was used for an air lock entrance.

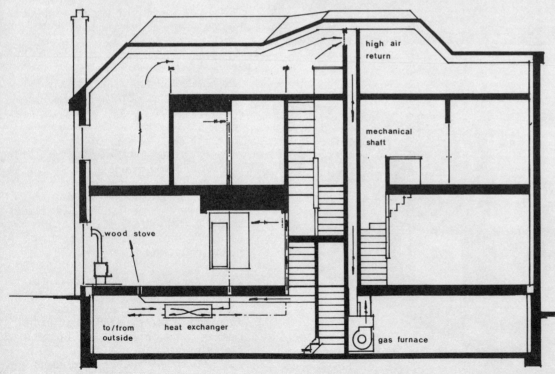

Terra Cotta House

An energy-efficient home
was built inside
the old stone farmhouse

LOCATION: Terra Cotta, Ontario
TYPE: Solid masonry , interior retrofit
SIZE: 3200 sq. ft.
DEGREE DAYS: 7200 (°F)
YEAR Constructed: 1861
        Renovated: 1981

This solid stone farmhouse, constructed in 1861, was in very poor condition when obtained by the present owner. Typically, the run-down building was not fitted with insulation and it was extremely leaky. The interior of the house was in need of a complete gutting to allow for the alterations required by the homeowner. The gutting of the structure allowed for the easy installation of a new energy-efficient envelope. The interior retrofit enabled the homeowner to maintain the original character of the exterior coursed limestone facade. The retrofit measures performed should result in a reduction in the space heating load of approximately 80 per cent.

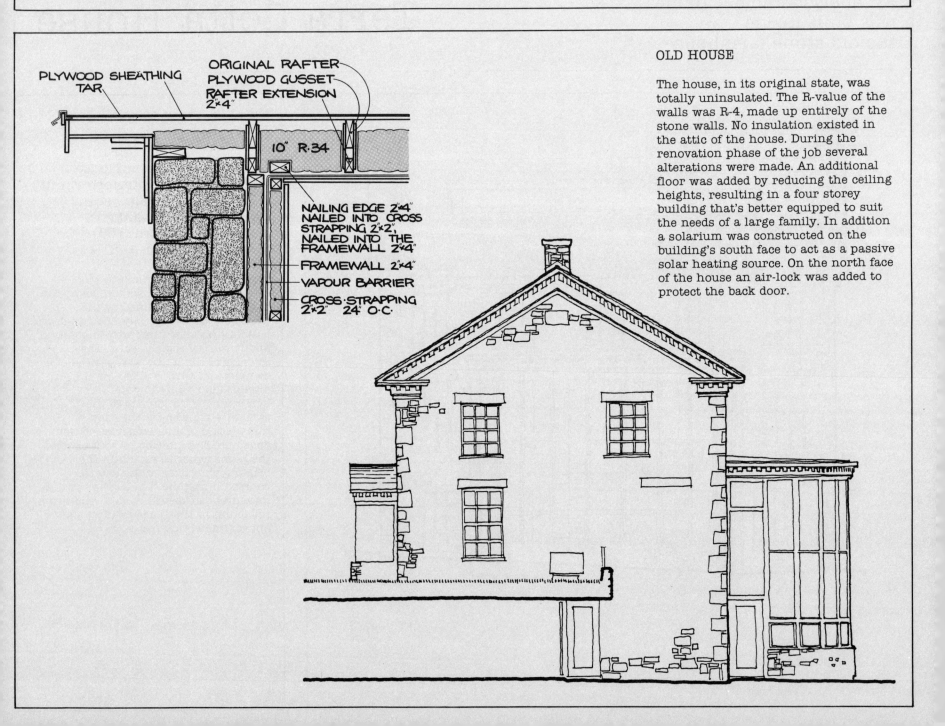

PLYWOOD SHEATHING
TAR

ORIGINAL RAFTER
PLYWOOD GUSSET
RAFTER EXTENSION
2"×4"

10" R·34

NAILING EDGE 2"×4"
NAILED INTO CROSS
STRAPPING 2"×2",
NAILED INTO THE
FRAMEWALL 2"×4"

FRAMEWALL 2"×4"

VAPOUR BARRIER

CROSS·STRAPPING
2"×2" 24" O·C·

OLD HOUSE

The house, in its original state, was
totally uninsulated. The R-value of the
walls was R-4, made up entirely of the
stone walls. No insulation existed in
the attic of the house. During the
renovation phase of the job several
alterations were made. An additional
floor was added by reducing the ceiling
heights, resulting in a four storey
building that's better equipped to suit
the needs of a large family. In addition
a solarium was constructed on the
building's south face to act as a passive
solar heating source. On the north face
of the house an air-lock was added to
protect the back door.

NEW HOUSE

In an ambitious programme the house was totally retrofitted. The gutting of the building afforded the homeowner access to the entire exterior envelope of the building. New frame walls were constructed throughout the building, and a complete air-vapour barrier was installed from the basement walls to the attic of the house. Reframing the interior of the house included not only the walls but also the floors and attics, allowing the air-vapour barrier to be stretched around the floor joists header. Although not measured, it is estimated that the infiltration rate has been reduced by 60 per cent.

The interior walls of the house were constructed with 2 x 4 framing with 2 x 2 cross-strapping laid horizontally over the framed stud wall cavities. The walls were insulated with 6 inches of fibreglass insulation resulting in an R-value of R-20.

The attic of the house was removed to allow more head space and the ceiling was dropped with gussets to allow for the installation of 10 inches of fibreglass insulation.

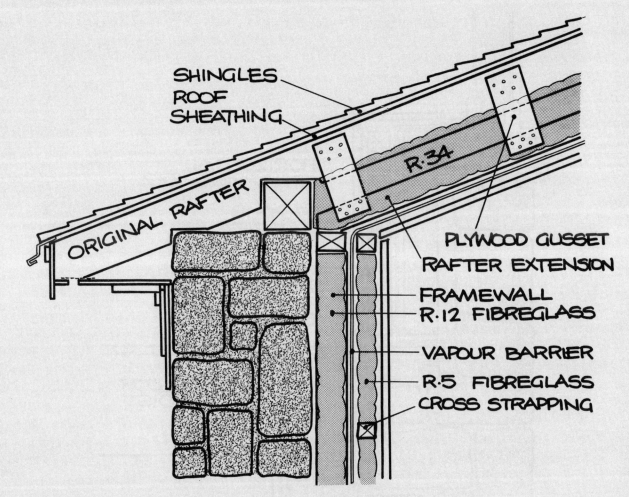

SHINGLES
ROOF
SHEATHING

R·34

ORIGINAL RAFTER

PLYWOOD GUSSET
RAFTER EXTENSION
FRAMEWALL
R·12 FIBREGLASS
VAPOUR BARRIER
R·5 FIBREGLASS
CROSS STRAPPING

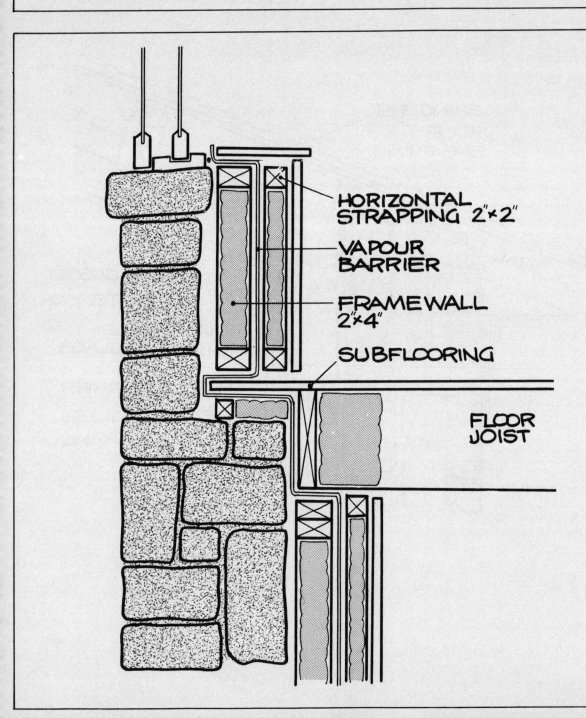

HORIZONTAL
STRAPPING 2"×2"

VAPOUR
BARRIER

FRAME WALL
2"×4"

SUBFLOORING

FLOOR
JOIST

WINDOW TREATMENT

The windows of the house had been upgraded to double-glazed status by a previous owner and were left in place and sealed and weatherstripped. The windows were equipped with insulating shutters to reduce night-time heat loss. Additional shuttering was installed in the south-facing solarium. Reflective Mylar shades are employed to reduce summer heat gains and winter heat losses.

HEATING SYSTEM

The original heating system of the house has been replaced with a small heat pump supplemented by an electric furnace. The original fireplaces have been rebuilt and upgraded to energy-efficient standards with the incorporation of steel liners and glass doors.

While not applicable to the majority of houses, the techniques employed in this super-insulated retrofit resulted in savings of close to 80 per cent. The reframing of the entire house interior allowed for significant improvements in the building's thermal envelope. Performing the retrofit on the interior allowed the homeowner to maintain the aesthetics of the century old farmhouse.

Access

Materials

Many well-intentioned retrofit jobs will fall short of the homeowner's expectations because of a lack of understanding about the materials needed for the job. The use of improper materials can result in a second rate retrofit, either because the homeowner is forced into bankruptcy, or because insignificant energy savings have resulted. The most important decisions to be made involve the type of insulation to be used, the framing materials for the new walls, the materials used for upgrading the windows, and the products needed to provide the house with an air-tight seal. This is not to suggest that the non-energy related purchases required for the super-insulated retrofit are unimportant. It is interesting to note that in many cases these components of the job will prove to be the greatest contributor to the total cost.

Proper purchasing habits can also have an important influence on the end product.

Take some time at the beginning of the job to assemble a complete shopping list and be sure that you find the best possible prices for the required materials. Proper purchasing will even result in energy savings as the gasoline required to get you to the hardware store and lumber supply outlet can be significantly reduced.

The investment of your time in the planning stages of the job can pay off handsomely, both in the short term in reduced capital costs and in the long term with your reduced fuel bills. Although we have made reference to some specific materials throughout the Do-It sections of the book, an overview of the various options for the retrofit will help the homeowner decide which products will serve to greatest advantage.

Purchasing Materials

Obtaining the best value for your money doesn't only entail shopping around for the best price in your local building supply outlet. Imaginative homeowners can perform the same job as a local contractor at only a fraction of the price. Using recycled materials or seconds can, in many cases, result in the same efficiency at less than half the cost. Time spent combing through the yellow pages of the telephone book looking for deals can yield surprising results. It is important to realize that value is not necessarily synonymous with the lowest price. Although in many cases using recycled materials or seconds will not involve any additional work, those people

who have spent countless hours trying to salvage lumber which is laden with nails will realize that a dollar figure must be attached to the man-hours required to perform a specific task.

Good values can often be obtained by going directly to the factory. Items which may have been slightly damaged during fabrication will not be sold at the conventional price. Fixed panes of glass, windows and doors, and even insulation materials can often be purchased at a reduced cost. Equally large savings can be found on the demolition market. In most parts of the country several large demolition firms enjoy the lion's share of the market. Yet you can often find smaller demolition firms who are trying to get rid of as much material as possible from the actual site. Check around for materials you might need.

Even when dealing with new building products, significant savings can result from some pre-planning. Economies of scale will often lead to large price reductions from most building supply outlets. Most suppliers will have a builders' price which allows for a 5 to 10 per cent reduction in the cost of the order if it totals over a certain dollar figure. For most retrofits, if the purchase is done in one bulk order, you should be able to swing these rates. Even larger savings should result if you can arrange your ordering with a friend who is also considering some construction work. In some cases you might arrange for large enough orders to bypass the retailer and order directly from the wholesale outlet. In general, the larger the order the greater the savings.

Lumber

One of the major decisions to be made by the homeowner relates to the size and amount of wood required for each specific component of the retrofit. As a general rule of thumb use as little lumber as possible. Every additional stud or piece of strapping takes away space which might accommodate insulation.

SPLIT ENDS LUMBER CO.

The lumber required for the super-insulated retrofit will not be responsible for bearing any of the structural loading of the building. This permits the builder to employ a lesser amount of lumber than would be traditionally called for. In most

cases 2 x 3's can be used instead of 2 x 4's in both the interior and exterior retrofits. This allows for the installation of more insulation and reduces the potential for thermal bridging from the interior to the exterior. It also means a reduced cost for the lumber.

The use of pressure-treated wood as an exterior lumber has been increasing at a rapid rate. In many areas it has pushed cedar out of its historically large share of the market. For the exterior retrofit it is advisable to use pressure-treated wood at any spot where snow build-up might lead to the deterioration of a less stable product. Any lumber within 16-inches of ground level should be pressure-treated wood or at least be treated with a preservative. We recommend that the bottom plate of a curtain wall assembly be constructed of pressure-treated wood to ensure the durability of the entire assembly.

Pressure-treated wood is being used by some homeowners as the framing lumber for attached greenhouses. Caution should be exhibited in this application, or in other locations in areas of high humidity where plants are located. One of the ingredients used in the pressure-treating process is highly toxic. Any condensate running from the rafters to the growing areas below can carry the toxic material into the growing beds and lead to contamination. Use the pressure-treated wood with caution. In most questionable cases cedar is the preferred option.

Recycled lumber is available in most of the country from demolition companies or the owners of run-down buildings. Several considerations should be borne in mind before jumping into a purchase prompted by cheap prices. Most recycled lumber will still have old nails immersed in the wood. These will need to be pulled, not only to facilitate the installation of new sheathing or wallboard, but to save your saw blades. Older lumber should also be checked for any insect infestation, fungal growths and dry rot. Precautionary measures will need to be taken in extreme cases. A relatively benign wood preservative which can be easily obtained is copper napthanate.

Another means of saving money involves arranging for shipments of lumber directly from a mill. While this may be more relevant to those homeowners in rural areas, in many cases arranging for the transport of these materials may still provide a cost reduction. In most retrofit applications rough sawn lumber can be used if the homeowner is willing to put up with the odd sliver. Problems might arise with the lack of curing time which lumber obtained directly through the mill will have undergone. As the lumber dries over time it will shrink and possibly warp, leading to the potential for nail pull-out and possible stretching of the air-vapour barrier. Also, if the wood is exceptionally wet when it is installed, the excess moisture could accumulate behind the vapour barrier leading to potential condensate build-up and deterioration of the insulating materials. Whether you have purchased your lumber from the mill or through a retailer, you should plan well enough in advance to allow for any wet wood to cure. The problems of wet wood are not limited to its use in a wood stove.

The type of wood used in the retrofit will vary according to availability and cost. For most aspects of the job you can use a low grade of lumber. There is little value to be gained by using an expensive grade of lumber which is hidden behind non-load bearing walls. Spruce and hemlock will generally be the least expensive option in eastern Canada, while cedar and redwood are more readily available on the West Coast.

Insulation

We have stressed the importance of properly installed insulation throughout the book. Filling all available spaces with insulation and obtaining as high a thermal resistance (R value) as possible must be emphasized. The choice of insulating materials should be based on a criteria that includes initial cost, availability of space, durability, water and vapour resistance (if not used with a vapour barrier) and the cost of the material per R value. As with almost all technologies, each of the options for insulating a house has its advantages and disadvantages.

The authors have let their biases be known throughout the text. In almost all locations within the retrofitted house we recommend

the use of fibreglass batts, with a smaller role for extruded polystyrene in limited applications. Your decision making criteria may lead to a different conclusion.

Insulating Material	¢/R/sq. ft.
Fibreglass Batts	1.5-1.6
Cellulose	1.7-1.8
Expanded Polystyrene	4.5-5.0
Extruded Polystyrene	6.5-7.5
Polyisocyanurate	7.1-7.5

Caulking Materials

A myriad different caulking materials are available to the homeowner through the local hardware stores and building supply outlets. Most people will purchase a caulking material without giving much thought to its potential use. This leads to the purchase of either the cheapest of material in the store or to one which the homeowner believes is the most durable. Without understanding that the cheapest of materials might soon become useless, or that the most expensive of caulks doesn't always provide the best seal, the homeowner is at a disadvantage when viewing the display of materials in the store.

In almost all cases the super-insulated retrofit can be performed with only a few different caulking materials. A specific type of caulk will be needed for each of the following tasks; sealing the air-vapour barrier; sealing fixed panes of glass; performing exterior weatherizing. The super-insulated retrofit, with its continuous wrapping of the house in a polyethylene sheet, eliminates the need for special caulks designed to seal specific areas of the house envelope.

Sealing the Air-Vapour Barrier

The requirements of the material used to seal the air-vapour barrier demand that it maintain its seal over an extended period of time and that it have adequate elasticity to allow for the movement of the polyethylene when the wallboard is installed. Several materials were tested for these properties under the direction of the Saskatchewan Research Council. As a first choice they recommend the use of an acoustical caulking material manufactured by Tremco. As a second choice either PRC Rubber Caulk #7000 or Tremco Butyl Sealant were suggested.

Some innovative developments have been undertaken in an attempt to heat seal the polyethylene air-vapour barrier. At best the acoustical caulking is expected to last for twenty years before it dries out and allows air to penetrate through the seams in the plastic. The theory employed in the use of heat-sealing technology is similar to the concepts used in sealing freezer bags or the bags provided in record stores. The application of heat to two sheets of plastic results in a bonding of the plastic. The problem confronted with the larger sheets of plastic used in the house relate to obtaining the right temperature needed for a good seal. Obvious problems will result if the heat applied to the overlapping plastic is either too cold or too hot.

The use of the acoustical caulk is not limited to the sealing of the polyethylene. It can also be used to seal around the edges of Styrofoam which is installed between the floor joists. Acoustical caulk can be used when caulking is needed to prevent air and vapour movement. Because of its unsightliness and stickiness it should only be used where it will be out of sight and out of touch.

The material does have two distinct disadvantages. It is extremely messy to work with and nearly impossible to clean from your clothes and hair. Second, it is currently available only in quart-sized tubes (versus the standard pint tube), so you will require a large caulking gun. It is hoped that with the additional consumer demand shown for the product, the manufacturer will respond by marketing the caulk in standard sizes.

Sealing Fixed Windows

To seal existing windows in place to reduce air infiltration around the edges, the homeowner will want a long lasting caulk which doesn't detract from the window's

appearance. In this case, and in others where the interior caulk should remain invisible, a clear silicone caulk will represent the preferred option. The silicone is extremely durable and has a high degree of elasticity which compensates for movement in the building's shell over time.

Exterior Weatherizing

As we have cautioned throughout the book, the application of caulking from the exterior of the house can lead to vapour lock within the house walls. All caulking which is designed to prevent air leakage should be performed from the inside of the house. There are cases where caulking will need to be installed on the outside to prevent damage from rain or snow. This will be especially true with the exterior retrofit where potential damage might result around windows and doors. Ensure that the material which you use for these applications is compatible with the siding material used on the house.

Caulking Materials

Tremco (Canada) Ltd.
220 Wicksteed Ave., Toronto, Ont.
M4H 1G7

P.R.C. Ltd.
226 Humberline Dr., Rexdale, Ont.
M9W 5X1

Dow Corning Canada Inc.
6747 Campobello Dr., Mississauga, Ont.
L5N 2M1

Weatherstripping

In the burgeoning field of energy conservation, new products are constantly being introduced. Weatherstripping materials are no exception. Whereas ten years ago one would have been hard pressed to find a good selection of these materials, even hardware stores now carry large stocks of weatherstripping that feature a variety of approaches.

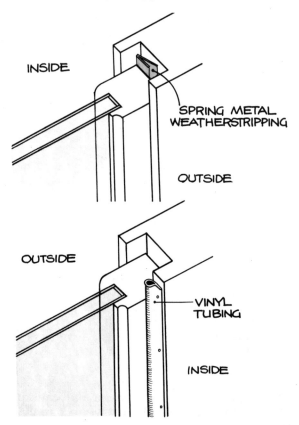

Historically, spring metal weatherstripping was accepted as the most efficient option. The spring metal is tacked into the casing of doors and windows using small brass tacks. Installation is relatively easy and the seal obtained can be excellent. More recently, spring vinyl weatherstripping with an adhesive backing has been introduced as a means of reducing installation time while maintaining the tight, durable seal. Both of the spring-type weatherstrippings can only be successfully employed on relatively tight-fitting windows and doors. Although large gaps in the exterior shell of the building have no place in the super-insulated retrofit, if they do exist a vinyl bulb will be needed.

Weatherstripping for windows and doors should be carefully installed. If the weatherstripping is too loosely installed air infiltration will not be stopped. If, on the other hand, the weatherstripping is fitted too tightly, the operation of the door or window can be severely hampered. This will also lead to a more rapid deterioration of the materials used to seal the air leakage.

Several specific materials have been manufactured to deal with the air leakage problems around vertical sliding windows. If properly installed these materials can defeat the need for counterweights for these windows, thus eliminating one of the blatant pathways for air movement through the buildings shell.

Durability of the materials installed should be ensured. Many of the cheaper weatherstripping options will not last over a single heating season. Those materials with adhesive backing should be stapled or screwed to the frame to maintain a longer lasting seal. Do the job right the first time and you'll reduce the amount of repair work needed.

Weatherstripping Materials

Schlegel Canada Inc.
514 South Service Road E., Oakville, Ont. L6J 5A2

3M Canada Inc.
1840 Oxford St. E., P.O. Box 5757, London, Ont. N6A 4T1

Quaker City Manufacturing Co.
705 Center Pike, Sharon Hill, PA, 19079

Air-Vapour Barriers

When one considers the importance of the dual role of the air-vapour barrier, several conventionally employed options should be discounted. Insulating materials with kraft paper backing have traditionally been considered adequate. More recently, builders have been employing 2 mil polyethylene sheets as the vapour barrier. Neither of these options will meet the criteria of the super-insulated retrofit. The paper-backed insulation does little to restrict the movement of air into and out of the home, and the thin polyethylene is extremely easy to tear or puncture during installation.

Several products, in conjunction with proper installation procedures, can provide an excellent seal to the retrofitted home. The first choice is 6 mil polyethylene. The plastic sheeting is available in large quantities at a reasonable cost (3¢ per square foot), has a very low permeance, and is sufficiently durable to withstand the abuse it will receive on the building site. The seams of the plastic can be properly sealed with an acoustical caulk and then stapled to the framing of the walls. The plastic is available in 10-foot widths to reduce the number of seams required.

Builder's foil is another effective air-vapour barrier option. The foil prevents the passage of any water vapour, will prevent any air infiltration or exfiltration if properly sealed, and has the ability to re-radiate heat to the interior of the house if sandwiched between two layers of still air. However, because the foil is generally available in smaller rolls (48-inches wide), more sealing of the seams is required. Also, the foil is considerably more expensive to purchase than polyethylene.

In many cases we have recommended the use of extruded polystyrene as a component of the building's air-vapour barrier. Although the permeance of Styrofoam is not quite as low as either the polyethylene or the builder's foil, the material constitutes an effective vapour barrier. If properly fitted and caulked around the edges the Styrofoam will provide an equally effective air-tight seal. Rather than suggesting its use throughout the home, we recommend it primarily for installation between the floor joists on the building's exterior shell. The material is relatively expensive and should only be used where a less expensive option cannot be employed.

To ensure an air-tight seal to the house several other techniques will need to be employed in conjunction with the air-vapour barrier installation. Specific problems arise when holes need to be cut into the vapour barrier to allow for the passage of electrical and plumbing fixtures, plumbing stacks and exhaust vents, and chimneys from furnaces and wood stoves. While the use of a cross-strapping technique can eliminate many of these problem areas, in some cases other products will be needed to ensure the complete sealing of the house.

Sealing Electrical Outlets: Commercially available boxes are manufactured as one means of reducing the work needed to adequately seal around electrical outlets in the exterior walls. Two products are currently available in Canada. 'Polypans' are produced by a Saskatchewan firm. These plastic boxes are designed to fit between blocking installed between studs on the exterior walls. A much smaller polyethylene pan is manufactured in Quebec. This pan fits directly over the standard electrical box and can be nailed directly to the vertical studs. Its limitations result from its size, especially when a large number of wires are running into and out of the box. Home made versions of these

products are detailed in the Do-It section of the book.

Sealing Around Flues and Chimneys: Building codes and common sense will dictate against placing any combustible materials close to chimneys. Using the standard practice of caulking a polyethylene sheet to a hole in the vapour barrier will result in melted plastic if performed around a chimney. Alternatively, a metal firestop should be installed around the chimney and the gap caulked with a muffler or stove cement. Cut the metal carefully to minimize the size of the gap between the chimney and the metal.

Air-Vapour Barriers

Tremco (acoustical sealant)
220 Wickstead Ave., Toronto, Ont.
M4H 1G7

Passive Solar Products (polypans)
2234 Hanselman Ave., Saskatoon, Sask.
S7L 6A4

Iberville Mft. Inc. (polypans)
100 Longtine St., Iberville, Quebec

Windows

The installation of new windows can be one of the largest expenditures in the super-insulated retrofit. If you are planning to install brand new operable windows, make sure that you are on good terms with your bank manager. As we have outlined in this section of the book, existing

windows can be upgraded at a significantly lower price.

If installing new operable windows, the casement or awning variety should be the preferred choice as they maintain a better seal over time. The homeowner should be aware that some window manufacturers produce a better product than others, when considering the infiltration losses around the edges. Pella, an American manufacturer, are acknowledged by many energy-efficient designers and builders as the 'Cadillac' of windows — with a price to back them. In many cases the homeowner will be restricted by budgetary limitations. This being the case, compare the infiltration rates of the windows within your price range and choose accordingly.

Although 'deals' may be hard to find when purchasing new operable windows, substantial savings can result when considering the installation of new fixed panes of glass. Be it tempered glass for a greenhouse addition or standard, double-paned sealed units, savings of up to 60 per cent can result. Most glass manufacturers, distributors and retailers will have odd sized or slightly faulted glass gathering dust in their warehouses. By altering your window openings to accommodate the size of the fixed units (or any operable units), large savings may be attained. An hour on the phone and some old fashioned bargaining, will result in an acceptable price for the homeowner and seller.

If you're considering the installation of an attached greenhouse or skylight, you'll need to be aware of your local building codes. Most municipalities will require that the glazing material be shatterproof. This will limit your options to tempered glass, wire glass, or one of the synthetic glazings such as fibreglass, acrylic or polycarbonate. Tempered glass is readily available in standard patio door sized units. Most manufacturers will stock sealed, double-glazed units in standard sizes — 34 inches x 76 inches, 34 inches x 74 inches, and 32 inches x 76 inches. As a rule, slightly flawed units can be obtained for a fraction of the cost. The flaws are not usually noticeable, but may consist of scratches on the glass, water stains or slight discolorations, all of which will have little bearing on the greenhouse.

Several alternatives to the conventional storm window are also being developed. Interior storms, made from plastics or acrylics, are now being marketed in Canada. These storms fit over the interior window trim and are tightly sealed with either a magnetic tape or a plastic channeling device. While these options are currently extremely expensive, it is assumed that prices will come down as research and development work continues.

Moveable Insulation

Insulating windows at night to reduce heat loss has become a more common practice over the past several years. Throughout North America more than twenty firms are producing insulating shades or curtains for the residential market. These devices range from low cost to extremely expensive, and from useless to highly efficient. Only a handful of the commercial systems have been made available on the Canadian market. Before purchasing any of the systems make sure that the energy savings which will result from the use of the device justifies the usually large capital outlay.

Several firms across the country will provide custom-made shuttering for the existing windows. These systems will generally be more expensive than their commercial counterparts, though both are prohibitively priced at $7.00 to $10.00 per square foot.

As a rule, a more justifiable expense will be incurred with one of the many owner-built options. Costs for these systems will range from 50¢ to $4.00 per square foot for the materials. The list below suggests some of the more frequently prescribed materials which can be employed by the homeowner.

Once installed, there are several ways you can finish the wood. For a pleasing surface the wall can be stained with Cuprinol or another longlasting durable material. If the siding is to be painted use a latex paint so that the exterior skin is able to breathe. Several built-up layers of enamel paint can constitute a vapour barrier, resulting in a vapour lock situation. As a rule, stains should be viewed as the preferred choice as they require less maintenance.

Movable Insulation
Commercially available systems:

Window Quilt — c/o Canadian Gem Instruments
3060 Lakeshore Road, Oakville, Ont.

Insulating Shade Co.
P.O. Box 406, Guildford, CT. 06437

Passive Solar Products
2234 Hanselman Ave., Saskatoon, Sask.
S7L 0W0

Materials:

Thermax c/o Westroc Industries Ltd.
2650 Lakeshore Road W., Clarkson, Ont.

Thinsulate — c/o 3M Canada (fibrous insulation)
155 Lesmill Dr., Toronto, Ont.

Plastiform — (magnetic tape)
available from local Magnet Distributors

Velcro
available from local dressmaking supply shops

Mylar — Dupont Canada Inc.
Most easily obtained as a space blanket from Camping Supplier.

Doors

When purchasing a new door check the insulation level in the core and try to determine the rate of infiltration around its casing. Pre-hung exterior doors will provide the best seal around the edges, but they usually come with a large price tag. Steel frame doors will provide the most durable of seals as they are not subjected to shifts in the building's shell or to deterioration over time. Several manufacturers are now producing well-insulated doors with R values greater than R-12. Once again, the better products have a greater cost, but they do represent a sound investment.

Doors

Stanley Door Systems Ltd.
42 Queen Elizabeth Blvd., Toronto, Ont.
M82 1M1

Premium Forest Products — Insul-Wood Doors
426 Ellesmere Rd., Scarborough, Ont.
M1R 4E7

Pease Doors, c/o H.A.S. Building Supplies
15 Teal Ave., Hamilton, Ont. L8E 2P1

Air-to-Air Heat Exchangers

With the advent of air-tight construction practices in new homes, several manufacturers are producing ventilation systems designed to extract a large proportion of heat from the exhausted air. These air-to-air heat exchangers have only recently become accepted on the market and in many cases 'bugs' are still being ironed out. If you're considering the purchase of an air-to-air heat exchanger we recommend that you deal with a local distributor who will be able to service the unit if problems arise. Several options are available across the country, ranging in cost from $600 to $1000 (not including installation).

Air-to-Air Heat Exchangers

Allen-Drerup-White Ltd. — Air Changer
334 King St. E., Studio 505, Toronto, Ont.
M5A 1K8

Enercon Industries Ltd.
2073 Cornwall St., Regina, Saskatchewan
S4P 2X6

Passive Solar Products
2234 Hanselman Ave., Saskatoon, Sask.
S7L 6A4

Van EE — c/o Conservation Energy Systems Inc.
Box 8280, Saskatoon, Sask S7K 6C6

Saskatchewan Home Built Version — Plans
Extension Division, University of Saskatchewan, Saskatoon, Sask. S7N 0W0

Tools

The following tools will be needed for the various aspects of the super-insulated retrofit. Most of the tools will be a part of a well-stocked tool box. Some of the tools are only needed for very specific components of the work and would best be rented from a local rent-all outlet. Along with the required tools, the homeowner should ensure that adequate safety precautions are taken.

Hammers	Hacksaw
Hand Saw	Chisels
Circular Saw	Safety Goggles
Carpenter's Square	Gloves
Chalk Line	Ladder
Tape Measure	Mitre Saw and Box
Framing Square	Bevel
Level	Staple Gun
Utility Knife	Filter Mask
Rasp	Keyhole Saw
Plane	Trowel
Vise Grips	Hard Hat
Caulking Gun	Steel Toed Boots
Router	Screwdriver
Electric Drill	

Conservation Gadgets

More and more items designed to save energy in the home are appearing in local hardware stores and building supply outlets. Some have a logical place in the energy-efficient home while others are little more than non-essential gadgets.

With an increased awareness of the substantial amount of energy required to provide hot water to the home, more and more products are entering the market to reduce energy consumption. Insulating jackets for hot water tanks are being pushed by utilities and manufacturers. Timed thermostats that regulate the heating supply are also being heavily promoted. In addition, several manufacturers are producing instantaneous demand heaters which can be located directly adjacent to a fixture, thus reducing heat loss through extensive plumbing runs. All of the above products can result in significant energy savings. In the same manner in which energy input to the domestic hot water of the house can be regulated through mechanical controls, energy savings can result from the use of thermostatic controls for the heating supply. Thermostat set-backs can be employed to automatically reduce the interior temperature at night and to re-establish an acceptable environment in the morning. Savings in the order of 5 to 10 per cent of the fuel bill can be realized with the proper operation of the house thermostat.

Domestic Hot Water

Deflecto (Insulating Jackets)
80 Carrier Dr., Rexdale, Ont. M9W 5R1

Exterior Siding

As discussed in the Do It section of the book, the largest single expense incurred in the exterior retrofit of a building occurs when re-siding the newly insulated curtain wall. This added expense can be avoided by re-using the existing siding of the house. Although this task may demand a substantial time commitment in order to take the siding off without destroying it, it will keep the cost of the entire retrofit job to a minimum. You'll want to investigate the feasibility of purchasing replacement panels for that siding which is beyond repair.

Do note that in many cases this option will be entirely unfeasible as the existing siding will be well beyond reusable condition. In other cases, such as solid masonry houses, if you pull down the siding you also pull down the house. Yet again, in many instances the home owner will want to install a different siding, be it for aesthetic reasons or to reduce the maintenance requirements on an annual basis.

If you have decided that you want to install a new siding over the curtain wall, you should analyse the various options available and determine which best suits your purposes.

Wood

Many different types of wood siding are available to the homeowner, ranging dramatically in appearance, ease of installation and cost. Prices will vary drastically depending on the local availability of lumber, the grade of wood required by the homeowner and the actual installation procedure. In some locales you may be able to find reasonably priced cedar or redwood, while in other parts of the country these options may stretch the bounds of your budget. As a rule, the lapped and bevelled siding options will cost considerably more than non-milled lumber. One of the cheaper options calls for the installation of a pine board and batten siding. The vertical siding will require the installation of cross-strapping to provide a nailing surface.

Pre-Finished Sidings

Several maintance-free siding materials are available through local building supply outlets. The most common material is aluminum siding. It can be pre-finished with an enamel coating suited to your colour requirements. The material is relatively easy to install and the various trim pieces can be pre-ordered to fit your house. The cost of the siding will range from 90¢ to $1.15 per square foot for the average home. The specific trim pieces (facia, soffits, trim for doors and windows) will add another 10 to 15 per cent to the overall cost of the installation.

More recently two other siding options have gained acceptance. Both vinyl and compressed chipboard are available as pre-finished horizontal siding. From an appearance perspective there is little difference between these options and the aluminum. You should be aware that both the vinyl and hardboard sidings are more susceptible to chipping or cracking during installation. Costs are comparable or slightly more than the aluminum siding.

Stucco

Stucco can be applied directly over a sheathing that's affixed to the new curtain wall. If properly installed it will require a minimal amount of maintenance, although over time it may need a new coat of paint or whitewash. Installing the stucco may demand some trial and error on the part of the neophyte. Improper installation may lead to cracking, buckling or chipping away from the wall. If stucco is applied over a smooth surface, a wire mesh will need to be placed over the wall to provide the necessary bond. The material is available in pre-mixed containers or in larger 'dry' bags. prices will range substantially depending on the type of material used and the surface to which it is applied. If installing the stucco over top of a newly framed curtain wall, the surface will first need to be sheathed. This cost should be considered in the economics.

Technical Appendix

Most people will shy away from performing detailed heat loss calculations, believing that a five year engineering degree is required to develop the necessary skill. In reality any individual equipped with a calculator and the basic heat loss equations can perform the work in a few hours.

These calculations allow the homeowner to determine the effects of retrofit measures on his/her fuel bill, resulting in an understanding of likely payback periods. This is not to suggest that all homeowners will base their decision to improve the thermal efficiency of their homes on heat loss calculations and projected payback periods. Many will simply decide to perform the work to provide a more comfortable living environment. It is very easy to get bogged down in calculations of payback periods, the present value of money, inflation rates and escalating fuel prices. Many homeowners will view the installation of new insulation in the same manner as the purchase of a new television. Who calculates the payback period of a new T.V.?

Heat loss calculations can be performed to determine the heat loss characteristics of a building at any given time, or over the course of the entire heating season. Performing the calculations for the coldest day of the year will allow the homeowner to determine the required sizing of the home's heating system, while the annual calculations will allow the homeowner to project the fuel bill over the heating season.

The calculations will also allow you to determine the heat loss characteristics of a specific component of the house, such as a window, in relation to the entire building.

The basic equation governing conductive heat loss is extremely simple to use:
Q (heat loss) $= U \times A \times (T_i - T_o)$, where:

- Q — heat loss across a material over an hour, expressed in BTU/hour.
- U — coefficient of transmission of a section
- A — the area of the section
- T_i — the interior temperature
- T_o — the exterior temperature.

Filling in the Blanks

Filling in the blanks in the above equation requires little more than an understanding of the construction practices used in your home and an ability to extract the right numbers from the charts below.

Step 1

The U in the equation refers to the conductive characteristics of the materials making up a section of wall, ceiling, window or door. The U value of a section of wall is the reciprocal of the more commonly used R value. The U value of an R-12 wall is determined by $U = 1/12$, where 12 represents the R value of the components of the wall assembly.

So we need to be able to determine the R value of an assembly before we can determine the U value to fit the equation. R

values are cumulative. If we know the values of each component of an assembly we can very simply add them together to find the total R value. In the case of a wall section, let us look at the drawing below.

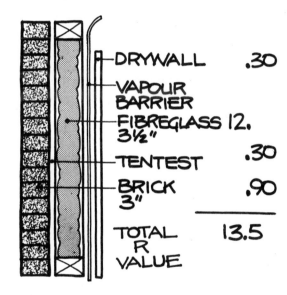

DRYWALL	.30
VAPOUR BARRIER	
FIBREGLASS 3½"	12.
TENTEST	.30
BRICK 3"	.90
TOTAL R VALUE	13.5

In this particular section, starting from the interior, we have a ½-inch layer of drywall, a plastic vapour barrier an R-12 batt of fibreglass insulation, ½-inch layer of tentest, and 3 inches of brick. By looking at the table below we can find the R value of each of the materials and add them together. In this case they add up to a total of close to R-13.5. To derive the U value, we then find the reciprocal: $1/13.5 = .074$. The U value for any component of the exterior shell can be obtained in a similar manner.

Step 2

In the initial equation A represents the area of the section to be calculated. Each component of the exterior shell of the house should be measured, and similar sections can be added together. In this manner you will know the amount of insulated wall space, the area of glazing, the area of the attic or ceiling and so on. Each of the components of the exterior shell should be itemized. A separate calculation will need to be done for each of the sections of the house.

Step 3

It will be necessary to know the design temperature in your specific region. The chart below provides the figures for most areas of the country, more specific information can be obtained from your local meteorological service. The design temperature refers to the coldest temperature which occurs during the heating season. The design temperature will only be exceeded for less than 1 per cent of the heating season. In calculating the peak heat loss through a section of the home, or to calculate the sizing requirements of a home's heating system, you will want to determine the temperature differential between the house interior and the exterior on the coldest day. This differential temperature $(T_i - T_o)$ fills in the last part of the initial equation.

Calculating the Design Heat Loss

We can now refer back to the equation $Q = U \times A \times (T_i - T_o)$ with a clearer understanding of how to relate the equation to your house. To calculate the conductive losses of the building you must perform a calculation on each component of the exterior shell. As an example we will take a typical, small house in Thunder Bay to show how all of this fits together. A quick check of the chart shows that the design temperature for Thunder Bay is —29°F (—33°C). Wandering around the house with a measuring tape gives us the various measurements for the specific components of the exterior shell.

This total of almost 45,500 BTU/hour relates to the conductive heat losses through the building's exterior. As we have stressed, a significant amount is also lost through the infiltration of cold air and the exfiltration of heated air. A separate equation is required to determine these heat losses;

$Q_i = 0.018 \times V \times (T_i - T_o) \times A.C./hr$, where;
Q_i is the heat loss attributable to infiltration as expressed in BTU/hr.
V, is the volume of air in the house
$(T_i - T_o)$, is the temperature differential between the interior and exterior
A.C./hr, is the rate of air changes within the building.

The major problem involved with the above equation relates to the difficulty of accurately determining the air change rate within the house. While technical means of monitoring the air change rate can assist in providing a more accurate assessment of the leakiness of a home, you will need to take an educated guess to determine the rate which applies in your case.

Recently a great deal of work has been performed in the technical field of building sciences. The attempt to gain a better understanding of infiltration and exfiltration has been led, most notably, by

Building Component	R Value	U Value	Area		$T_i - T_o$		Q
Exterior Walls	8	.125	x 1028 sq. ft.	x	94	=	12,079
Basement Walls (above grade)	4	.25	x 174		94	=	4089
(below grade)	4	.25	x 825	avg.	35	=	7218
Basement Floor	4	.25	x 1076	avg.	20	=	5380
Attic	20	.05	x 1076		94	=	5057
Windows	.95	1.05	x 107		94	=	10,560
Doors	3	.33	x 38		94	=	1,178
							45,561

the Division of Building Research in Canada and the Energy Research Group at Princeton in the U.S.A. Through the use of tracer gas experiments and depressurizing fans, we are beginning to understand these new developments. Yet, a great deal of controversy still exists regarding the air change characteristics of the average house. Estimates range from .50 air changes per hour (A.C.H.) to 1.0 A.C.H. for the average pre-1976 dwelling. To illustrate the spectrum, it is estimated that a leaky farmhouse would have a rate of air change of up to 8 A.C.H. on a windy day while at the other extreme a new super-insulated home might have a rate of less than .05 A.C.H.

We can work from the assumption that the average house — minimal insulation, caulking and weatherstripping, and a furnace burning oil or gas — has a rate of 1 A.C.H. Older houses will have a higher rate if no upgrading has been performed, and newer homes or those buildings which have been thermally upgraded will have a rate of between .4 — .8 A.C.H. Of course, without the more sophisticated equipment, this evaluation can be no more than a 'guesstimate'. As this component of the total heat loss equation for the house might amount to as much as 40 per cent of the fuel bill, some of the frailties of standard heat loss estimations become apparent.

Getting back to our 'average' house located in Thunder Bay. We will assume an air change rate of 1 A.C.H. The volume of the house has been calculated to be 14,400 cubic feet. Using a temperature differential of 94°F we can now continue with our calculations. By filling in the blanks of the equation for infiltration heat losses we arrive at the following total:

$$Q = 0.018 \times 14,400 \times 94°F \times 1 \text{ A.C.H.}$$
$$= 24,330 \text{ BTU/hour.}$$

When added to the total conductive heat losses from the building (45,500 BTU/hr), we arrive at a design heat loss of slightly less than 70,000 BTU/hr. This means that on the coldest day of the year a heating system would need to supply that amount of heat to the building each hour.

Using the procedure outlined above, you are now capable of guesstimating the design heat load of your house, or of any component of the building's shell. Using that information to find the seasonal or the monthly heat loss characteristics of the building involves a simple alteration to the overall equation.

To assist in characterizing the heating and cooling load in any given location, a degree-day factor has been developed. A degree-day accrues for every degree the average outside temperature over a 24 hour period is below the inside temperature of 65°F (18°C). For instance, if the average temperature during a 24 hour period is 64°F, the degree-day factor would be 65-64 = 1. If the average temperature is 0°F, the degree-day factor would be 65 — 0 = 65. Degree-day figures are recorded for most cities and towns throughout the country on a monthly and yearly basis.

To determine your heat loss characteristics over a period of time, we use the equation:
$$Q = U \times A \times 24 \times DD, \text{ where:}$$
  Q, is the heat loss from the building as expressed in BTU
  U, is the reciprocal of the R value of a wall section
  A, is the area of the section
  24, is the number of hours in the day
  DD, is the degree-day factor for a specific period.

If you have already performed the heat loss calculations for the design temperature as outlined above, the task can be simplified. To calculate the heat loss per degree-day use the equation:
$$Q \text{ (per DD)} = \frac{Q \text{ (Design load)}}{\text{Design Temperature}} \times 24$$

Our Thunder Bay example has a calculated design load of 70,000 BTU/hour at 94°F. To find the heat loss per degree-day:
$$Q \text{ (per DD)} = \frac{70,000 \times 24}{94}$$
$$= 17,872 \text{ BTU/DD}$$

In January 1,792 DD (F°) accrue in Thunder Bay. We can now multiply 17,872 BTU x 1,792 to determine the heat loss from the house in Thunder Bay during the month of January, resulting in a monthly heating load of 32,000,000 BTU. The appended chart provides degree-day factors for many Canadian and northern U.S. locations. More detailed figures for your specific location should be available from your local meteorological station.

Calculating Dollars and Cents From Heat Loss Figures

In most cases we are able to determine the cost of providing X BTU to the home. To perform these calculations we need to know: the type of fuel being consumed; the price of the fuel; and, the efficiency of converting the fuel to heat.

The relative price of oil, natural gas and electricity will vary considerably depending on your location across the continent. Check with your local utility or fuel supply company to determine the exact cost of the fuel in your area. Similarly, the efficiency of converting the fuel to usable heat will range from 55 per cent for a poorly maintained oil furnace to 100 per cent for electrical heating. If you are not sure of the relative efficiency of your heating system, a qualified service mechanic should be able to offer you a sound estimate. The average oil or gas furnace will range in efficiency from 60 to 65 per cent on a seasonal basis.

The energy content of each fuel is listed below. These figures provide the maximum theoretical energy available to the homeowner.

Oil — 166,000 BTU/gallon
Natural Gas — 1,000 BTU/cubic foot
Electricity — 3,414 BTU/kwh

When we multiply these figures by the average efficiency of their conversion, we end up providing to the house:

Oil — 166,000 BTU/gallon x .65 (seasonal efficiency) = app. 107,000 BTU/gallon of usable heat
Natural Gas — 1,000 BTU/cubic foot x .65(seasonal efficiency) = 650 BTU/cubic foot (650,000 BTU/mcf)
Electricity — 3,414 BTU/kwh x 1.0 (seasonal efficiency) = 3,414 BTU/kwh

In Thunder Bay the costs of the various fuels are as follows:

Fuel Oil — app. $1.20/gallon
Natural Gas — app. $4.65/mcf
Electricity — app. 4¢/kwh

By slipping these figures into the calculations we find that the cost to the homeowner for heat derived from the various sources becomes:

Oil — $1.10 per 100,000 BTU
Gas — $0.71 per 100,000 BTU
Electricity — $1.13 per 100,000 BTU

For our Thunder Bay house with a heat loss in January of 32,000,000 BTU, the heating costs with the various fuels would be:

Oil — $352.00
Gas — $227.20
Electricity — $361.00

Heat Gains

Several factors will result in a reduced heating load. The Primer has discussed the concept of internal gains — the heat supplied from activities within the building envelope. In an average house internal gains will amount to approximately 94,000 BTU per day:

Source	BTU/day
Dryer (1 hr/day)	17,000
Refrigerator (24 hours/day)	24,000
Television (3hrs/day)	2,000
Water Heater (24 hrs/day)	12,000
Cooking (2hrs/day)	14,000
Lights (4 hrs/day)	11,000
People (4 @ 16 hrs/day)	14,000
Total	94,000

In January, therefore, 2.9 million BTU (31 x 94,000) will be produced from internal gains, reducing the heating load in an average house by as much as 10 per cent.

Passive solar gains will contribute an even larger amount of heat to the house throughout the heating season. Sun shining through the south-facing windows of the house will result in a reduction in the heating load of approximately 15 per cent in the average house.

Detailed calculations regarding the number of BTU's of heat gained from solar radiation can be calculated by employing available radiation charts. Good sources of information include Atmospheric Environmental Services and *The Well-Tempered House* . Using these sources, we can calculate that in Thunder Bay, in a house with random window orientation, approximately 1.2 million BTU's will be gained in the form of solar radiation. If the house had only 50 square feet of south-facing glass, the number of BTU's would increase by 25 per cent. The corresponding gains in the month of March would provide 2.1 million BTU and 2.5 million BTU, respectively.

By adding the internal gains and the solar gains for the month of January in Thunder Bay, we attain 4.1 million BTU's free heat. Our heat load, initially calculated at 31.9 million BTU, is thus reduced to 27.8 million BTU.

Building Component	R-Value	U-Value	Area	T_i-T_o	Q
Exterior Walls	28	.035	1028	94	3,382
Basement Walls (above grade)	24	.041	174	94	670
Basement Walls (below grade)	24	.041	825	avg 35	1,185
Basement Floor	16	.062	1076	avg 20	1,345
Attic	40	.025	1076	94	2,528
Windows	2.7	.37	38	94	253
				Total	13,082

Infiltration = .018 x 14,400 x 94 x .3 (ACH)   7,309

Total Heat Loss   20,391 BTU/hr.

Heating Load Reduction Resulting from Retrofit Measures

We can use the same procedure outlined above to determine the heat load features of the retrofitted building. In this case we are assuming the house has been the recipient of the super-insulated retrofit. The walls of the house have had R-20 added, the same to the attic. The windows of the building were upgrade to triple-glazed status and a new R-14 door was installed. The installation of a tight air-vapour barrier resulted in a 66 per cent reduction in the infiltration rate of the building.

Our new January heat loss is then derived using the same process outlined above:

$$Q \text{ (per DD)} = \frac{Q \text{ design load} \times 24}{\text{Design Temp.}}$$

$$= 5206 \text{ BTU/DD}$$

1792 degree-days will occur in Thunder Bay in January resulting in a monthly load of 9.3 million BTU. Considering the free heat gains from internal sources and the available solar radiation, there will be a constant 4.1 million BTU in the month of January. Our new requirements for space heating will be 5.2 million BTU's or the equivalent of 48.5 gallons of fuel oil, 8 mcf of natural gas or 1523 kwh. in that month.

Compared with the pre-retrofit heat load of 27.8 million BTU in January, the retrofitted heat load represents an 84 per cent reduction.

Summary of Methodology

To calculate the Design Heat Load:
For each separate component of the building's envelope use the equation $Q = U \times A \times (65°F — \text{Design Temperature})$; Total the conductive losses and add the infiltration losses as determined by: $Q = .018 \times V \times (65°F — \text{Design Temperature}) \times ACH$. The totals of the conductive and convective heat losses will be expressed in BTU/hour.

To calculate the Heating Load monthly or seasonally:
Take the design heat load of the building and divide it by the difference between the interior temperature and the design temperature. Multiply the figure by 24 to obtain BTU/DD. Multiply by the number of DD to obtain the heat loss over the specified period of time. Subtract from this figure the estimated internal gains and passive solar heat. This will give you the total auxiliary energy needed to be supplied.

To calculate Costs of Heating:
Determine the efficiency of your heating system and the costs of the fuel you use. Multiply the energy content of the fuel by the efficiency of your heating system to determine the available heat per unit of fuel.

Charts

Thermal Resistance Values of Common Building Materials

Material	R/inch	RSI/ mm
Insulation		
Fibreglass batt	3.17	.022
Rock wool batt	3.32	.023
Fibreglass loose (blown)	2.16	.015
Fibreglass loose (poured)	3.03	.021
Rock wool loose (blown)	2.74	.019
Rock wool loose (poured)	3.03	.021
Cellulose (blown)	3.61	.025
Cellulose (poured)	3.46	.024
Vermiculite	2.31	.016
Polystyrene (loose)	2.88	.020
Expanded Polystyrene	3.89	.027
Extruded Polystyrene	4.62	.032
Polyurethane (rigid or foamed)	6.06	.042
Fibreglass sheathing	4.47	.031
Wood fibre	3.32	.023
Wood shavings	2.45	.017
Glass fibre roof board	4.04	.028
Mineral aggregate board	2.60	.018
Fibreboard	2.74	.019
Cladding Materials		
Fibreboard siding	.45-.57 (³/8″)	.10-.08 (9.5mm)
Softwood lapped siding		
drop —	.80 (³/4″)	.14 (18mm)
bevel —	.80-1.0 (¹/2″-³/4″)	.14-.18 (12-19mm)
Plywood	.57 (³/8″)	.10 (9mm)
Wood shingles	1.0	.17
Brick	.30-.42 (4″)	.053-.074 (100mm)
Stucco	.20 (1″)	.001 (25mm)
Metal clapboard with backing	1.40	.246

Material	R/inch	RSI/ mm
Sheathing Materials		
Softwood plywood	1.25	.008
Mat-formed particleboard	1.25	.008
Insulating fibreboard	2.45	.017
Gypsum sheathing	.89	.006
Sheathing paper	.06	.0004
Polyethylene vapour barrier	—	—
Structural Materials		
Softwood lumber	1.25	.008
Cedar logs and lumber	1.33	.009
Concrete		
— high density	.06	.0004
— medium density	.19	.001
— low density	1.00	.006
Concrete Block (3 oval core)		
— sand and gravel aggregate	1.14 (8″)	.20 (200mm)
	1.25 (12″)	.22 (300mm)
— cinder aggregate	1.70 (8″)	.30 (200mm)
	1.87 (12″)	.33
— lightweight aggregate	1.99 (8″)	.35 (200mm)
	2.27 (12″)	.40 (300mm)
Common Brick		
— clay or shale	.40 (4″)	.07 (100mm)
— concrete mix	.28 (4″)	.05 (100mm)
Interior Finishing Materials		
Gypsum board	.45 (¹/2″)	.08 (13mm)
Gypsum plaster (sand)	.10 (¹/2″)	.018 (13mm)
(lightweight)	.32 (¹/2″)	.05 (13mm)
Plywood	.40 (¹/4″)	.07 (7.5mm)
Hardboard	.18 (¹/4″)	.032 (6mm)
Fibreboard	2.39 (1″)	.42 (25mm)
Drywall	.45 (¹/2″)	.08 (13mm)

Material	R/inch	RSI/mm
Flooring Materials		
Maple or Oak flooring	.68 ($^3/_4''$)	.12 (19mm)
Pine or Fir	.97 ($^3/_4''$)	.17 (19mm)
Plywood	.80 ($^5/_8''$)	.14 (16mm)
Wood Fibre Tiles	1.12 ($^1/_2''$)	.21 (13mm)
Tile or Linoleum	.08 ($^1/_8''$)	.014 (3mm)
Carpeting		
— with fibre underlay	2.10 (average)	.37
— with foam underlay	1.31 (average)	.23
Roofing Materials		
Asphalt roll roofing	.15	.026
Asphalt shingles	.44	.078
Wood shingles	.97	.170
Windows (including air films)		
Single glass	.85	.15
Double glass (sealed units)		
$^1/_4''$ airspace	1.53	.27
$^1/_2''$ airspace	1.70	.30
$^3/_4''$ airspace	1.89	.33
Triple glass (sealed units)		
$^1/_4''$ airspace	2.15	.38
$^1/_2''$ airspace	2.78	.49
$^3/_4''$ airspace	2.84	.50

Air Surfaces	R	RSI
Horizontal surface (upward heat flow)	.61	.11
Horizontal Surface (downward heat flow)	.92	.16
Vertical Surface (Horizontal heat flow)	.68	.12
Moving air 7.5 - 15 mph	.17-.25	.03-.04

Permeance Ratings of Common Building Materials

Material	Average Perm Rating	
	Kg/Ns (10^{-11})	*grain/hrft²* (*in. Hg*)
Vapour Barriers		
1 mil. aluminum foil	0.00	0.00
6 mil. polyethylene	0.34	0.06
4 mil. polyethylene	0.46	0.08
2 mil. polyethylene	0.92	0.16
1 mil. polyester	4.0	0.69
Asphalt kraft paper	4.3	0.74
Paint and Wallpaper		
1 coat latex vapour barrier paint	3.4	0.59
vinyl wallpaper	5.7	0.99
2 coats oil based paint on plaster	11	1.90
3 coats latex paint on wood	57	9.90
ordinary wallpaper	115	20.00
Insulation		
25mm (1″) polyurethane	5.7	0.99
25mm (1″) extruded styrofoam (blue)	3.5	0.60
25mm (1″) beadboard	23	4.0
100mm (4″) cellulose	172	29.9
100mm (4″) fibreglass	172	29.9
Other Materials		
13mm ($^1/_2''$) plywood CDX	2.9	0.17
100mm (4″) brick	5.7	0.99
200mm (8″) concrete block	11	1.90
19mm ($^3/_4''$) wood	17	2.90
6.8kg (15 lb.) tarpaper	103	17.90
plaster	115	20.00
drywall	287	49.90

Degree-Days

Listed beside each city is the Design Temperature and the Latitude.

The Design Temperature indicates the probable lowest temperature on the coldest day. This temperature will be lower only 1 per cent of the time.

The monthly numbers given are the degree-days. A degree-day accrues for every degree the average outside temperature for a 24 hour period is below 65°F. This information can be used to determine the annual heating requirements of buildings.

Canadian Degree — Days

J	F	M	A	M	J	J	A	S	O	N	D	Total
Yellowknife, N.W.T. -49°F 62°28′N												
2601	2223	2048	1399	783	320	137	227	599	1073	1741	2317	15,468
Whitehorse, Yukon -45°F 60°43′N												
2055	1599	1438	985	625	323	243	336	575	985	1468	1908	12,550
Victoria, B.C. 20°F 48°30′N												
840	718	691	504	341	204	136	140	225	462	663	775	5,699
Vancouver, B.C. 16° F 49°11′N												
862	723	676	501	310	156	81	87	219	456	657	787	5,515
Kamloops, B.C. -16°F 50°40′N												
1314	1057	818	462	217	102	22	40	189	546	894	1138	6,799
Prince George, B.C. -33°F 53°53′N												
1612	1319	1122	747	468	279	236	251	444	747	1110	1420	9,755
Grande Prairie, Alta. -38°F 55°11′N												
1976	1554	1426	847	449	240	135	193	426	778	1319	1747	11,090
Calgary, Alta. -27°F 51°66′N												
1575	1379	1268	798	477	291	109	186	402	719	1110	1386	9,703
Edmonton, Alta. -29°F 53°40′N												
1810	1520	1330	765	400	222	74	180	411	738	1215	1603	10,268
Medicine Hat, Alta. -29°F 50°00′N												
1696	1344	1203	665	348	148	36	66	300	603	1076	1441	8,926
Prince Albert, Sask. -42°F 53°12′N												
2103	1763	1559	867	446	219	81	136	414	797	1368	1872	11,630

J	F	M	A	M	J	J	A	S	O	N	D	Total
Swift Current, Sask. -36°F 50°20′N												
1800	1469	1366	787	449	210	68	108	370	684	1142	1562	10,015
Regina, Sask. -33°F 50°26′N												
1965	1687	1473	804	409	201	78	93	360	741	1284	1711	10,806
Saskatoon, Sask. -35°F 52°07′N												
2034	1626	1462	828	410	163	50	90	383	693	1269	1705	10,713
Brandon, Man. -31°F 49°50′N												
2059	1682	1496	815	438	155	44	83	351	688	1258	1782	10,871
Winnipeg, Man. -31°F 49°50′N												
2008	1719	1465	813	405	147	38	71	322	683	1251	1757	10,679
The Pas, Man. -36°F 53°N												
2232	1853	1624	969	508	228	59	127	429	831	1440	1981	12,281
Churchill, Man. -42°F 58°45′N												
2558	2277	2130	1569	1153	675	360	375	681	1082	1620	2248	16,728
Thunder Bay, Ont. -29°F 48°25′N												
1792	1557	1380	876	543	237	90	133	366	694	1140	1597	10,405
Sault Ste. Marie, Ont. -18°F 46629′N												
1605	1484	1302	801	503	215	99	111	310	575	953	1404	9,362
North Bay, Ont. -22°F 46°22′N												
1680	1463	1277	780	400	120	37	90	267	608	990	1507	9,219
Windsor, Ont. -1°F 42°16′N												
1231	1080	1055	526	252	51	5	14	113	363	732	1102	6,529
Toronto, Ont. -3°F 43°40′N												
1233	1119	1013	616	298	62	7	18	151	439	760	1111	6,827
Ottawa, Ont. -17°F 45°25′N												
1624	1441	1231	708	341	90	25	81	222	567	936	1469	8,735
Chicoutimi, Que. -26°F 48°25′N												
1997	1721	1486	943	535	217	107	172	395	720	1120	1762	11,175
Montreal, Qué. -15°F 45°35′N												
1540	1370	1150	700	300	50	10	40	180	530	890	1370	8,130
Sherbrooke, Que. -22°F 45°24′N												
1541	1352	1139	693	349	100	24	63	231	526	868	1366	8,252
Quebec City, Que. -18°F 46°50′N												
1695	1495	1276	814	427	140	41	82	286	613	984	1517	9,372

	J	F	M	A	M	J	J	A	S	O	N	D	Total
Rimouski, Que. -17°F 48°27'N													
	1617	1421	1278	850	542	221	106	153	358	657	963	1448	9,614
Edmunston, N.B. -20°F 47°23'N													
	1707	1454	1285	821	445	176	52	106	315	630	995	1520	9,511
Fredericton, N.B. -17°F 45°57'N													
	1541	1379	1172	753	406	141	78	68	234	592	915	1392	8,671
St. John, N.B. -11°F 45°20'N													
	1370	1229	1097	756	490	249	109	102	246	527	807	1194	8,219
Nappan, N.S. -9°F 45°46'N													
	1415	1293	1160	810	503	224	61	92	268	551	823	1250	8,450
Halifax, N.S. 0°F 44°39'N													
	1213	1122	1030	742	487	251	58	54	180	457	710	1074	7,361
Sydney, N.S. -1°F 46°10'N													
	1262	1206	1150	840	567	276	62	71	219	518	765	1113	8,049
Charlottetown, P.E.I. -8°F 46°19'N													
	1380	1274	1169	813	496	204	40	53	198	518	804	1213	8,164
Corner Brook, Nfld. -10°F 48°58'N													
	1358	1283	1212	885	639	333	102	133	324	643	873	1194	8,978
St. John's, Nfld. 3°F 47°37'N													
	1262	1170	1187	927	710	432	186	180	342	651	831	1113	8,991

U.S. degree-day data

	J	F	M	A	M	J	J	A	S	O	N	D	Total
Astoria, Oregon 27°F 46°12'N													
	772	613	611	459	357	222	138	111	146	338	537	691	4,995
Bismark, N. Dak. -24°F 46°47'N													
	1730	1464	1187	657	355	116	29	37	227	598	1098	1535	9,033
Blue Hill, Mass. -4°F 42°13'N													
	1178	1053	936	579	267	69	0	22	108	381	690	1085	6,368
Boise, Idaho 4°F 43°34'N													
	1169	868	719	453	249	92	0	0	135	389	762	1054	5,890
Boston, Mass. 6°F 42°22'N													
	1113	1002	849	534	236	42	0	7	77	315	618	998	5,791
Caribou, Maine -18°F 46°52'N													
	1745	1546	1342	909	512	201	85	133	354	710	1074	1562	10,173
Cleveland, Ohio 2°F 41°24'N													
	1101	977	846	510	223	49	0	9	60	311	636	995	5,717
East Lansing, Mich. 2°F 42°44'N													
	1277	1142	986	591	287	70	13	33	140	455	813	1175	6,982
Fairbanks, Alaska -53°F 64°49'N													
	1240	1089	1082	858	685	471	149	296	612	1163	1857	1190	10,692
Glasgow, Mont. -25°F 48°13'N													
	1683	1408	1119	597	312	113	14	30	244	574	1086	1570	8,690
Great Falls, Mont. -20°F 47°29'N													
	1311	1131	1008	621	359	166	24	50	273	524	894	1194	7,555
Lander, Wyo. -16°F 42°48'N													
	1494	1179	1045	687	396	163	7	23	244	632	1050	1383	8,303
Madison, Wis. -9°F 43°08'N													
	1417	1207	1011	573	266	79	10	30	137	419	864	1287	7,300
Medford, Oreg. 21°F 42°23'N													
	862	627	552	381	207	69	0	0	77	326	624	822	4,547
New York, N.Y. 11°F 40°46'N													
	995	904	753	456	153	18	0	0	39	263	561	908	5,050
Portland, Maine -5°F 43°39'N													
	1373	1218	1039	693	394	117	15	56	199	515	825	1237	7,681
Rapid City, S. Dak. -9°F 44°09'N													
	1361	1151	1045	615	357	148	32	24	193	500	891	1218	7,535
St. Cloud, Minn. -17°F 45°35'N													
	1690	1439	1181	663	331	106	32	53	225	570	1068	1535	8,893
Sault Ste. Marie, Mich. -12°F 46°28'N													
	1587	1442	1302	846	499	224	109	126	298	639	1005	1398	9,475
Schenectady, N.Y. -5°F 42°50'N													
	1349	1207	1008	597	233	40	0	19	137	456	792	1212	7,050
Seattle, Wash. 28°F 47°27'N													
	831	655	608	411	242	99	34	40	147	384	624	763	4,838
Spokane, Wash. -2°F 47°40'N													
	1243	988	834	561	330	146	17	28	205	508	879	1113	6,852

Cross·Views

UNINSULATED FRAME HOUSE

- INTERIOR AIR SURFACE .68
- ½" DRYWALL .45
- 3½" AIR SPACE .68
- ½" SHEATHING .62
- ½" SIDING .80
- TOTAL R VALUE 3.23
- THIS IS A NOMINAL VALUE

WITH INSULATION

- 3½" FIBREGLASS 12.
- WITH EXISTING WALL 15.23
- 3½ ROCKWOOL 10.50
- WITH EXISTING WALL 13.73
- 3½ CELLULOSE 12.50
- WITH EXISTING WALL 15.73

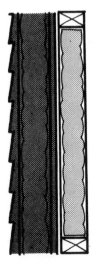

INTERIOR FRAMEWALL WITH 4" FIBERGLASS

- FIBREGLASS 12.
- EXISTING WALL 15.23
- TOTAL R VALUE 27.23

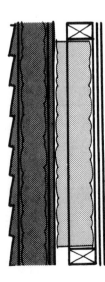

INTERIOR FRAMEWALL WITH 6" FIBREGLASS

- FIBREGLASS 20.
- EXISTING WALL 15.23
- TOTAL R VALUE 35.23

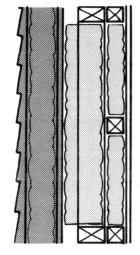

INTERIOR FRAMEWALL
AND CROSS·STRAPPING
- FIBREGLASS (6"+2") 28.
- EXISTING WALL   15.23
- TOTAL R VALUE   43.23

EXTERIOR
6" CURTAIN WALL
- FIBREGLASS   20.
- EXISTING WALL   15.23
- TOTAL R VALUE   35.23

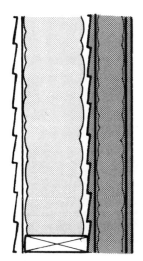

EXTERIOR
8" CURTAIN WALL
- FIBREGLASS   28.
- EXISTING WALL   15.23
- TOTAL R VALUE   43.23

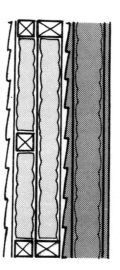

EXTERIOR STRAPPING
AND CROSS·STRAPPING
- FIBREGLASS (2½"+2½") 18.
- EXISTING WALL   15.23
- TOTAL R VALUE   33.23

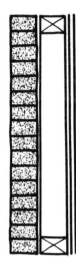

BRICK VENEER
- INTERIOR AIR SURFACE .68
- ½" DRYWALL .45
- 3½" AIR SPACE .68
- 4" BRICK .90
- EXTERIOR AIR SPACE .17
- TOTAL R VALUE 2.88
- THIS IS A NOMINAL VALUE

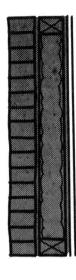

WITH INSULATION
- 3½" FIBREGLASS 12.
- WITH EXISTING WALL 14.88
- 3½" ROCKWOOL 10.50
- WITH EXISTING WALL 13.38
- 3½" CELLULOSE 12.50
  WITH EXISTING WALL 15.38

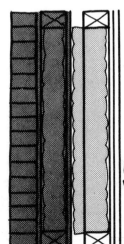

INTERIOR FRAMEWALL WITH 6" FIBREGLASS
- FIBREGLASS 20.
- EXISTING WALL 14.80
- TOTAL R VALUE 34.80

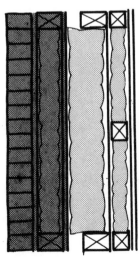

INTERIOR FRAMEWALL AND CROSS·STRAPPING
- FIBREGLASS (6"+2") 28.
- EXISTING WALL 14.80
- TOTAL R VALUE 42.80

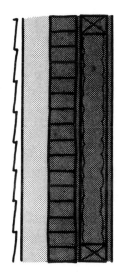

EXTERIOR WITH 4″ EXTRUDED POLYSTYRENE

- POLYSTYRENE   20.
- EXISTING WALL   14.80
- TOTAL R VALUE   34.80

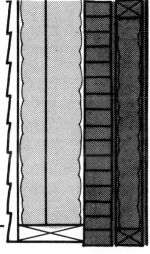

EXTERIOR 6″ CURTAIN WALL

- FIBREGLASS   20.
- EXISTING WALL   14.80
- TOTAL R VALUE   34.80

DOUBLE BRICK WITH LATH AND PLASTER

- INTERIOR AIR SURFACE .68
- ½″ LATH   .32
- ¾″ AIR SPACE   .68
- 8″ BRICK   1.80
- ½″ AIR SPACE   .68
- EXTERIOR AIR SURFACE .17
- TOTAL R VALUE   4.33
- THIS IS A NOMINAL VALUE

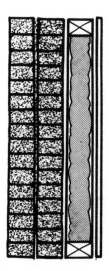

INTERIOR FRAMEWALL WITH 4″ FIBERGLASS

- FIBREGLASS   12.
- EXISTING WALL   4.30
- TOTAL R VALUE   16.30

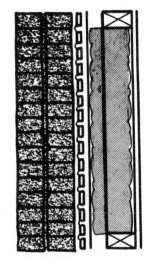

INTERIOR FRAMEWALL WITH 6" FIBERGLASS

- FIBREGLASS   20.
- EXISTING WALL   4.30
- TOTAL R VALUE   24.30

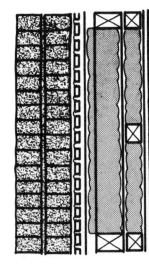

INTERIOR FRAMEWALL AND CROSS·STRAPPING

- FIBREGLASS (6"+2")   28.
- EXISTING WALL   4.30
- TOTAL R VALUE   32.30

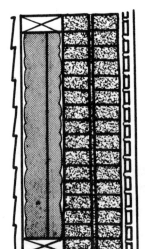

EXTERIOR 6" CURTAIN WALL

- FIBREGLASS   20.
- EXISTING WALL   4.30
- TOTAL R VALUE   24.30

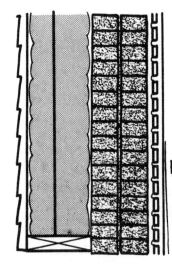

EXTERIOR 8" CURTAIN WALL

- FIBREGLASS   28.
- EXISTING WALL   4.30
- TOTAL R VALUE   32.30

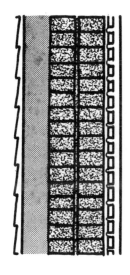

EXTERIOR WITH 4" EXTRUDED POLYSTYRENE

- POLYSTYRENE   20.
- EXISTING WALL   4.30
- TOTAL R VALUE   24.30

FOUNDATION UNINSULATED

- POURED CONCRETE   1.50
- CONCRETE BLOCK   1.14

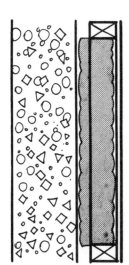

INTERIOR FRAMEWALL WITH 6" FIBREGLASS

- FIBREGLASS   20.
- EXISTING WALL   1.50
- TOTAL R VALUE   21.50

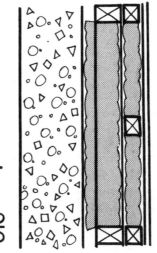

INTERIOR FRAMEWALL AND CROSS-STRAPPING

- FIBREGLASS (6"+2")   28.
- EXISTING WALLS   1.50
- TOTAL R VALUE   29.50

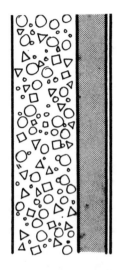

INTERIOR STRAPPING 4" EXPANDED POLYSTYRENE

- POLYSTYRENE   20.
- EXISTING WALL   1.50
- TOTAL R VALUE   21.50

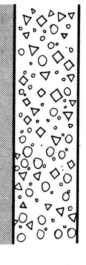

EXTERIOR WITH 4" EXTRUDED POLYSTYRENE

- POLYSTYRENE   20.
- EXISTING WALL   1.50
- TOTAL R VALUE   21.50

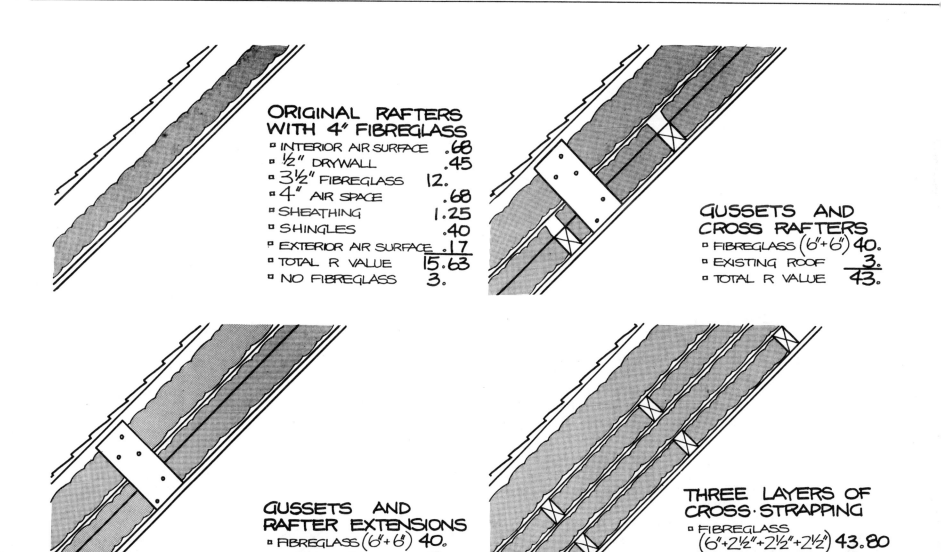

ORIGINAL RAFTERS WITH 4" FIBREGLASS
- INTERIOR AIR SURFACE .68
- ½" DRYWALL .45
- 3½" FIBREGLASS 12.
- 4" AIR SPACE .68
- SHEATHING 1.25
- SHINGLES .40
- EXTERIOR AIR SURFACE .17
- TOTAL R VALUE 15.63
- NO FIBREGLASS 3.

GUSSETS AND CROSS RAFTERS
- FIBREGLASS (6"+6") 40.
- EXISTING ROOF 3.
- TOTAL R VALUE 43.

GUSSETS AND RAFTER EXTENSIONS
- FIBREGLASS (6"+6") 40.
- EXISTING ROOF 3.
- TOTAL R VALUE 43.

THREE LAYERS OF CROSS-STRAPPING
- FIBREGLASS (6"+2½"+2½"+2½") 43.80
- EXISTING ROOF 3.
- TOTAL R VALUE 46.80

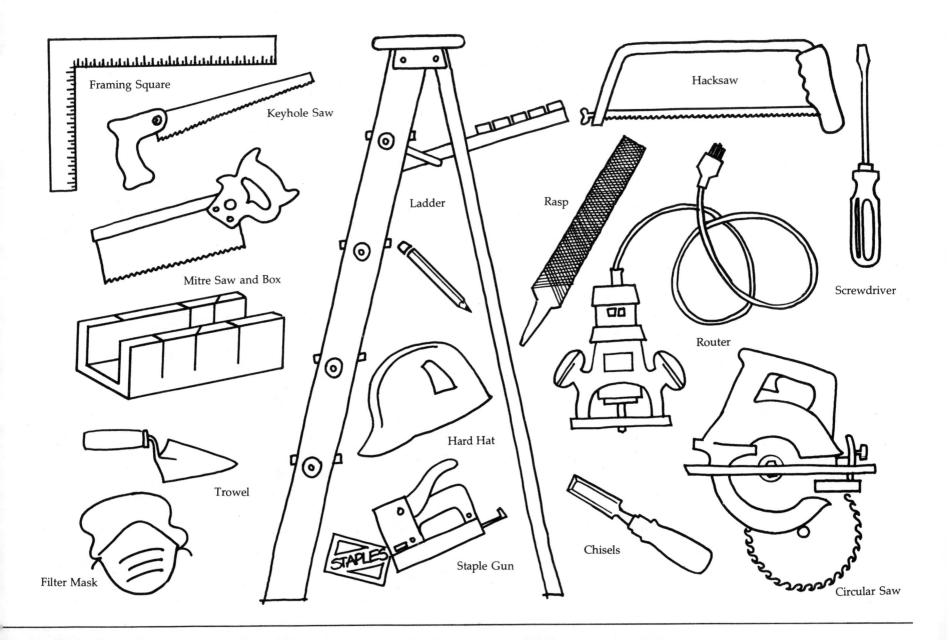

Framing Square

Keyhole Saw

Mitre Saw and Box

Trowel

Filter Mask

Ladder

Hard Hat

Staple Gun

STAPLES

Rasp

Router

Chisels

Hacksaw

Screwdriver

Circular Saw

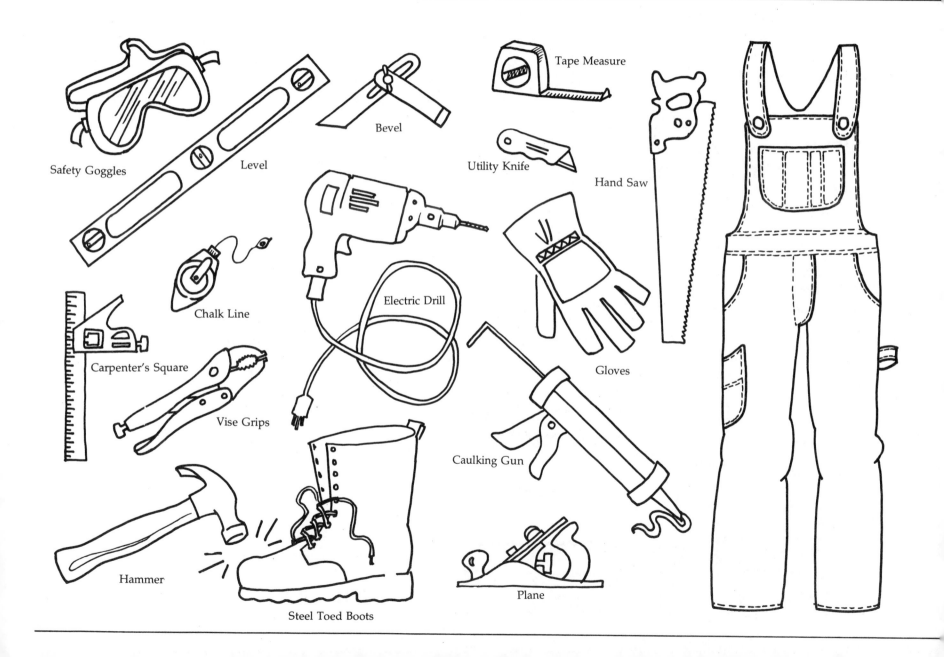

Safety Goggles

Level

Bevel

Tape Measure

Utility Knife

Hand Saw

Chalk Line

Electric Drill

Gloves

Carpenter's Square

Vise Grips

Caulking Gun

Hammer

Steel Toed Boots

Plane

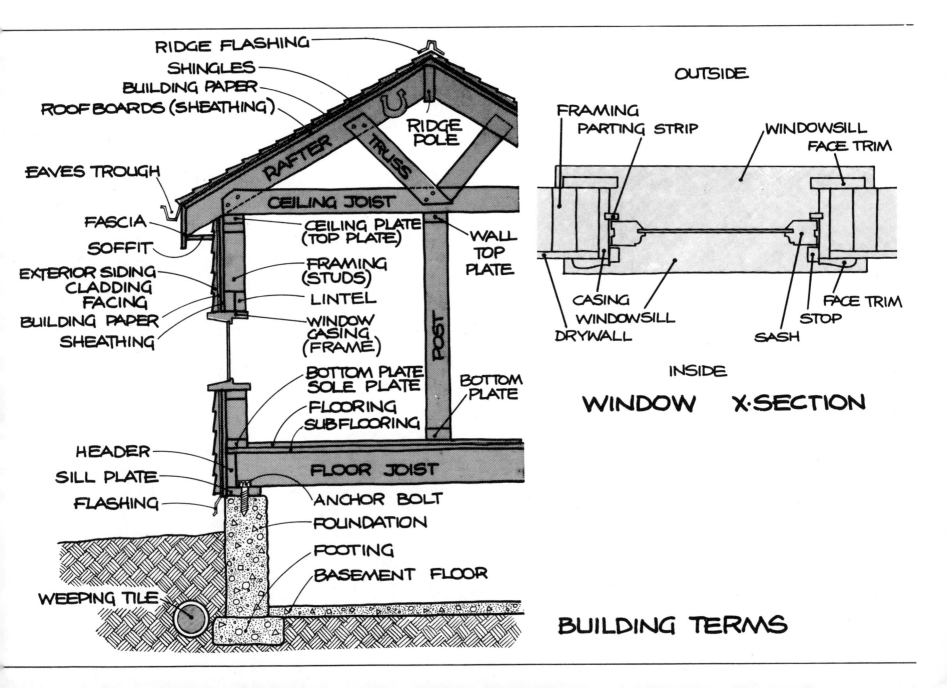

RIDGE FLASHING
SHINGLES
BUILDING PAPER
ROOF BOARDS (SHEATHING)
RIDGE POLE
RAFTER
TRUSS
EAVES TROUGH
CEILING JOIST
CEILING PLATE (TOP PLATE)
WALL TOP PLATE
FASCIA
SOFFIT
EXTERIOR SIDING CLADDING FACING
FRAMING (STUDS)
LINTEL
BUILDING PAPER
SHEATHING
WINDOW CASING (FRAME)
POST
BOTTOM PLATE SOLE PLATE
BOTTOM PLATE
FLOORING SUBFLOORING
HEADER
SILL PLATE
FLASHING
FLOOR JOIST
ANCHOR BOLT
FOUNDATION
FOOTING
BASEMENT FLOOR
WEEPING TILE

OUTSIDE
FRAMING
PARTING STRIP
WINDOWSILL
FACE TRIM
CASING
WINDOWSILL
DRYWALL
FACE TRIM
STOP
SASH
INSIDE

WINDOW X·SECTION

BUILDING TERMS

CONVERSION TABLES

Multiply	by	To Obtain
feet	0.3048	metres
inches	25.4	millimetres
square feet	0.0929	square metres
gallon (Imp.)	4.55	litres
gallon (U.S.)	3.79	litres
litre	0.001	cubic metres
cubic feet	0.0283	cubic metres
pounds	0.4535	kilogram
lb/cubic foot	16.03	kg/cubic metre
Btu	1054.35	Joules
Btu	0.0002929	Kilowatt-hours
Btu/hr	0.293	Watt
Btu/ft^2	.0113	MJ/m^2
Btu/hr/ft^2/°F (R)	0.176	W/m^2/°C (RSI)

Multiply	by	To Obtain
metres	3.2808	feet
millimetres	0.0393	inches
square metres	10.76	square feet
litre	0.2197	gallon (Imp)
litre	0.2638	gallon (U.S.)
cubic metres	1,000	litres
cubic metres	35.33	cubic feet
kilogram	2.204	pounds
kg/cubic metre	.0623	lb/cubic foot
Joules	.0009485	Btu
Kilowatt-hours	3,414.4	Btu
Watt	3.412	Btu/hr
MJ/m^2	88.05	Btu/ft^2
W/m^2/°C (RSI)	5.679	Btu/hr/ft^2/°F (R)

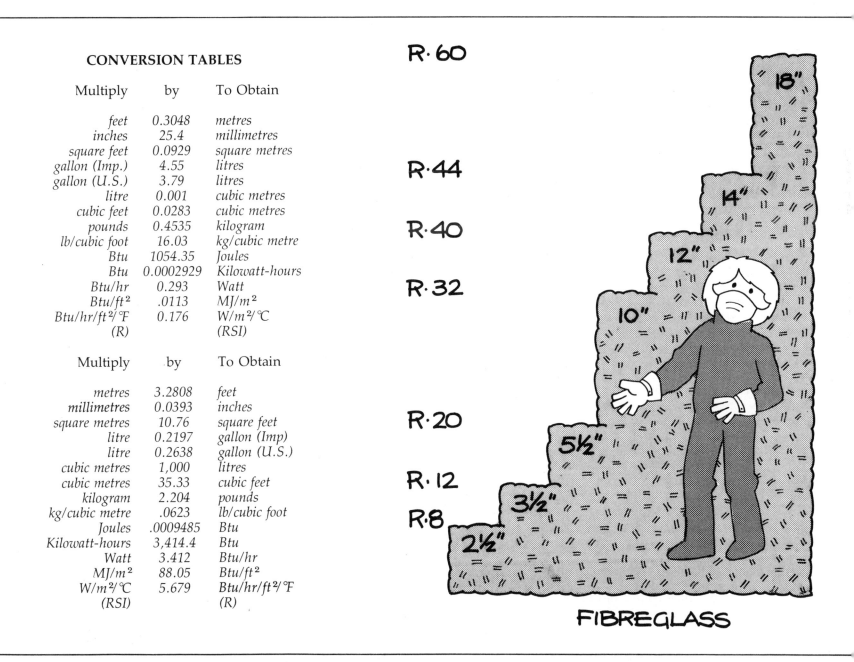

FIBREGLASS

Glossary

Angle Bolt   A steel bolt used to secure a structural member (such as sill plate onto a foundation wall).

Angle Iron   An L-shaped steel section used to support masonry over a window or door opening.

Awning Window   A window that hinges from the top.

Balloon Framing   Window-frame construction method in which the studs extend in one piece from the foundation sill to the roof top plate.

Baseboard   A molded board that conceals the joint between the floor and the wall finish.

Batten   A narrow strip of wood that covers joints between boards or panels.

Beam   A horizontal structural member used to support vertical loads.

Bearing   The part of a joist, rafter, truss or beam which rests on a support and the area of support on which it rests.

Bearing Wall   A wall that supports a vertical load.

Beer Labour   A common form of exchange offered to friends for their Saturday afternoons.

Bottom Plate   A lower horizontal member of a frame wall which is nailed to the bottom of the wall studs and to the floor framing members.

Brick Veneer   A single course of brick-facing which carries no structural load.

Bridging (Cross)   Small members inserted diagonally between adjacent floor or roof joists.

Casement   A type of window that hinges open from one side.

Chimney Flue   The passage in the chimney that carries smoke and gases to the exterior.

Crawl Space   A shallow space between the lowest floor of a house and the ground beneath.

Curtain Wall   A non-supporting wall used to increase wall thickness and provide nailing support for siding.

Degree-Days   A measurement of the total number of degrees occurring each day below a set temperature. Also shown as DD

Double-Glazing   Two panes of glass in a window or door separated by air gap.

Drywall   An interior wall and ceiling finish other than plaster.

Fascia Board   A finished piece around the face of eaves and roof projections.

Flange   A projecting edge, rib or rim.

Flashing   Sheet metal or other material used to shed water.

Footing   The widened section, usually concrete, at the bottom of a foundation wall or column.

Foundation   Usually concrete or masonry (including the footings) which transfers the load from the building to the ground.

Furring   Strips of wood applied to a wall as nailing support for the finished material, or to thicken the wall.

Grade   The ground surface around the foundation wall.

Gusset   A plywood (in most cases) support used to strenghten two joining members.

Header   A wood member at right angles to a series of joists or rafters where the joists or rafters terminate.

Jamb   The side post or lining of a doorway, window or other opening.

Joist   One of a series of horizontal wood members (usually 2 x   ) used to support a floor, ceiling or roof.

Kerf   The groove formed in wood by a saw cut.

Lagged   To mechanically affix or to bolt onto a member.

Ledger Plate   A strip of lumber fastened along the bottom of the side of a beam on which joists rest.

Lintel   A horizontal member that supports the load over an opening such as a door or window.

On Centre   The point from one member to an adjacent member. Used to measure spacing.

Rafter   The structural member of a roof used to support roof loads but not ceiling finish.

Sash   The wooden (in most cases) support of a window onto which the glazing is affixed.

Sheathing   A cladding (in most cases) material used to give added support to stud members.

Sheathing Paper   Paper treated with tar or asphalt used under exterior wall cladding as weather protection.

Shim   A thin wooden piece used as a wedge to support or level a member.

Sill   The horizontal member that forms the bottom of an opening such as a door or window.

Sill Plate   A structural member anchored to the top of a foundation wall upon which the floor joists rest.

Soffit   The underside of building elements such as roof overhang.

Strapping   Fixing wood members horizontal to existing members to increase thickness or provide nailing support.

Stud   A wood structural member used as supporting elements in walls and partitions.

Subfloor   Boards or sheet material laid on joists under a finished floor.

Toe Nailing   Nailing at an angle to the first member (such as a stud) to ensure penetration into a second member.

Top Plate   The horizontal member nailed to the top of the partition or wall studs.

Truss   A prefabricated support system that can replace joists or rafters.

Vapour Barrier   Material used to retard the passage of water vapour or moisture.

Vapour Lock   The condition in which vapour and moisture are trapped between two vapour barriers.

Weephole   A small hole, i.e. at the bottom of a window, to drain water to the exposed face.

Wind Loading   The positive and negative pressure on a wall created by the wind.

Bibliography

An Air-to-Air Heat Exchanger for Residences *Extension Division, University of Saskatchewan, Saskatoon, Sask. S7N 0W0, $1.00, June 1980.*
This pamphlet is for the do-it-yourselfer and those wishing to learn more about air-to-air heat exchangers. It contains detailed information on how to build a low-cost counter-flow heat exchanger for residential use.

From The Wall In *Charles Wing, Atlantic Monthly Press, 1979, 217 pages, $12.95.*
This book explains how retrofitting will improve the energy-efficiency of existing homes. While he stops short of the super-retrofit, Wing carefully explains the why's and how's of dealing with older houses.

Keeping The Heat In *Energy, Mines and Resources, Ottawa, 1976, 98 pages, Free.*
Subtitled 'How To Re-insulate Your Home And Save Energy And Money (And Be Comfortable Too)'. This excellent introduction describes how to assess your house, re-insulate and weatherseal. It features well-illustrated "how-to" sections.

Energy-Efficient Housing — A Prairie Approach *Alberta Energy and Natural Resources & Saskatchewan Mineral Resources, 1980, 31 pages, Free.*
This excellent booklet examines methods to help reduce the energy needs of (mainly) new housing. It examines in detail air-tightness, super-insulation and shuttered south-facing windows.

First, Seal Your House *Renovation and Energy Conservation Unit, Ministry of Municipal Affairs and Housing, Queen's Park, Toronto, 1981, 15 pages, Free.*
This pamphlet presents the why's and how-to's of sealing a house. It presents a detailed description of these critical first steps before re-insulation. It examines attics, basements, doors, windows, vents, outlets and other sources of air leakage and heat loss.

The Solar Greenhouse Book
ed. J. McCullagh, Rodale Press, 1978, 328 pages.
A good book on designing and building energy-efficient greenhouses. It covers a wide range of approaches, including freestanding, attached and pit solar greenhouses.

The Solar Water Heater Book *R. Bryenton, et. al., Renewable Energy in Canada, 1980, 96 pages, $6.95.*
Subtitled 'Building and Installing Your Own System', this is a well-illustrated, step-by-step guide to building solar water heating systems. It describes systems that have been successfully operated throughout Canada and the United States.

The Well-Tempered House *R. Argue, Renewable Energy in Canada, 1980, 222 pages, $11.95.*
Subtitled 'Energy-Efficient Building For Cold Climates', this is an introduction to super-insulated and passive solar heated housing. It features the work of 12 well-known solar architects and builders, a primer, appendix, access information and a survey of 14 outstanding energy-efficient houses.

Super-Insulated Houses and Double-Envelope Houses *William Shurcliff, Brickhouse, 1981.*
This is a detailed examination and comparison of the super-insulated and double-envelope approaches to low-energy housing. Super-insulation comes out the winner.

Thermal Shutters and Shades *William Shurcliff, Brick House, 1980, $16.95.*
This is a comprehensive guide to simple, low-cost window insulation techniques. It includes many homemade and commercially available systems.

Movable Insulation *William Langdon, Rodale Press, 1980.*
An excellent detailed discussion of heating and cooling losses through windows. Covers insulation options for greenhouses, windows, glass doors and skylights.

Air-Vapour Barriers *D. Eyre; D. Jennings, Saskatchewan Research Council, 1981, 105 pages, $6.50.*
This is an excellent guide to the issue of air-tightness in residential buildings. It provides the details necessary for vapour barrier installation in new homes.

Solarizing Your Present Home *ed. Joe Carter, Rodale Press, 1981, 672 pages, $24.95.*
This book presents the details of 30 different solar retrofit projects you can add to existing homes. Each project is well-illustrated and includes step-by-step instructions.

Winter Greens *ed. Mark A. Craft, Renewable Energy in Canada, April 1982, 250 pages, $11.95*
Subtitled 'Solar Greenhouses for Cold Climates', this book explores the design, construction and maintenance of greenhouses for use as both heaters and growing spaces. It also examines in detail plant management in northern climates.

Periodicals

Canadian Renewable Energy News
Box 4869, Station E, Ottawa, Ontario K1S 5J1, $14.00/year.
This superb monthly newspaper will keep you up-to-date on the national as well as international renewable energy scene. It covers policies, politics and new technologies.

Fine Homebuilding *The Taunton Press, Inc., Newtown, CT 06470, $14.00/year.*
This quality bi-monthly publication has articles on various aspects of home building including solar and energy-efficient construction. A recent issue had articles on site-built collectors, a passive solar house and several interesting book reviews.

New Shelter *Rodale Press, Emmaus, PA 18049, $11.00/year.*
This magazine (9 issues per year) explores the solar and energy conservation world with well-researched articles, commentary and do-it-yourself details and projects.

Index

Acknowledgements

Editor
Rick Wilks

Illustration
Gram Campbell

Cover
Valdis Lapsa

Research and Production
Karen Klett
Mary Lovett
Diane Harford
Ints Plampe
Rapid Typesetting
Acme Stat
Elizabeth White
Nancy Nares
Rob Dumont
Greg Allen
Harold Orr
Annick Press
Henry Schefter
Alastair McCallum
Bruce Gough
David Neufeld
Don Wharton
Jan Neuman
David Coon
Karen Englander
Crown Fish & Chips

Photo Credits
Allen-Drerup-White Ltd.
158, 159
Conservahome, Sask.
166 (ul)
Dept. of Agriculture, Alta.
145, 146, 147, 148, 165 (ur)
Division of Building Research, NRC,
Prairie Region
166 (br, cr, ur)
Ecology House
150, 151, 152, 167 (cl, bl, br)
Bruce Gough
154, 155, 156
David Neufeld
141 (b), 143
Ints Plampe
168 (br)
Other photos by Robert Argue

This book has a permeance rating of approximately 1.7 grains/hr ft^2.

Authors

Robert Argue is a graduate of Environmental Studies at York University, Toronto. He works as a consultant and publisher, documenting the emerging renewable energy field and low energy building industry.

He is a co-author of The Sun Builders; A People's Guide To Solar, Wind and Wood Energy In Canada, and The Well-Tempered House; Energy-Efficient Building in Cold Climates.

Bob conducts courses and seminars across North America on low energy building and solar heating.

Brian Marshall is a graduate from York University in Toronto. He spent three years teaching high school in the Yukon, where he learnt the true meaning of cold.

After a year of contracting and renovating, Brian joined Energy Probe as a researcher into conservation and renewable energy sources. This led to his role as co-ordinator of Ecology House during its design and construction phase. It was here that he fine-tuned his retrofitting skills.

Brian teaches and conducts a variety of courses on retrofitting and energy conservation. He lives with his wife and son in a super-insulated retrofit home in Newmarket, Ontrio.

Other titles from Renewable Energy in Canada:

The Well-Tempered House
Energy-Efficient Building for Cold Climates (July 1980) $11.95

The Solar Water Heater Book
Building and Installing Your Own System (July 1980) $6.95

Winter Greens
Solar Greenhouses for Cold Climates (April 1982) $11.95